Tie the Knot
on a SHOESTRING

Tie the Knot on a Shoestring

Leah Ingram

ALPHA

A member of Penguin Group (USA) Inc.

To all the engaged couples who don't want to mortgage their financial future for a wedding. I hope you find the advice in this book beneficial to your bottom line.

ALPHA BOOKS

Published by the Penguin Group

Penguin Group (USA) Inc., 375 Hudson Street, New York, New York 10014, U.S.A.

Penguin Group (Canada), 10 Alcorn Avenue, Toronto, Ontario, Canada M4V 3B2 (a division of Pearson Penguin Canada Inc.)

Penguin Books Ltd, 80 Strand, London WC2R 0RL, England

Penguin Ireland, 25 St Stephen's Green, Dublin 2, Ireland (a division of Penguin Books Ltd)

Penguin Group (Australia), 250 Camberwell Road, Camberwell, Victoria 3124, Australia (a division of Pearson Australia Group Pty Ltd)

Penguin Books India Pvt Ltd, 11 Community Centre, Panchsheel Park, New Delhi—110 017, India

Penguin Group (NZ), cnr Airborne and Rosedale Roads, Albany, Auckland 1310, New Zealand (a division of Pearson New Zealand Ltd)

Penguin Books (South Africa) (Pty) Ltd, 24 Sturdee Avenue, Rosebank, Johannesburg 2196, South Africa

Penguin Books Ltd, Registered Offices: 80 Strand, London WC2R 0RL, England

Contents

Introduction

Just before I began writing this book, the folks who publish *Brides, Modern Bride,* and *Elegant Bride* magazines (the Conde Nast Bridal Group) published their American Wedding Study for the year. This study is an overview of the wedding industry and the demographics of the people getting married these days.

Although it's easy to gloss over some of the mundane information in the study, such as how old the average bride and groom are, when I first saw the study I couldn't help but pause at the heart-stopping information about how much weddings cost these days.

Are you sitting down? I hope so.

Are you aware that the average wedding in the United States costs more than $27,000? That's more than some people's starting salary out of college! Granted that figure includes the average cost for an engagement ring (about $4,000) but even without the ring factored in, one thing is clear—getting married in the twenty-first century is a big financial deal.

With 2.3 million Americans saying "I Do" each year to the tune of $27,000 on average, we're talking $62.1 billion (with a "b") spent on weddings each year. I don't know about you, but those kinds of numbers scare me.

Here's something even scarier for engaged couples to consider: unlike years past, when the bride's parents paid for a wedding, these days more and more couples are footing the bill for their big day. Only 30 percent of parents pick up their kids' wedding tab—meaning that, as engaged people, the big numbers mentioned above are going to fall on your shoulders.

So why am I telling you all this? Because I want you to know how much you "could" spend on your wedding—and why I've written a book on how not to spend that kind of cash on a one-day event.

It's easy to get sucked into the world of weddings and end up spending way more on your big day than you'd planned. (The Conde Nast Bridal

Group people found that 36 percent of couples do just that—blow their budget.) But you don't have to, and obviously you don't want to or you wouldn't be holding this book.

I'm here to tell you that it is possible in this day and age to plan a fabulous wedding for about $5,000—and that's without compromising on a whole lot. In fact, that's the purpose of this book—telling you all the secrets of having a cheapo wedding that doesn't look cheapo.

Keep in mind, though, that to tie the knot on a shoestring, you're going to have to invest a bit of time and effort into finding the best deals possible. And buying this book is a great way to get started. Why? You can't just ring up your local four-star restaurant and expect them to feed your 200 guests for $200. You need to think about things like an open bar or the month when you get married, and how elements like these can hurt your budget or help it.

Are you willing to do your homework and think outside the wedding box? If so, then I'm confident you're going to be able to plan an event that's going to blow that $27,000 wedding statistic to bits. You'll still have a memorable day with the people you love, and you won't end up at your fifth anniversary, still paying off your wedding bills.

Acknowledgments

Thank you to agent Marilyn Allen, who brought this project to me. If it weren't for her, I'd never have written this book.

I also need to thank writer Jennifer Pirtle for putting Marilyn Allen in touch with me in the first place, many years ago.

Thanks also to the married men and women at various online communities (ASJA, FLX, Profnet) who shared their expertise and anecdotes with me for the "Thrifty Thoughts" sections of this book. I believe that reading other people's first-person accounts helps make advice more believable—I hope the reader agrees with me on this—and I couldn't have included any of this real-life advice if people hadn't generously shared it with me.

Thank you to Margo Donohue at The Conde Nast Bridal Group for sharing statistics from the American Wedding Study with me. These numbers gave me a great basis from which to work when writing this book.

As always, I appreciate the support and love of my family and friends, who don't understand how the heck I can write a book in just a few months flat but despite shaking their heads at me, do whatever they can to help me make my deadlines.

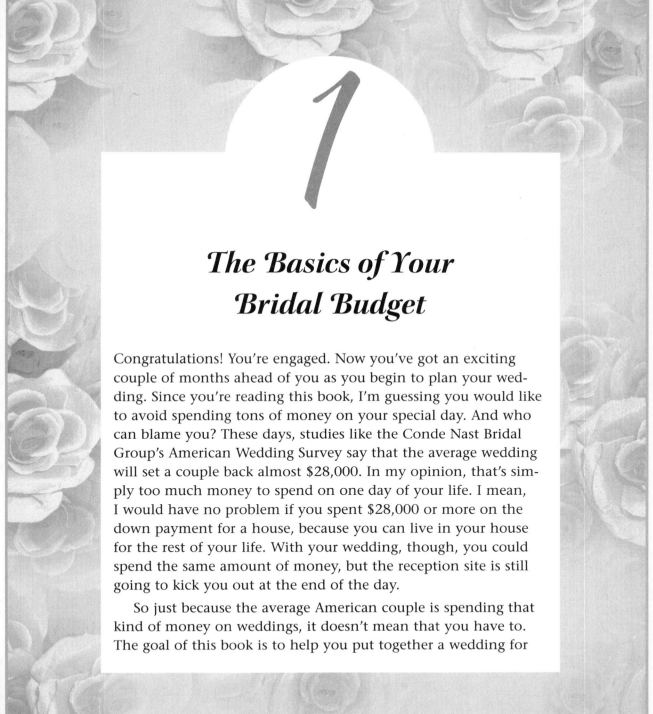

1

The Basics of Your Bridal Budget

Congratulations! You're engaged. Now you've got an exciting couple of months ahead of you as you begin to plan your wedding. Since you're reading this book, I'm guessing you would like to avoid spending tons of money on your special day. And who can blame you? These days, studies like the Conde Nast Bridal Group's American Wedding Survey say that the average wedding will set a couple back almost $28,000. In my opinion, that's simply too much money to spend on one day of your life. I mean, I would have no problem if you spent $28,000 or more on the down payment for a house, because you can live in your house for the rest of your life. With your wedding, though, you could spend the same amount of money, but the reception site is still going to kick you out at the end of the day.

So just because the average American couple is spending that kind of money on weddings, it doesn't mean that you have to. The goal of this book is to help you put together a wedding for around $5,000—maybe a little less, maybe a little more. Every chapter in this book keeps that amount in mind, so as you plan your big day, you can make the smartest decisions possible for your budget.

What Things Cost

Before we get into the specifics of making your budget work for you—or the creative things you can do to tweak your decisions in your financial favor— I think it's important to explain exactly what things cost in today's wedding world. Keep in mind that I'm using the latest version of the aforementioned American Wedding Survey as my guide. You may discover that goods and services cost significantly more or less where you live, but I want you to understand up front what a big business weddings have become, so you can get over your sticker shock now and then use this information to make knowledgeable choices later on.

So what are the average bride and groom spending on their weddings these days? Here's a breakout of some of the main categories, rounded to the nearest dollar:

- ✆ Reception—$10,110

- ✆ Wedding rings—$2,000

- ✆ Ceremony location and officiant fees—$390

- ✆ Photography—$2,000

- ✆ Videography—$705

- ✆ Flowers—$1,100

- ✆ Bridal attire—$1,355

- ✆ Entertainment (reception and ceremony music)—$1,070

- ✆ Stationery (save the date cards, invitations, table card, programs, thank-you notes)—$528

- ✆ Transportation (limousine)—$260

- ✆ Day-of makeup and hair—$370

Now that you know what things cost, you may be wondering how this will affect you. Well, for starters, you don't have to pay what the studies say the typical bride pays. However, it's important to keep in mind how the typical bridal budget breaks out. A recent issue of *Modern Bride* magazine suggests you use this bridal budget template for your spending:

- 50 percent for the reception
- 10 percent for photography
- 10 percent for music and entertainment
- 10 percent for flowers
- 10 percent for wedding attire
- 4 percent for stationery
- 6 percent for other purchases like rings, favors, and gifts

While not every event will follow this structure, it's a good starting point for budgeting your wedding. In fact, when you're thinking about this book's $5,000 wedding budget goal, here's how those numbers get divvied up:

- $2,500 on your reception
- $500 on photography
- $500 on music and entertainment
- $500 on flowers
- $500 on attire
- $200 on stationery
- $300 on everything else

Of course, this budget template doesn't show how couples either increase or decrease their spending in certain categories, based on what's important to them. What do I mean by that? Well, a couple who wants to rock out to live music at their reception will likely want to dedicate more than $500, or

10 percent, of their budget on entertainment, and then decrease spending in other areas to even things out. Another couple may decide the photography is what matters most, so they up their spending in that category. Then they'll adjust their budget accordingly. Later on in this chapter, I'll help you figure out where your wedding priorities lie so you can plan your spending without going over budget.

Who Pays for What

It used to be the bride's family picked up the tab for the whole wedding, with the groom's parents paying for the rehearsal dinner. Man, did this arrangement let the groom's parents get off easy. According to studies, a typical rehearsal dinner costs about $750 where, as you know, the average wedding celebration is in the $20,000 range.

But now parents of brides everywhere can breathe a sigh of relief—only about a third of engaged couples expect their parents to pay for their wedding. The rest hope their parents will help out where they can but understand that in this day and age, more and more couples are assuming the cost of their wedding. In my opinion, that makes the most sense, and that's probably why you're reading a book about planning a wedding on a shoestring.

Even with good intentions, though, not every couple can swing even $5,000 for an affair. That's why I want to let you know there's nothing wrong with approaching your respective parents and asking them for financial help. In fact, it's not uncommon for parents to pay for a specific element of the wedding—say the photography—and then say to their child, "This is our gift to you." Why should your parents buy something off your registry when the gift you really need is help paying for the wedding?

If you think your parents would be open to this arrangement, definitely discuss it with them soon after you get engaged. It's best to talk about these kinds of details as far in advance as possible. Don't spring this sort of thing on your parents at the last minute when, suddenly, you realize you've gotten in over your head with the cost of your wedding. Your parents are going to feel better about giving you this "gift" when you've given them sufficient time to plan for it.

Setting Financial Priorities

I mentioned earlier how, when looking at your wedding budget, you need to determine up front what is important and what's not a priority. Why is this key? Well, when you're trying to plan a wedding for about $5,000, you can't just take everything you'll need to buy or the people you'll need to hire at face value—literally.

DON'T TRIP
on your **SHOESTRINGS**

> It may not be in your nature to save money, but if you want to end up avoiding debt while planning your wedding, you should plan to cut back on some everyday expenses. Some easy ways to do that is to make coffee at home instead of buying it, brown-bag your lunch instead of eating out, and rent films instead of going to the movies. These small changes could easily add up to hundreds of dollars of savings each month, all of which you can funnel into a wedding savings account.

For instance, your best friend may have hired a fantastic photographer for her wedding and has recommended you speak to him. When you call him up and find out he charges $1,000, you can't just say, "Book 'em, Dano." You need to ask yourself the following:

- How important is photography to me?
- What exactly will I be getting for this $1,000?
- What are my other priorities for my wedding?
- With these priorities in mind, is it worth spending 20 percent of my budget on pictures?

Once you have a sense of where you'd like your money to go, you can begin planning how you'll spend money on your wedding.

Must Haves/Things You Can Do Without

When you got engaged, probably one of the first things you did was go to your local newsstand or bookstore and stock up on bridal magazines. I know, I've been there and done that, and it's fun to flip through the pages of magazines that are as big as a phone book and see all the gown choices and everything else these wedding magazines suggest you should have for your wedding.

However, just because the editors of a magazine recommend all these extras, like truffles for favors, or suggest an elaborate train on your gown, that doesn't mean you have to have them. As you read this book, you're going to learn tricks and tips to make your wedding look expensive when you don't spend a lot.

For example, no rule says your wedding must be a sit-down dinner with chicken, fish, or beef. You can plan an elaborate brunch or luncheon for your guests for a lot less than a Saturday night dinner, yet the event will still seem substantial.

Here's another for instance: at the ceremony you may think you need to have extra decorations because that's how things look in those "real weddings" the bridal magazines feature. But if you're getting married in a setting that can hold its own visually—a lovely old church with beautiful wood details or the local botanical garden—there's no reason to spend a lot of money prettying up a place that's already pretty.

I don't want you to feel like you're getting ripped off with your wedding by suggesting you forego the pew bows or flowers as your centerpieces. If these are things you really want, then by all means have them. But when you're planning a wedding on a budget or with limited funding, you'll have to make sacrifices somewhere, and that's why it's important to know ahead of time what you can do without.

How Your Timeline Affects Your Choices

As you set your financial priorities for your wedding and think about what you want and what you can live without, it's important that you also keep your "to do" timeline in mind. Although you may have phoned the photographer first, for example, unless you've determined photography is your number-one priority for your wedding, you probably shouldn't book him yet.

In most instances, you first should have your guest list in place and some dates in mind. Then begin calling ceremony and reception locations. Make these your first two "to do's" on your booking list, because you want to make sure that both your ceremony and reception locations can accommodate your guest list. You also want to make sure these places are available on your targeted dates.

If your reception location doesn't come with a caterer or your ceremony space doesn't have an officiant, you'll need to hire these folks next. Then you'll get into the next level of "to do"—finding a photographer, florist, entertainer, and so on.

The Deal with Deposits and Written Agreements

Now that you've figured out what elements of your wedding are important to you and how much you would be willing to spend on each of them, you've got to start booking people and preparing to dole out dollars. Every person or company you're going to be dealing with is going to want a deposit, so don't be surprised when asked to secure someone's time and services with a down payment.

In a perfect world, when you begin paying deposits, you should also be signing a written agreement with each of your vendors. This agreement should spell out all the terms you've agreed to for this person or the company's services. Key elements to look for in an agreement include the following:

- ✆ Date of event
- ✆ Time vendor will be on-site and, if applicable, how long vendor will be working
- ✆ Fee you've agreed to pay, including deposit
- ✆ Number of personnel you've agreed the fee will cover
- ✆ Outline of services to be provided

Every professional you work with should present a written agreement for you to sign. If he doesn't, you can't just assume everything will go according to plans. Generally folks are not out to rip off brides and grooms, but should something go wrong, you'll have no recourse if you don't have anything in writing. So if your vendors don't have a written agreement for you to sign, you should present one for them to sign. (See Appendix D for a sample agreement.)

Okay, so let's say a vendor balks at the notion of putting your agreement in writing and says something like, "Don't you trust me?" Well, in my book, when someone asks me if I trust him, it's a red flag that says I shouldn't trust him. Neither should you. I don't care how great a band or photographer is or how yummy the food is at a reception locale, if the person refuses to sign a written agreement, then you should refuse to do business with him. In fact, it would be smart to ask up front, when interviewing potential vendors, "Can I see a copy of your agreement?" If they don't have one, bring up the notion of your providing one, and then see how they react. This will let you know right away if this is the kind of person or business you want to do business with for your wedding.

Paying with Cash, Check, Debit, Credit, or Equity

Now that you're to the point of putting down deposits, you need to figure out exactly how you're going to pay for everything. Hopefully, you and your fiancé have already begun discussing finances. Luckily, you have a number of options for paying for your wedding. However, each of these options has its pros and cons.

Lots of couples like the idea of saving up for their wedding and then paying for everything with cash, debit, or check. You may think this is a great way to avoid going into debt: when you pay by cash or check, you don't have to worry about that credit card bill that's going to show up next month with all these charges on it. However, while cash, debit, and checks may make sense from a debt point of view, they don't always make sense from a protection point of view—once you pay someone this way, your money is gone. And if you find out that suddenly your vendor has skipped town, you can't recoup costs. And this brings me to the next option—credit.

I'm a big fan of paying for wedding-related goods and services by credit card because you've got the Fair Credit Billing Act backing you up. This little piece of federal legislation says that if you need to dispute a charge on the delivery of goods and services you've received based on a credit card payment, the law is on your side—meaning you don't have to pay for anything you've called into question. Also, many credit card companies have a similar policy of letting customers dispute something they're not happy with or that didn't turn out as expected that was paid for by credit card. That's why it's a good idea to use credit cards for your wedding.

DON'T TRIP
on your SHOESTRINGS

> Here's a bit more about The Fair Credit Billing Act and how it can help you in your wedding plans. This piece of legislation ensures that consumers don't have to pay for goods or services that were paid for with a credit card and then not delivered as promised. The Federal Trade Commission (FTC) enforces the Fair Credit Billing Act. There are a couple of caveats that you need to keep in mind, in case you need to take advantage of this law. First, your purchase must be for at least $50 and the transaction must have occurred within your home state or within 100 miles of your credit card billing address. And second, you should have made a good-faith effort to resolve the dispute first before contacting the FTC. (Keep copies of all correspondence to show your effort.) For more information on the Fair Credit Billing Act, visit the FTC's web page devoted to it at www.ftc.gov/bcp/conline/pubs/credit/fcb.htm.

Let's say you order your wedding dress and it doesn't come in on time. Now you're stuck without a dress, and you've got to scramble to find something to wear to your wedding. Okay, you'll figure that out, but what about the charge for the wedding dress that never materialized? You shouldn't have the added stress of having to pay for it, and when you pay by credit, you likely won't have to. If you dispute this kind of charge, most credit card companies will put a hold on payments and won't charge interest or finance charges on the amount until the issue is resolved.

If you are averse to using your credit card, think about it this way—you can still set aside cash to pay for your wedding but keep it in the bank until your credit card bill arrives. Then you can use the cash to pay off the bill in full. That way you can have the double benefit of paying with protection without incurring any debt you can't afford.

Now let's say you can't afford to put aside the cash to pay for your wedding. One financing option that may make more sense than relying on credit cards is equity—that is, taking out a home equity loan or line of credit on your house. The interest on these kinds of liens is tax-deductible, which is a benefit right there. (Note: I am not an accountant so please check with yours on the financial benefits and drawbacks of a home equity loan or line of credit.) If you do decide to go the equity route, you can adopt a similar plan as someone who wants to pay by credit card but not end up in debt. You can still use your credit card to pay all deposits and bills, so you've got protection, and then you can use the lump sum from your loan or a portion of your line of credit to pay your bills. Later on, you'll pay off what you borrowed against your home's equity.

Is Bartering an Option?

Although bartering might be an old-fashioned concept, plenty of modern business folks use bartering to get what they need when they can't afford to pay full price. Not familiar with the notion of bartering? Here's how it works: one person trades his services for another person's service. So a guy who owns a lawn service and needs his house painted might find a house painter who would be willing to paint the lawn service guy's home in exchange for a summer's worth of lawn mowing. See how easy that is?

If you've got a skill or talent that someone in the wedding industry might find valuable, could you arrange a barter for goods and services? A writer I know was able to get the limousine for her wedding for free (a $400 value) in exchange for penning a brochure for the limousine company. I used bartering when planning my honeymoon. At the time I was doing photography on the side, and I found out the resort where my husband and I were going to honeymoon needed new photographs for their marketing materials. I negotiated a deal where they would take 50 percent off our weeklong stay in exchange for my photographing the grounds. This ended up saving us about $1,500.

Does one of you design websites? Are you an accountant? Is one of you a dentist? As you begin interviewing vendors for your wedding, find out if they would be willing to do your wedding for a reduced fee or even for free. In return you can offer website design, tax returns, teeth cleaning, or whatever skill you may have to offer that a vendor may want or need.

Do You Know Anyone in the Business?

Another way to secure terrific discounts or free services for your wedding is knowing someone in the business. And when I say "in the business," I don't just mean someone who owns a business. If you know people who freelance or do wedding-related jobs on the side or as a hobby, perhaps you can tap into their talent without having to pay full price.

You will see plenty of examples in this book where knowing people in the business really helped couples stretch their wedding budgets. Brides who had friends who baked wedding cakes in their spare time were able to get a cake that looked like something out of a Martha Stewart magazine without having to pay Martha Stewart prices. Grooms who knew guys who did deejaying on the side were able to secure reception entertainment for peanuts. Other examples I've heard of include a friend of the groom whose dad owned a tuxedo shop, so the groomsmen were all able to get their rentals at deep discounts. Also, the former boss of a bride who used to work in a flower shop wanted to do all of her wedding flowers for her—for free. Then there were the groom's parents who owned an Italian restaurant. They ended up hosting the couple's rehearsal dinner at their restaurant and didn't charge them a dime.

Just as you would network to meet people who might help you in your career, do the same with your wedding. Don't be afraid to ask people for recommendations for vendors they might have a personal connection with and who would be willing to negotiate some sort of discount or deal with you.

Considering a Sponsored Wedding

One of the newest trends for making a wedding affordable is the sponsored wedding. In this kind of wedding, vendors provide their goods and/or services to the couple for free or a reduced price, with the promise that the couple will advertise and promote the companies before, during, and after the wedding. This usually means the wedding invitations will feature the sponsoring companies' names and websites. At the wedding, the guests will find the same kind of advertising on their ceremony programs or at the reception tables. After the wedding, the advertisers' messages might appear on the back of the thank-you notes the bride and groom use.

Why would a vendor agree to such an arrangement? Well, if they're a fledgling business or don't have a budget for advertising, this might be a great opportunity to reach new customers.

Of course, in order to get a company to sign on to a sponsored wedding, you have to prove that doing so is going to be worth their while. In essence, you should put together a sales presentation to convince your would-be sponsors to get on board. Your presentation might show, for example, how many guests you anticipate will be at your wedding, how far away those guests live from a certain business, and why you believe the guests might be interested in learning about that business.

So if you're having a wedding for 200 people and you say in your presentation that 50 percent of these guests are going to be planning a wedding, bar mitzvah, or other special event in the next year, a company that provides services for these kinds of get-togethers might be keenly interested in promoting itself to this "target audience," even at the cost of providing something for your wedding for free.

Also be sure to mention the promise of free publicity. These kinds of weddings are still so novel that I'll bet if you called your local paper or TV station, they would be interested in covering the story of your sponsored wedding. Not only will this get you publicity and perhaps additional vendors, but also it will be free advertising for the vendors that have already agreed to sponsor your wedding.

Money in Your Pocket

So you're thinking of trying a sponsored wedding? Here's how one couple I know pulled that off.

Neither the bride nor the groom had any experience in sales, but once they started adding up how much it was going to cost to have their wedding in their hometown, Philadelphia, they knew they needed to get creative. They started calling around to businesses to see if they would go for the notion of sponsoring the wedding. "We promised to advertise the company through an insert in the invitations and thank-you notes, a blurb in the program, and a mention during the toast," the groom recalls. In all, they were able to line up 24 companies. And while the groom says he was a little embarrassed reading off the list of sponsors when he made a toast, in the end that embarrassment was worth it—they'd lined up $32,000 worth of services and paid nothing for them.

Savings for you: $32,000   **Running total: $32,000**

Wedding-Related Celebrations and How They Can Affect Your Budget

You'll be attending plenty of parties long before your wedding day arrives. These include your engagement party, bridal shower, and rehearsal dinner. The good news is the couple usually doesn't have to pay for any of these celebrations. The bad news is that all these parties can still put a dent in your bottom line.

How, you may be wondering, can these free-for-me events cost me money? Well, the parties aren't exactly free when having to attend them affects you in the following ways:

- ✆ Travel, especially if you don't live nearby where the party is happening

- ✆ Clothing, if you want to wear a new outfit to each of these get-togethers

- ✆ Other primping, if you've gotten into the habit of getting a manicure or eyebrow waxing before every social event

I'm not saying that you can't buy yourself a new dress or treat yourself to a manicure before your wedding shower, but you've got to plan for these expenses if you're going to stick to your budget. So get yourself a new skirt but maybe figure out a way to wear it with a shirt you already own. Want to get your nails done? Can you do them yourself and save the manicure splurge for before your wedding? See where I'm going with this?

Don't use these events as an excuse to blow your budget, because the more money you keep in your pocket now, the easier it will be for you to plan a wedding you can truly afford later.

Dollar-Saving Do's and Don'ts

Here's a recap of how you can find savings even in the smallest bridal budget:

- ℒ Don't think that just because the "average" wedding costs about $28,000, you have to spend this kind of money. It is possible to plan a fab wedding for about $5,000, and that's what this book is all about.

- ℒ Don't worry about what bridal magazines say you should have at your wedding. Plan only for the things you like and that fit your budget.

- ℒ Do consider asking your parents if they'll pay for a certain portion of your wedding as their gift to you.

- ℒ Don't start spending money on vendors until you've gotten your financial priorities in line.

- ℒ Do make sure to get a written agreement with each vendor before you give him a deposit—no contract, no doing business with them.

- ℒ Do keep in mind the kinds of protections paying with a credit card can bring you.

- ℒ Don't think that just because you pay with a credit card you have to go into debt for your wedding. You can save your cash and then use it to pay off your credit card bills in full.

✆ Do consider bartering for certain wedding goods and services, especially if you have a talent to share.

✆ Don't be afraid to ask friends and acquaintances if they know someone in a wedding-related business who might be able to give you a friends or family discount.

✆ Do think about trying to put together a sponsored wedding if you've got grand ideas for your event but a miniscule budget.

✆ Don't let all of the wedding-related parties you go to blow your budget. You don't need to buy a new outfit or splurge on a manicure for each event.

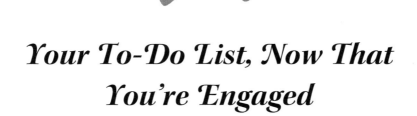

Your To-Do List, Now That You're Engaged

Although you're excited about getting married, you're probably also feeling overwhelmed by everything you have to accomplish between today and your wedding day. In this chapter, I'll start revving your engagement engines by getting you going on some of your pre-wedding tasks, which include doing an engagement photo and announcement inexpensively and taking a stab at your guest list—all with your bottom line in mind. I'll help you begin to think about the time and location of your wedding and at what stores and businesses you might want to register for gifts. I'll also talk about the cost of insuring that brand-new engagement ring you're wearing. Finally, I'll show you how a wedding website can help you save money.

Engagement Photo and Announcement

There are a number of things that I love about the modern world and how it affects weddings. For starters, I love that society doesn't expect formal engagement photos anymore and that the etiquette of these photos has loosened considerably in the past few years for those who choose to have them taken. Whenever I look in my local paper at the engagement announcements, I rarely see what looks to be a studio shot.

I also love that engagement photos and announcements are optional these days. Most people continue to send them out, simply as a nod to tradition, but it's not really necessary. However, having had my engagement announcement appear in my hometown paper, I do understand how fun it is to see your name and picture in print announcing your upcoming wedding.

So what does this all have to do with saving you money? Well, for starters, because you don't need to pay for a formal engagement photo, you can get away with having a friend or family member take a picture of the two of you. Cost to you? Nothing, except for developing and printing the pictures. Next, most local papers will publish engagement announcements for free, whereas others may charge a nominal fee. For example, *The New York Times* charges about $20 for a paid engagement announcement. It's a small price to pay, to be sure, but perhaps that's a cost you can get your parents to pick up—since, technically, they're the ones who are going to be announcing your engagement.

Finally, if this all seems too much to bother with, the good news is you don't have to do the photo or announcement at all. The wedding gods won't frown on you if you skip right over this engagement formality. And if you do skip it, you'll end up with one less thing on your "to do" list!

Determining Your Guest List

Probably one of the hardest things you're going to do in planning your wedding is finalize your guest list. Other tasks might require more brainpower, but creating a guest list is often fraught with emotions, expectations, and, sometimes, disappointment. It's the one area of the wedding where parents and other relatives are going to share input with you, whether you asked for or want it. Your parents may insist you invite their friends, whom you haven't seen in years, and your single friends might push you to let them bring a date. Also, making your guest list is the one act that is going to most affect how much you spend on your wedding.

To get you started on this task, I suggest both you and your fiancé create a draft guest list. Approach this first take with a "perfect world" scenario in mind—that is, don't worry about head counts and costs right now; instead, put everyone on the list that you'd like to attend your wedding. You can write down everyone from the sister you grew up with to the sorority sister you haven't seen in 10 years. At the same time ask each of your parents to do the same with their version of the guest list. Once these lists are finished, compare them. Start by crossing off any overlapping names, which are usually relatives you've both written down. This will likely get rid of 10 to 20 percent of the total names.

Now count the number of names. This will give you a first draft of your guest list.

DON'T TRIP on your **SHOESTRINGS**

> When you're making your guest list, don't forget some important players—yourselves, your parents, and the people in your wedding party. You wouldn't believe how many couples forget to add themselves into their head count, which not only affects the total bill but also how many chairs, for example, you will need at the reception.

Next I want you to consider this: a really good deal on a sit-down meal at a wedding reception is about $25 a person in middle America. (In big cities, on the other hand, that number balloons to at least $100 a person, so keep that in mind.) Many receptions, however, cost way more than this. Although the reception isn't the only cost associated with your wedding, it will likely comprise 50 percent of your spending, so multiply the number of people on this first draft of your guest list by $25. Now double that number, since the $25 per person is for your reception only—and, like I just said, the reception tends to be about 50 percent of your total costs.

The figure you now have is a good estimate of how much you may end up paying to entertain this many guests at a wedding. How does this number look? Are you ready to have a heart attack? Or are you feeling an overwhelming sense of inner calm? If you still don't feel like these numbers mean anything to you, read on.

Let me show you an example of how this exercise can work in the real world. I'll use my long-ago wedding as an example.

When my husband and I were first planning our wedding, we each created drafts of our guest list, and we asked our parents to do the same. After we put our lists together with our parents' and crossed off all of the repeats, we were left with 250 names on the list. If I were to use the formula I've described, we would have been looking at $6,250 at the very minimum. Remember, this number is an estimate for the reception only, which would be 50 percent of our total costs. So if we doubled that number, we were looking at $12,500 for a wedding. Ouch!

Not only did we want to whittle down our numbers for the sake of our bank account, but we didn't want to deal with the meet and greet that goes along with having this many guests at a wedding, either. Imagine 250 guests moving through a receiving line. You would be there for hours! And if you wanted to mingle and see everyone at the reception, by the time you'd made your way through the room, it would be time for the last dance.

To cut down those numbers, we revisited our guest list with an "A" list and "B" list approach. We put an "A" next to the names of people we had to invite—grandparents, cousins, and the like. Then we put a "B" next to the names of people who it would be nice to have attend our wedding, but it wouldn't be the end of the world if they didn't. Once we accomplished that, we did a recount, and our "A" list had 175 names on it. To us that was a more manageable number and, in fact, that's how many people we ended up inviting.

In getting back to your need to formulate a guest list, you should do a similar exercise. If the number of names on your first draft feels too big, take the "A" and "B" list approach like I did. Then see how the numbers add up.

Keep in mind that another issue that will affect your guest list, beyond "A" and "B" lists and budgets, is where you'll hold your wedding—and whether or not it's big enough to hold the number of people you want to invite. Briefly, if you want to get married in your hometown chapel that can hold only 150 people and you're planning to invite 250 people to your wedding, you've got to do one of two things—forego the chapel and book a place that can accommodate 250, or whittle your guest list down to the 150 range so everyone can fit. But I'll discuss this all in more detail in Chapter 3.

Go Figure

To give you a rough estimate of how much your wedding might cost you, you need only do some simple arithmetic. This worksheet helps you do that. (Remember, these numbers are just an FYI. If you live in a big city or are planning to get married in an upscale locale, you would be hard pressed to find a caterer charging $25 per person.)

Step 1: Number of people on your guest list _____

Step 2: Multiply Step 1 by 25 _____

Step 3: Double total from Step 2 _____

Your total preliminary cost for your wedding _____

Another area to think about when trying to keep the number of guests under control is in relation to kids: do you want to have them at your wedding? If you're going to invite kids, will you invite everyone's children or only the kids of people in your wedding party? How will you draw that line? There is no rule that says you must invite kids to your wedding, although, in fact, some caterers may offer a reduced price for smaller guests. However, if you're facing space constraints and need fewer people on your list, you'll need to decide who takes precedence—your sister's children or your college roommate?

You may find that giving your lists this new set of criteria helps everyone to rank people differently and gets you closer to your target list size. Of course, once you have the new number, do the math again, using the $25 per person figure, double it, and then see where your tentative budget is in relation to the size of your guest list.

Thinking About the Time and Location of Your Wedding

I just mentioned that if you want to get married in a smaller space but you've got a bigger guest list, you're going to have to compromise on something—either guest list size or wedding location. In Chapters 3 and 4, I talk more in depth about choosing the right place for your ceremony and reception, but for now you should keep in mind that five-star hotels and expensive country clubs are going to be—surprise, surprise—expensive places to have a wedding. If you'd like to stick to this book's premise of a wedding for about $5,000, then you need to look at places that aren't going to charge you an arm and a leg. These less costly places would include a house of worship where you are a member, which may have space for your ceremony and reception. Oftentimes, having your ceremony and reception in the same place is a big money saver. Or you could look to local township halls for an affordable reception. Another place to look for a bargain is at the college or university from which one of you or a family member graduated, or if one of you has a job on a campus.

As far as the timing of your wedding, there is one truth in weddings—Saturday night is the most expensive time of the week for a special event. Other truths apply to how the time of year can make your wedding expensive or affordable. For example, in states with four seasons, the months of June and September are pricey, regardless of the time of day of your wedding. That's because June and September are the top two months for weddings. In the South, months in early fall and spring are the most popular and, therefore, the most expensive. So if you've been dying to have a Saturday night wedding in the middle of June in a Northeastern location, you can forget about planning a wedding for about $5,000. That will be nearly impossible to pull off. However, if you change your ideas slightly, say choose a Friday night wedding in April, you'll probably have more leeway in your budget.

I'll talk more in depth in Chapter 4 about how the time of year can work in your favor in negotiating affordable prices for your wedding.

How Gift Registry Choices Can Cut Your Wedding Costs

It's important for newly engaged couples to register as soon as possible, because you may find yourselves the guests of honor at an engagement party or other celebration at which people would like to give you gifts. To avoid unnecessary returns or "what the heck are we going to do with this gift?" reactions, you should select one or two stores where you can ask your guests to get you things you actually need.

I do not believe in turning a gift registry into a shopping free-for-all, yet at the same time I don't think you should hold back on registering for things you could really use. In fact, if you plan things carefully, you could conceivably register for—and receive before your big day—goods and services that you'll need for your wedding. People may give you these gifts at your engagement party or bridal shower. By registering for them, you will cut your wedding bill because someone else will have bought them for you. In case this is confusing, let me explain.

If you register for—and receive at your shower, for example—an iPod or MP3 player, you can avoid the cost of a band or deejay by using your new iPod or MP3 player as your digital deejay. Similarly, if you add a digital camera and/or video camera to your registry list—and someone gets you both as an engagement gift—you can consider skipping the professional photographer or videographer if someone you know is good behind the lens—and then he or she can use your new equipment for the job. Once you upload the pictures to your computer, you can use your new photo printer and paper to make free prints. Other examples include registering for, receiving, and cashing in a gift certificate for spa or beauty treatments as a way of getting your hair and makeup done for your wedding, again, for free; and having your guests help to chip in for your honeymoon through your registry. (More on honeymoon registries in Chapter 12.)

Money in Your Pocket

You may be wondering just how much money registering for an iPod or MP3 player can save you on your wedding bill. Well, consider this: according to the Conde Nast Bridal Group's American Wedding Survey, the average couple spends about $843 on reception entertainment. On the other hand, at Apple. com, you can get a fully loaded iPod, with room for thousands of songs, for about $300. Now Apple may not have a registry, but places like Amazon.com does, and they sell iPods, too. And if you register for and get this iPod, not only will you save money on reception entertainment, but you'll also be able to enjoy the iPod long after your wedding is over.

Savings for you: $543   **Running total: $32,543**

You may think of other ways your registry preferences can benefit your bottom line, by "giving" you goods and services you might otherwise have to pay for. Think creatively as you prepare to register, and see if you can't find other ways to have your gift registry help cover your wedding costs.

Of course, taking this approach brings with it inherent risks, and you need to determine ahead of time what you're going to do if, say, you registered for an iPod, never booked a band, and you never got the iPod. Will you buy the iPod yourself? Try to find a band at the last minute? It's wonderful to hope for the best and save money in the process, but if you try to stockpile gifts to take the place of certain wedding vendors, do have a Plan B in place just in case.

How Where You Register Can Put Cash in Your Pocket

In addition to figuring out what you need to register for, you should also give some careful consideration to the places where you register. Normally, my advice in this respect is about making the lives of your guests easier by regis-tering in stores convenient for them. That's still true. However, since the goal of this book is to make the most of your hard-earned dollars—and to help you avoid spending them whenever possible—you need to approach your gift registry store selections from a slightly different angle.

Probably the most important thing to keep in mind is making sure you choose stores that have lenient and flexible return policies. You don't want to get stuck with overstocks from your registry and have no way of returning them. Many stores automatically give a gift receipt with a purchase off of a registry, and if your gifts come with one, don't lose it. Other stores are a bit more generous with returns from registries. Some will take back anything from your registry, even if the person didn't buy it at that store, and give you store credit. Others may not only take back an item from your registry purchased elsewhere but also give you cash for that return instead of credit.

One bride in Florida had this experience. She'd registered at Bed Bath & Beyond, and like many brides, ended up with more registry items than she needed. Many guests had gone to other stores and bought brand-name goods on her list—likely because they found them cheaper somewhere else or because there wasn't a Bed Bath & Beyond near them. When the bride went to take back the extras after her wedding, the store took everything back and gave her cash in return. The bride reports that she made returns in two South Florida Bed Bath & Beyond locations and received the cash-back option at both.

What a wonderful way to end up with additional cash in your pocket after your wedding! Of course, I'm not suggesting you commit gift registry fraud by registering for more than you need and returning stuff just to get the cash. That would be wrong. Nonetheless, you should make sure that when you're thinking about the stores where you're going to register, you know what their return policy is. If you can end up with a few more greenbacks like this bride did, that would be wonderful.

Registering for Charity Saves Everyone Money

Lots of couples these days are choosing to forego the traditional registry altogether—most likely because they have enough stuff and don't want to get gobs of gifts at the wedding. Many of these couples are choosing to register with a charity, in that they ask their family and friends to make a donation to their chosen good cause in lieu of boxed gifts. Organizations like The I Do Foundation can help you set up this kind of registry.

So how can registering for charity save everyone money? First, you'll save money on gas because you won't have to drive from store to store to register your preferences. Second, you won't have to drive back to all of these stores after the wedding to return and exchange gifts, for which you might only get store credit and not cash. And third, your guests will save money because they'll be able to make a donation in whichever denomination they choose, and I'm guessing that amount would probably be a lot less than they would have spent on a "regular" gift.

The Cost of Insuring Your Engagement Ring

So what does insuring an engagement ring have to do with saving money? Well, it's simple. If you don't insure your engagement ring and something happens to it or you lose it, guess what? You'll have to pay to get a new one. And if your engagement ring is anything like the ones most brides these days are getting, having to pick up the tab for a new ring is going to hurt your pocketbook.

The first thing you have to do when insuring an engagement ring is to have it appraised. That means taking your ring to a jeweler and having him determine how much it is worth. You'll pay about $50 for an appraisal. Next, you need to get insurance for the ring. In some instances your homeowner's insurance will include coverage of your ring. However, if your ring is worth a significant amount of money, you may have to add a rider (an extra protection policy added to an existing policy) to your insurance. We pay about $20 a year to insure my ring, which isn't a lot to spend when you consider the thousands of dollars we'd have to spend for a replacement.

I wish I could tell you here which kind of expensive jewelry needs a rider, but it's not that simple. Homeowner's policies vary from insurance company to insurance company, and each state has different rules on what can be covered under a homeowner's policy and what requires a rider. You'll need to investigate these options on your own.

Bottom line: make getting your ring appraised and insured a priority. Speak to your insurance agent about whether or not your homeowner's policy will cover your ring. And if for some reason you don't have any such insurance, it would be wise to get it now.

Setting up Your Wedding Website

In this day and age of techno-savvy brides and grooms, having a wedding website has become an almost expected part of an engagement. This is especially true if you're planning a destination wedding and need to communicate a lot of information to your guests over a period of time. Even if you're not planning this kind of wedding, you may find some cost-saving benefits from having a wedding website.

For starters, having a website can cut your postage costs significantly. If you need to mail information about lodging to your guests in advance, for example, you're going to have additional postage costs to deal with. However, if you have a wedding website, with links on it to information online, you can let your guests know, via e-mail, how and where they can get this information, with nary a stamp purchased.

Speaking of e-mail, to save yourself from having to pay return postage on your RSVP cards, you can offer an e-mail link to your wedding website where guests can RSVP. Or create some kind of online guest book, like an Evite.com invitation does, where people can log in a "yes" and "no" RSVP answer. I realize that this suggestion is pushing the wedding etiquette envelope to its limits, but if you're serious about saving money on your wedding, you may want to seriously consider this e-mailed RSVP idea.

Another benefit of having a wedding website: you can link information from your gift registry.

Now what about the cost of the website itself? Well, there doesn't have to be any cost at all. Online wedding advice sites like TheKnot.com offer free wedding websites to their registered users. In addition, some companies that offer a honeymoon registry will give you a free wedding website as well. I'll talk more about that in Chapter 12.

Of course, if you want to register your own domain and set up your own site, then you're going to have to invest some money into the venture. The idea here, though, is to get the wedding website you want without spending money you don't have. If one of you works in IT or web development and can figure out a way to get the website up and running for pennies, then by all means go for it. Or take a truly modern approach to this trend: ask your parents or the gals in your bridal party to buy you a website subscription as their gift to you.

Dollar-Saving Do's and Don'ts

There are plenty of ways to get your pre-wedding "to do" list done and save money in the process. Here's a recap of some of this chapter's advice:

- Don't spend money on a formal engagement photo. Just have someone take a nice shot of the two of you.

- Do see if your parents will pick up the tab for a paid engagement announcement in your local paper if there is a fee.

- Don't worry if you're not into doing an engagement picture or announcement; these days, they're optional.

- Do think about how the size of your guest list is going to affect your overall cost. Use the formula I've provided to figure that out.

- Do consider if you want to deal with the social responsibilities that come with having a big guest list.

- Don't forget to include yourself and your wedding party in your guest list to keep your figures accurate.

- Do create "A" and "B" lists to get a better handle on the size of your guest list.

- Do think about how the location and the timing of your wedding can affect the price.

- Do brainstorm ways you can register for gifts to cover some of your wedding costs.

- Do choose to register in stores with lenient return policies so you won't end up with extra gifts you can't get any credit for.

- ✆ Do think about registering with a charity as a way to save everyone money.

- ✆ Do make insuring your engagement ring a priority on your to-do list.

- ✆ Do investigate how having a wedding website can help cut down on your postage costs.

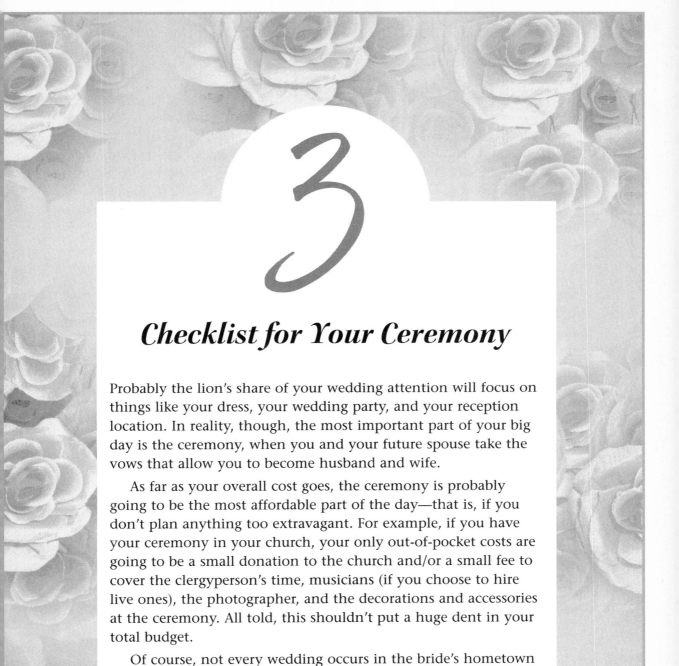

3

Checklist for Your Ceremony

Probably the lion's share of your wedding attention will focus on things like your dress, your wedding party, and your reception location. In reality, though, the most important part of your big day is the ceremony, when you and your future spouse take the vows that allow you to become husband and wife.

As far as your overall cost goes, the ceremony is probably going to be the most affordable part of the day—that is, if you don't plan anything too extravagant. For example, if you have your ceremony in your church, your only out-of-pocket costs are going to be a small donation to the church and/or a small fee to cover the clergyperson's time, musicians (if you choose to hire live ones), the photographer, and the decorations and accessories at the ceremony. All told, this shouldn't put a huge dent in your total budget.

Of course, not every wedding occurs in the bride's hometown church where she can probably do things cheaply. That's why in this chapter, I'll help you figure out other options for where to hold a ceremony and have you consider the economics of having a civil or religious wedding. I'll offer advice on choosing your officiant and your attendants, plus help you determine how to secure all the other necessary items and objects for a wedding (rings, vows, decorations, accessories, musicians, and flowers) without putting yourself into debt. And if you're wondering why I haven't mentioned anything about hiring musicians for the ceremony, it's because I cover that topic in Chapter 8.

Wedding Location Options

While the typical Hollywood wedding involves a magical walk down the aisle of a breathtaking cathedral, in real life a wedding ceremony can occur just about anywhere. Knowing this allows you to explore all of your options and choose the location that's not only right for you but also for your budget.

Let's start with the house of worship you attend, assuming you attend one. This is probably your most affordable ceremony location because you likely won't have to pay anything extra to "rent" the church or temple. Sure, you may have to pay the priest, minister, or rabbi to officiate at the wedding, but that's usually only a couple hundred dollars, if that, though sometimes if you're a parishioner, they'll waive the fees altogether. And no matter where you get married or by whom, you'll have to pay someone to officiate.

If you want to have your wedding in someone else's house of worship, chances are you'll pay a location fee, which the facility may mask as a "donation." Whatever they call it, you'll pay extra for the use of this space unless someone in your family is a member. Then you may be able to negotiate a discount.

Another place family connections may come in handy is at a college chapel. When my husband and I were first considering where to get married, we looked at the campus chapel where my future father-in-law had graduated. As the children of an alumnus we could have gotten the space, with officiant, for $250. Considering we were planning a ceremony for about 150 guests, we thought that was a pretty good deal. I'm sure we would have found similar deals at the nondenominational chapels on the campuses of our respective alma maters as well.

Finally, many couples choose to keep their ceremony costs down by having it in the same place as their reception—whether that be a hotel, a private club, public gardens, or any other location that allows weddings. Often you can negotiate one price for the whole shebang, and in the end pay less for both the ceremony and the reception.

The Costs of a Civil Versus a Religious Ceremony

The type of ceremony you choose, civil or religious, shouldn't affect your bottom line that much because either way you're going to have to pay someone to officiate at your ceremony.

However, a really cheap way to have a civil ceremony is to make the ceremony a separate part of your wedding. That is, you'll go to a local courthouse to get married and then have your wedding reception on an entirely separate day. This is the option that my husband and I eventually chose. By getting married at a government building, we negated the need for musicians, decorations, and more. (I did splurge on a bouquet of fresh-cut flowers, but I picked them up at the local market for $20.) We paid $50 to have the justice of the peace marry us in the presence of our parents, siblings, and attendants. And then on another day we had the reception.

You, too, could plan for an inexpensive civil ceremony at your local courthouse or government building where marriage licenses are issued. Log onto your county's website, and search for "marriage license" for more information. You should be able to track down the details of getting married on-site.

Finding an Inexpensive Officiant

If you're getting married in a house of worship that requires you to use its spiritual leader, then the work of finding an officiant is done. But what if you need to find someone else to officiate at your wedding? How can you do so affordably?

Start by asking around. Ask the people at your house of worship whom they can recommend for a wedding ceremony that's not being held there. Question your colleagues, friends, and family members about any officiant they may know who is a decent person and is decently priced. Pick the brain of the person at the place where you're having your ceremony and/or reception. The wedding experts at hotels, reception halls, and other venues that deal with weddings on a regular basis often keep lists of local officiants, or they can make recommendations if need be.

Believe it or not, an individual doesn't have to wear a white collar or be a judge to marry people. A friend of ours got licensed as a justice of the peace through the Internet, and then married his sister and her fiancé for free as his gift to them.

It's actually easier to get ordained than you might think. You can do so instantaneously via websites that offer this service. For example, the Universal Life Church (www.ulc.org), a multidenominational church based in Arizona, gives out free ordination papers to anyone who takes the time to register on the website. However, just having papers doesn't mean you can perform at a wedding. What you need to do next to become "legal" is take that ordination paper to your local county clerk's office, where you'll receive a certificate saying that you are an ordained officiant. Some counties require a "letter of good character" or something similar, along with the ordination paper, to issue the certificate. Rules vary from county to county so make sure you know what you're getting yourself into—and what's required of you—before investigating how to become a bona fide officiant.

Of course, you can always resort to using online resources to locate an officiant nearby. Some websites that offer referral services include www.weddingofficiants.com and, if you're marrying someone of a differing religion, you can try www.rcrconline.org (Rabbinic Center & Research Counseling) or www.interfaithofficiants.com. If you do use the Internet to track down your officiant, make sure you check the person's references. If an officiant (or any other vendor, for that matter) doesn't come with a personal recommendation or stellar references, I wouldn't recommend hiring him or her, no matter how good their prices seem.

Choosing Attendants (Penny) Wisely

A lot of psychology goes into deciding who will be in your wedding and who won't. But as far as tying the knot on a shoestring goes, the fewer attendants you have, the easier your financial life is going to be. Just think about all of the added costs that go along with having multiple attendants. These include:

- ✆ Clothing, if you decide to pick up the tab for it
- ✆ Lodging, if you're paying for that, too
- ✆ Flowers for bouquets and boutonnières
- ✆ Pictures of the wedding party, which can run up your photo tab
- ✆ Thank-you gifts for your attendants

For these reasons alone, I recommend limiting the number of people you have in your wedding party. I'm not suggesting you have no one stand up there with you. Rather, if you are tempted to recreate the von Trapp family with your wedding party, I suggest going for something more like "The Brady Bunch" with three girls on one side and three guys on the other, if not fewer than that.

Even better, just have a maid of honor and a best man, and call it a day. You can honor the special people in your life in other ways, such as having them do a reading at the ceremony or asking them to give a toast at the reception. Trust me on this one—your bank account will benefit if you have fewer attendants. Plus, if you've ever been in a wedding, you know it's not always a financial cakewalk. I'm confident your friends and family members (and their 401k accounts) will thank you if you don't include them as bridesmaids or groomsmen.

Wedding Rings

An easy way to keep your wedding rings affordable is to keep them simple: for the most part, the fancier your rings are, the more expensive they'll be. Take my wedding band, for example. It's a simple circle of white gold with an ever-so-slight swirl around the outer edge. I spent about $60 for it. What would have made my ring more expensive wouldn't have been more details on it but rather if I'd selected a more precious metal for it, like platinum.

Money in Your Pocket

If you want to keep your wedding budget in check, you can't go overboard with wedding ring spending, especially since the average couple spends about $2,000 on both rings. Yikes—that's just way too much! One of the best ways to keep your ring costs down is to go with less expensive metals. One couple I know did just this—she went with a solid band of platinum and he chose white gold. They bought the same design ring, but hers cost $400 and his $150. Even with his being the bigger version of the ring, his cost significantly less because of his metal choice. This shows how a less expensive metal can really keep your ring costs down. So for this couple, instead of spending the national average of about $2,000 for rings, they spent $550.

Savings for you: $1,450   **Running total: $33,993**

My husband's wedding band was even cheaper; it's his grandfather's ring, which his grandmother gave us, with her blessing, before our wedding day. Is there a sentimental piece of jewelry in your family's history you can use as your wedding band? If so, your only expense for your rings will be having them resized, if necessary.

DON'T TRIP on your **SHOESTRINGS**

Keep in mind that the cost of your ring will increase as you add semi-precious and precious stones to it and/or if you upgrade the metal—from gold to platinum. If you really must have a fancy wedding ring, wait for it. Wait until your fifth anniversary, when you'll likely be on better financial footing and can afford to splurge on this piece of jewelry. For now, though, make your budget your priority as you shop for rings.

Another option is to visit a jewelry wholesaler or a jewelry district, where storefronts compete with each other to offer the best prices to customers. One such place is New York City's 47th Street, which is known as the Diamond District for its great prices on diamonds. But you can get fantastic deals on all other kinds of jewelry, too. That's where I got my wedding ring.

Other cities have "diamond districts," too, though they might be called something else. For example, in Philadelphia, this area of the city is called Jeweler's Row. Also, some of these "districts" might be housed in a single commercial building in a neighborhood, like it is in Boston, instead of encompassing an entire street like in New York City. If your city has such an area, check it out as a place to get great deals on wedding jewelry.

Finally, going online could save you a ton. Jewelry retailers like BlueNile. com or even eBay may be where you get the greatest deals on your wedding jewelry. However, like those who buy their wedding gown from eBay, you'll be buying sight unseen. Are you comfortable doing this with a piece of jewelry you're going to wear every day? If so, then definitely scope out the bargains on the Internet.

Vows

Did you know there's a growing cottage industry of writers-for-hire for weddings? Couples are using them to write their vows and any speeches they need to give during the wedding. For someone like you, though, looking to plan your wedding for as little as possible, having someone write your vows for you (for a fee, no less) should be a financial last resort.

I realize that for people who don't write for a living, writing vows can be a daunting task. But if you want to avoid unnecessary expenditures, then figure out the easiest and cheapest way to put together heartfelt vows. Here are four suggestions:

- ✆ Talking out loud about how you feel about your future spouse is a terrific way to capture your thoughts. Tape yourself as you brainstorm or write your thoughts down, then read it back aloud and see how it sounds.

- ✆ If you have a friend or family member who is a writer, you might ask him or her to work with you on this very important task.

- ✆ Check out online sites where you can find sample wedding vows.

- ✆ Ask your officiant for a vows template that you can work off of. You may just discover that his basic vows are perfect as is for your big day.

Bottom line—if you want to keep your wedding budget in check, vows should be the last thing you spend your hard-earned bucks on.

The Lowdown on Decorations and Accessories

If flowers are going to eat up about 5 percent of the average wedding budget (or about $1,850), that doesn't mean you have to end up doing everything yourself just to save money. Sometimes a florist can be a bride's best friend— and an economical one, too—as long as two things happen. One, you are upfront with the florist about the limitations of your budget, and two, your florist is willing to work within your budget guidelines. Most are, so don't be shy about asking.

When you meet with a florist, right away say, "I can only spend a certain amount on my bouquets, boutonnières, and corsages." That way the florist will know to be creative with choices and offer cost-cutting ideas to get you the flowers and decorations that you want and need for your reception.

"I would recommend using vendors like a florist who works out of his or her home. That's what we did, and we found they did as good a job, if not better, than larger vendors with fancy (and expensive) storefronts. Because they didn't have large overhead costs to cover, they were able to give us a great deal."

—Jessica, Minnesota

This is exactly what one bride did; she told her florist she had $250 budgeted for flowers and ceremony decorations, and she asked the florist to figure out a way to make it work.

She did by choosing mostly in-season blooms with a few exotic stems mixed in. For that $250 the florist created the bride's bouquet of alstromeria, marguerite daises, and purple dendro, with similar bouquets for her two bridesmaids. In addition, that $250 covered boutonnières for the groom and his two attendants, as well as boutonnières for the fathers and grandfathers and corsages for the mothers and grandmothers. One of the ways the florist made the most of her miniscule budget was getting the bride's permission to use carnations in the boutonnières and corsages—who looks at them closely anyway? she reasoned—while reserving the more expensive flowers for the three bouquets. Also, this price covered a vase full of white daisies to put on the table outside the ceremony, and two gigantic tulle bows on poles to decorate the altar.

This goes to show you that even when you're buying flowers for 14 people, plus some decorations, it's possible to do so for only $250.

I can't promise that you, too, will be able to do all of your flowers and decorations for $250, but do read on for economical ways to deal with this part of your wedding plans.

Decorations and Accessories

Before you go crazy shelling out funds for aisle runners, pew bows, and yarmulkes, stop and ask yourself: are all these items really necessary? Do you think it will make your wedding a more memorable event if you walk down the aisle on a veritable sidewalk of white fabric? Will your guests feel more welcomed if a white, tulle bow greets them as they enter their pew? Is it really necessary to have you and your husband's name and your wedding date stamped inside hundreds of skullcaps? If you answer "yes" to all of these questions, then by all means spend the money on these decorations and accessories, but understand how all these extras can put an extra dent in your budget.

Sometimes you can find actual savings within the house of worship. They might have a "props closet" on-site where they stock pew bows, aisle runners, chuppahs, and other accessories that brides frequently use in a wedding. If so, they might loan these items to you for free.

However, if you decide you really don't need these things—and can you tell that I'm leaning toward this option?—then you'll have gone a long way toward saving yourself a ton of money. I mean, if your house of worship has a lovely aisle, why cover it up? Do you really want to have someone in your family tying bows on the pews in the hours before the wedding when they could be spending that time with you? (And if it's not your family member, then you're going to pay someone to do it, which is not good for your budget!) And if you're getting married in a Jewish ceremony, what's wrong with the generic yarmulkes most synagogues stock? If you're a germaphobe and want new ones, fine, get them. But be frugal about it, and don't bother with personalization or any fancy colors. Go with your basic black—black matches everything, right?

Best Bets on Bouquets and Boutonnières

If there's one constant at a wedding, it's that the bride carries flowers as she walks down the aisle. Many brides like to match their flowers to their wedding colors or choose shades that complement their wedding setting. For example, one bride I know held foliage-inspired flowers in reds and oranges for her fall wedding in a local botanical garden.

You, too, can achieve a beautiful bouquet that reflects your wedding colors and/or the wedding season, without spending a lot of money doing so. The average bride spends about $300 on her bouquet, but you don't have to, if you keep the following notions in mind.

Choose In-Season Blooms

The easiest way to keep your bouquet budget in check is to use flowers that are in season and abundantly available at the time of your wedding. That's what the bride mentioned earlier in the chapter did, and look at what a great deal she got. The reason the in-season approach works comes down to simple economics. Peonies, for example, are in ample supply in June, and therefore are an affordable flower for a June bride to choose. However, if you're getting married in December and want peonies, expect to pay a higher price. Because peonies are out of season in December, they will likely have to be flown in from somewhere faraway to fulfill your order, and that's why you'll pay more for peonies (or any other flower) when they're out of season.

Here's a rundown of each month of the year and some familiar flowers that are considered to be in season:

- ⚭ **January:** calla lily, sweet pea, tulip
- ⚭ **February:** calla lily, sweet pea, tulip
- ⚭ **March:** calla lily, sweet pea, tulip
- ⚭ **April:** calla lily, sweet pea, tulip

- **May:** calla lily, lily of the valley, sweet pea, tulip

- **June:** freesia, hydrangea

- **July:** freesia, hydrangea

- **August:** freesia, hydrangea

- **September:** freesia, hydrangea

- **October:** calla lily

- **November:** calla lily, tulip

- **December:** calla lily, sweet pea, tulip

I pulled this information from a variety of sources, and in doing so found three great websites I would recommend you visit while researching in-season flowers: www.romanticflowers.com (search for the "flower chart"); www.aboutflowers.com (this is the website of the Society of American Florists); and www.ccfc.org (the website of the California Cut Flower Commission, a trade association of flower growers). Also, keep in mind that there are a number of wonderful flowers that are available year-round. These include roses, gerber daisies, and eucalyptus.

Armed with this information, you can talk intelligently with your florist or local gardening center about when certain flowers are in bloom and when they're not. That way you can plan your floral choices—and your expected spending on flowers—accordingly.

DON'T TRIP on your **SHOESTRINGS**

When placing your order for corsages, bouquets, boutonnières, and other ceremony flowers, know how many items you'll actually need. At the same time, don't procrastinate putting in your flower order. Because a florist has to order flowers in advance, he may tack on a surcharge for any late additions or orders received too close to the wedding date. And those surcharges could break your floral budget like a stepped-on flower stem.

Keep It Simple, Silly

Who says a bride has to have a cascading bouquet of flowers? You know what looks really elegant—and is really inexpensive? A bride who walks down the aisle holding just three or four calla lilies or a few sprigs of her favorite flower. She can provide the same for her maid of honor and brides-maids or have them hold a single stem each.

Think about the cost savings you'll enjoy when you have to purchase less than two dozen flower stems versus the same number of multiflower bouquets. You'll still outfit your entire wedding party with flowers, but you won't spend a lot doing so.

Let me explain this in terms of simple dollars and sense. Recently, I found 20 fresh calla lily stems sold on the Internet for $79.99. That comes out to about $4 a stem. Compare that with a calla lily bouquet I found at a national floral retailer. This bouquet of only four blooms cost $96. If you were to purchase from the first florist and buy four stems only, you would have paid $16 instead of $96, saving yourself $80 in the process!

In addition to going with loose stems of calla lilies, another way to create an elegant-looking bouquet that doesn't cost a bunch is to go for something like a hand-tied ribbon around a cluster of tulips. When it comes to bou-quets, sure you're paying for the flowers but you're paying for labor, too. If you can cut down on the intricacy of your bouquet, you'll cut your costs at the same time.

Visit a Nontraditional Florist

Have you been to a mega-supermarket lately? Did you notice the flowers they have? Not only do many supermarkets sell fresh cut flowers these days, but they may have added a florist to their staff—a florist who might do your wedding flowers a lot cheaper than the competition. The same thing may apply to warehouse stores, like Sam's Club, Costco, or BJ's Warehouse. They, too, may have an affordable florist on hand to work with you.

Both a supermarket florist and a warehouse club florist may be able to offer you drop-dead flower arrangements for dirt-cheap prices. However, like with most things at these clubs, you've got to buy in bulk to get your biggest savings. Case in point: you can get all the bouquets and centerpieces you need for your wedding at Costco, but you have to be planning a big wedding for their bargain to be worth your time. For example, one floral package that Costco offers is a sunflower arrangement that includes the following:

- ⚭ 9 bouquets

- ⚭ 12 corsages

- ⚭ 12 boutonnières

- ⚭ 6 centerpieces

- ⚭ 1 basket of yellow petals for the flower girl to throw

The cost? $879.99, which may seem like a lot, but when you break it down, that adds up to about $20 per arrangement. In the world of flowers, that's fantastic. Also, what you're getting isn't too shabby, either. The bridal bouquet, for instance, includes four big sunflower blooms, hand-tied with Queen Anne's lace and eucalyptus. A similar-looking bouquet at a chain florist costs $55.

Not only can these clubs offer you floral packages, but they can act as your flower wholesaler as well—good to know if you're going to be doing your flowers yourself. Recently, I saw 80 gerber daisy stems, also at Costco, for $45, or about 50¢ a bloom.

So the next time you stop in to your favorite warehouse club for bread, milk, or a 120 pack of toilet paper, look at what the floral department has to offer. You may be surprised by the deals.

Go With Nature

If you, your fiancé, a friend, or a family member is an avid gardener and has the flowers to show for it, why not consider using hand-picked flowers from their garden for your wedding? Yes, that's right, I'm suggesting you don gardening gloves and boots and pick your own wedding flowers.

Think about it this way—it's a free option. Also, it's exactly what I did on the morning of my wedding. My mother and I visited her heirloom garden (my mom is a master gardener, so her garden is pretty impressive) and picked a variety of flowers that were in bloom. Then with colored wire and ribbons, which we picked up at a craft store for a few bucks, we quickly put together the ribbon-wrapped bouquets we needed for the big day.

If you don't have a garden, do you know someone who does? Might that person allow you to pick your flowers and some greenery from her garden? Another idea would be to contact your local gardening club, and see if you can work out a deal with them that will give you access to their gardens. You can find a local club by visiting the National Gardening Association's website at www.garden.org.

Consider Dried Flowers

One of the saddest things about wedding flowers is that in a week (or even by the end of the day), they're a wilted mess. It's sad because they don't live very long, and it's sad because if you spent a lot of money on your flowers, you will have only enjoyed them for a short period of time. But what if you could make your wedding flowers last forever—a sort of cryogenics for your bouquet? And what if this option was actually cheaper than fresh flowers? Then you should consider using dried flowers for your bouquet. One bride I know was able to arm 20 people with bouquets and boutonnières for only $60 because she chose to use dried flowers.

DON'T TRIP on your **SHOESTRINGS**

When leafing through bridal magazines, it's important to remember that bridal magazine spreads of flowers are often done without your budget—or any budget, for that matter—in mind. Keep your wits about you as you fold down the corners of pages or tear them out to take with you to the florist, because that bouquet you loved on the pages of the magazine might just cost more than your car payment. One bride from Pennsylvania fell in love with a bouquet she'd seen in her favorite bridal magazine and ordered an exact replica from her florist. This bouquet featured pink roses and hot pink feathers and cost her more than $200—the amount she'd hoped to spend on everyone's flowers, not just her own.

Believe it or not, an association of florists, called the International Freeze Dry Floral Association, specialize in dried flowers. You can use this association's website at www.ifdfa.org to search for florists near you that work in dried flowers, or you can simply ask your local florists if they work with dried flowers.

If you've never seen dried flowers, I suggest you find a nearby florist who can show you how great they look. If you visit the IFDFA website and click on a link to a local florist, you'll often find examples of their work online.

Go Figure

Use the following worksheet to figure out how many sets of flowers and floral arrangements you'll need to buy for your wedding ceremony.

How many women need bouquets (bride included)   _____

How many women need corsages   _____

How many men need boutonnières   _____

How many pews/chairs will need flowers   _____

How many altar flowers are necessary, if needed   _____

What miscellaneous flowers are needed (arrangements for entrance, powder room, etc.)   _____

Total number of floral orders you need to place with florist   _____

Checking Out Ceremony Flowers

A good reason to have your ceremony in a pretty location is that you won't have to decorate with ceremony flowers—or anything else, for that matter! Take my cousin Cara, who held her wedding in the Brooklyn Botanical Gardens. Because her wedding was outside and surrounded by the entire flora in the gardens, all she needed for her ceremony were the chairs for guests to sit on and her wedding canopy or chuppah. That's it. Given that the gardens supplied the chairs, her ceremony decoration bill added up to a big fat goose egg—or $0.

"We got married in December and spent zero dollars on decorations. Everything was already decorated with poinsettias for the holidays at the church and the restaurant where we had the reception."

—Stephanie, North Carolina

I know Christian brides who've waited until Christmas to get married so their church already would be decorated with poinsettias for the holidays. But what if you aren't getting married around the time of a holiday? Often houses of worship are decorated with flowers throughout the year, giving them a fresh appearance regardless of the weather outside. I implore you to take a critical look at your ceremony space and see if you really do need to add any flowers or other kinds of decorations to it. You may be surprised to discover that your ceremony location can hold its own without any accoutrements.

Why Recycling and Reusing Flowers Makes Sense

Now let's say you do need or want to have ceremony decorations. Well, you can still do it on the cheap, if you plan ahead to recycle them. Case in point: you can put fresh cut, dried, or silk flowers in standing containers, which you can pick up for a nominal price at a craft store. Use these flower-filled containers to line the ceremony aisle. When your ceremony is over, have a bridesmaid, usher, or family friend transfer those containers to the tables at the reception where they'll moonlight as your centerpieces. (Turn to Chapter 4 for more information on receptions, including table centerpieces.)

My cousin recently did this at his wedding, with pillars topped with calla lilies. First, these pillars lined the ceremony aisle. An hour later they stood at the center of the reception tables. And it wasn't obvious that these were the same decorations from the reception—I'm guessing I'm the only one who noticed because of the kinds of books I write for a living! Since your guests probably aren't wedding experts, chances are they'll never notice a doubly used decoration.

Another way to recycle ceremony decorations is to use someone else's. Yes, I'm talking about hand-me-down flowers. Here's how to do it.

Ask your ceremony location about any wedding that might be occurring the day before or the morning of your own wedding. It's possible that there is a ceremony before yours that is being extravagantly decorated. Once that wedding is over, the previous couple may be leaving the flowers and other decorations behind, which means "cha-ching" for you. Ask if it would be okay to keep those decorations in place so that you'll come into a fully furnished ceremony location that was free (for you) to decorate. Plus, the location will save some money on their cleaning bill—since they won't have to discard the decorations between ceremonies. That might be incentive enough for them to let you use the previous bride's decorations.

My friend Jeanne pulled this off as she was planning her traditional Jewish wedding. During a conversation with her florist about how she wanted to decorate her chuppah with fresh flowers, he remarked that he was going to decorate another bride's chuppah for her wedding in the same synagogue the night before Jeanne's. Since the bride wasn't interested in taking the chuppah with her, the florist offered the reuse of it to Jeanne. This chuppah, made of wisteria branches and decorated with fresh flowers, was costing the other bride about $2,000. The only catch was the florist wanted to charge Jeanne $100 to freshen the flowers the day of her wedding. Jeanne negotiated him down to $60.

Ask About a Congregation Discount

Oftentimes houses of worship will have an established relationship with a florist—usually if the church or synagogue gets fresh flowers delivered each week for the sanctuary. If so, ask your contact at the house of worship if you could place your floral order through them. Doing so might net you their volume discount. A bride I know in New Jersey got her flowers this way. Thanks to that discount, available to parishioners only, she secured all of the flowers she needed for only $180.

Transportation Options

Getting to the church (or synagogue) on time is key for a wedding to go off without a hitch, but there's no reason to book the Hummer limousine to get there. Besides, have you seen the prices of those things? And with gas costing what it does these days, I shudder to think about how that kind of extravagance could deep-six your financial plans.

There are a number of ways to get a great car to take you to and from your wedding. For starters, you can get that limo you love, just don't tell the company that you're using it for a wedding. It's amazing how much more companies will charge brides and grooms. For example, at a limousine company near me, the price for a six-person, stretch limousine jumps from $60 an hour, with a three-hour minimum—or $180—to $275 for three hours when you book that same car for a wedding. True, with the latter price you get a tuxedoed driver, plus free soda, ice, and water in the car. But is a driver and some refreshments really worth almost $100?

"We chose a party van rather than a limo and rented it from a local agency. It was so much cheaper, because with our big wedding party, we would have needed at least two cars to take everyone from the ceremony to the reception. This way we all fit in the van."

—Kim, Ohio

Another idea is to rent a car instead of, basically, renting a car and driver. Recently, I discovered that you could get a Lincoln Town Car (the vehicle most traditional limos are built on) for about $90 for 24 hours. Sure, you have to drive it, but you'll be paying for an entire day what it would have cost you per hour ($90) to get that wedding limousine mentioned earlier. If you like the idea of renting a car, you can have some fun with the car you choose. I know plenty of brides who arrived at their wedding in a PT Cruiser, VW Beetle, or Mini Cooper. And who says the car has to be white? Brides today choose cars in an array of colors—from basic black to flaming red.

There's nothing wrong with thinking frugally about your wedding transportation. And if you're having your ceremony and reception in the same place, why bother spending money on a fancy car at all?

If you'll likely arrive well ahead of your guests, or everyone will already be inside by the time you get there, why make a big deal with a fancy car that will put a big dent in your budget? No one is going to see your mode of transportation anyway.

Walking is also an option if your ceremony and reception locations are nearby. In fact, it's a fantastic option for the frugal bride because it's free! Just invest in some umbrellas at the dollar store in case it rains, or have someone's car on standby if you'd rather ride in the rain (a good idea so you don't ruin your dress).

Dollar-Saving Do's and Don'ts

Even if your ceremony doesn't end up costing as much as your reception, it's still a smart move to use your budget wisely as you plan everything. Here's a recap of some of the ceremony savings ideas from this chapter:

- ✆ Do think first about having your ceremony in your own house of worship. It's often your cheapest option for a religious setting.

- ✆ Do consider a college chapel for your ceremony, especially if you qualify for an alumni discount.

- ✆ Don't fret over an officiant's fee, especially if it's reasonable. No matter where you tie the knot, you'll likely have to pay someone to officiate at it.

- ✆ Don't assume a large wedding party is a must. Smaller is often cheaper when it comes to attendants.

- ✆ Do think about how your metal choices and the use of semi-precious stones can affect the cost of your wedding rings.

- ✆ Don't waste your money on having someone write your vows when your officiant can supply them for you for free.

- ✆ Don't go crazy buying ceremony decorations and accessories just because you think you have to have them. Your wedding will be just fine without the aisle runner or the pew bows.

❧ Do figure out ahead of time how many items you'll need to order from the florist. Adding arrangements or additional bouquets as time goes on can run up your bill with surcharges.

❧ Do keep the notion of in-season flowers in mind as a cost-saving option. While most flowers these days are available year-round, you will pay more for your favorite bloom when it's not in season. So if you're sweet on sweet peas and want to have that flower in your bouquet, you'd best have your wedding sometime between December and May, when sweet peas are readily available and cheaper to buy.

❧ Do tell your florist your floral budget and ask her to stick to it.

❧ Don't disregard the notion of less is more. Sometimes a bride can look more elegant holding a single flower than a huge bouquet that looks overwhelming.

❧ Don't think that fresh flowers are your only option. Freeze-dried flowers are a great alternative for the bride on a budget.

❧ Do look into creative and affordable ways to get to and from your wedding, such as renting a car instead of renting a limo.

4

Getting Ready for Your Reception

For certain families, weddings follow tradition, no questions asked. You get married at the house of worship where everyone else in the family has been married; you register in the same stores as your forefathers and foremothers; and you hold your reception where all of your relatives have held theirs. I'm guessing that if you've bought this book, this doesn't describe you or your family. Good. Not that anything's wrong with following tradition, but it doesn't leave a lot of wiggle room for shopping around or negotiating.

By shopping around, you can score some really great deals for reception locations or caterers. When I was planning my wedding, I probably interviewed and tasted the food of three or four local caterers. I had my heart set on one of them, who, I'll admit, was a bit above our budget, but he came with such great recommendations I was willing to bite the budget bullet. Then a friend told me about a great caterer she'd just used for a corporate event, someone located clear across the county and completely off my radar screen.

I called this caterer, brainstormed menus, and liked what I heard. When my husband and I finally met with her (and devoured the samples she'd set out for us), we were smitten—with her food and her prices. She was able to put together a more extensive menu, with more creative items on it, for about half what the other guy had said he would charge. Bringing this gal on board would mean we could cut our wedding expenses in half.

The same thing happened with Chris and Carley, who wanted to hold their reception in a restaurant in Connecticut. Every place they visited kept quoting $50 a head for a buffet dinner. The couple was disappointed that the best they could do was $50 per person.

At the point when they were almost ready to give up, they stumbled upon a restaurant with good reviews, great food, and a menu comparable to the competition—but with competitive prices: $20 per person. "We had about 135 people at the wedding and were prepared to pay $6,750 to feed them. But when we found this place at $20 and discovered we'd be saving $4,000 in the process, we booked the place on the spot," recalls Chris.

But Chris and Carley's story is even sweeter because, like any smart couple planning a wedding, they got everything in writing in a contract, including the per-head price that had convinced them to book the place. A few months later the restaurant doubled its price to $40 per person, but because of the contract, they honored the $20-a-head price. Their reception only set them back $2,700.

An Offbeat Locale Can Save You Tons of Money

Besides shopping around for good prices, a clever way to make your reception affordable is to hold it in an offbeat location. For example, I recently learned of a couple who had met at camp during their teen years and decided to hold their wedding back at the camp. They were married in the summer when the camp was in session, but on the weekend; they were able to take advantage of the existing tables, china, silverware, and everything else they needed to feed their guests. Yes, theirs was a more casual reception than most, but when the final bill came in, they'd shelled out less than their parents had spent to send them to summer camp so many years ago!

Money in Your Pocket

Want to hear something really scary? Most couples planning a wedding reception these days can expect to spend about $9,300. Granted, this price includes the reception space, food, liquor, linens, and more, but it doesn't include everything else that goes into a reception, such as the music (more about that in Chapter 7). And when you consider the mission of this book is to help you plan a wedding for around $5,000, spending almost double that on just the reception really gives you pause.

Like everything else I'll discuss in this guide, you don't have to take a follow-the-masses approach to your reception. Just because the average American couple spends close to $10,000 on a reception, that doesn't mean you can't do yours for significantly less. There are ways to bring your reception costs in well under that number without compromising on food or setting, or cutting your guest list.

One bride was able to pull off her wedding for 100 for only $3,500. How? For starters, she booked her reception at the local college, which has a special events space. In addition, this college includes a culinary arts and hotel management program, so they really know how to do food-oriented special occasions well. Best of all, the $35-a-head price included everything she would need for a reception—caterer, servers, tables, chairs, linens, cutlery, drinks, and more.

In fact, many couples who figure out how to do their reception affordably have figured out that reception locations that don't nickel-and-dime you about add-ons, like linens or liquor, are the places where you're going to find the best deals.

Savings for you: $5,800   **Running total: $39,793**

Another bride knew she'd be having a bunch of children at her wedding and didn't want them to be bored at the reception. Not content to hire babysitters or a clown to entertain the kiddies, this bride decided to take her guests to an unexpected place for the reception—a local water park! Granted, most brides probably wouldn't willingly wear a bathing suit for their reception celebration, but the deal this bride was able to negotiate was just too good to pass up. For $1,500 she was able to pay for a BBQ meal, plus drinks and dessert, for her 50 guests, along with all-day passes to the park (rides included)! Talk about your memorable, albeit wet, wedding reception.

When considering offbeat locations, don't automatically think that museums are a bride's best budget friend. Many museums have discovered the big business to be had in weddings, and now they're a really expensive venue for most events. (Having to pay for killer insurance to protect the art during your affair doesn't help, either.)

However, don't automatically write off other kinds of historical or artistic spaces, either—you know, as long as they're not the Metropolitan Museum of Art in New York City or the Capitol Rotunda in Washington, D.C.

You can still find deals at smaller historical spots, especially the kinds run by a city or town's recreation department, which really isn't in the business to make money off of special events. I know a bride who booked just such a place near her home in Northern Virginia. The space came complete with tables, linens, china, and an in-house caterer. This is important, because most "empty" spaces like museums make you rent those separately and then charge you an arm and a leg for the honor. All told, she was able to have her five-hour reception for more than a hundred friends for about $900. When she found out that most brides in her area couldn't even rent a space, let alone feed everyone, for less than $3,000, she knew she'd gotten a really good deal.

"We had our wedding reception at my in-laws' house, which happens to have a professional-grade kitchen in it. To keep our food costs down, we simply purchased food in bulk from Sam's Club—cheese plates, fruit platters, crackers, tamales, pasta, you name it—and used that to serve our 80 guests. We stocked up on beer, wine, and champagne, too. All told, we were able to have our fabulous reception for less than $600."

—Susanna, Colorado

If you're interested in discovering the historical and cultural buildings an area has to offer, I would recommend getting in touch with chambers of commerce, tourism organizations, and historical societies. Some have likely already checked out places that are appropriate for weddings and may even have a resource booklet to share with you.

Churches and Fire Halls Can Offer Affordable Options

If you are members of a house of worship, have you considered holding your reception in the fellowship hall? It may not be the most fashion-forward place to throw a party, but chances are it's going to be a great deal. One couple booked such a space when they discovered that, as members of the congregation, they could rent the place for free!

What also makes a fellowship hall or even a fire hall an attractive option is they are usually fully stocked for something like a wedding reception—in that they usually have tables, chairs, linens, silver, china, and an industrial-size kitchen, meaning you won't have to bring in anything but the man-power to make your reception a reality.

Likely the only work you'll have to do is dressing up the space, since fire halls don't look like fancy hotels on the inside. Potted plants, clusters of balloons, and fresh flowers can accomplish this. See if the fire hall even has these kinds of dressing-up props on hand that you can use for a small fee or free. Some fire halls will let you take your decorating one step further by taking down all their framed photos of fire chiefs, and replacing them with your own framed family wedding pictures from home.

How Time of Day Can Save You Money

When you have a wedding ceremony that begins late in the afternoon, with a reception occurring around dinner time, your guests are going to expect a full meal—and rightly so. They're going to be hungry, and you should feed them. But if you're looking to scale back on your reception spending, think carefully about your timing.

"We had a morning wedding, so no one expected a large meal or alcohol at the reception," says Ramona, a bride in Colorado. "Instead, we purchased simple meat trays and bread so everyone could make light sandwiches." In addition to light sandwiches, Ramona and her husband served their guests fruit and dessert. It was a simple, inexpensive, and classy reception.

Another bride I know did something similar with a ceremony a little later in the day. After saying "I do" at 2 P.M., everyone went to the reception. However, since her guests had arrived at the wedding having already eaten lunch, by the time they got to her reception at 4 P.M., they were a little hungry but not quite ready for dinner. That's how she was able to get away with an hors d'oeuvres-only affair.

And we're not talking just a few deviled eggs passed around before the cake. This bride had arranged for an hour's worth of finger food, with more than a dozen selections circulating the room; there was more than enough food to fill everyone up. Also, people weren't just standing around. There were many small, round tables and chairs for everyone to sit down and enjoy the revolving door of food.

The only formally served food occurred after they'd cut the cake, when servers placed plates of slices out for the guests to take. Again everyone sat down and enjoyed the food. It's no wonder this bride was able to pull off a wedding reception for 180 for only $3,000!

Here's another way time of day can save you money: most people want to have a wedding on a Saturday night, and if you do, too, you're going to pay premium prices. However, if you move your reception to a Friday night, Saturday afternoon, or even Sunday night (great if you're getting married on a holiday weekend), you'll likely find more flexibility in caterers' prices. I've had catering managers admit to me that they can cut their prices by 30 percent or more when you choose a nontraditional night in an off-season month.

Why Weddings Are Cheaper in the Off-Season

You'll find similar flexibility, or rather negotiability, if you approach caterers or other reception locales about having your wedding during the off-season.

Since most people want to get married in either June or September, that's when weddings cost the most. Weddings in the months surrounding June and September can be pricey, too, since couples often consider May, July, August, or October the second-best time to tie the knot. So what does that mean? November through April is the time when you could probably find terrific deals on receptions, if not every other aspect of your wedding, but there are exceptions to the off-season months, too. For example, because families like to gather together for Thanksgiving, the weekends before and after Thanksgiving usually come with premium prices. In addition, because brides and grooms will be competing with office holiday parties for function space in December, there may be less availability and higher prices. Finally, New Year's Eve is a popular night to tie the knot, regardless of the day of the week. So if you've dreamed of ringing in the New Year with an exchange of rings, your shoestring budget may not be able to accommodate your dreams.

Think about the off-season this way—it's simply a case of supply and demand. There is a lot of demand from brides and grooms in the warm-weather months, so the people who supply the services can charge higher prices. However, in the off months, the balance of power flips to your advantage. Because there isn't as great a demand, suppliers, who want to make ends meet, will likely be more open-minded about negotiating their prices. Of course, this may not be true in all cases, but in all my years of writing about weddings, I've found the couples that get the best deals on their weddings do so when they know they have the stronger negotiating position; i.e., they're getting married during a less busy time of the year.

One other tip that might not make your groom happy but your bank account jump for joy: Super Bowl Sunday is often the cheapest day of the year to have a wedding. One expert told me that places have slashed their fees by up to 70 percent on this one day, because no one thinks about having a special event.

Mouthwatering Menus and Meal Plans That Don't Cost a Lot

As I mentioned in the previous section, time of day saved one bride a ton of money on her reception, and it worked for me, too. When my husband and

I decided to make our reception a Sunday brunch versus a Saturday night dinner, our prices plummeted and rightly so. It is way cheaper to have your caterer prepare muffins, omelets, and fresh fruit rather than chicken, beef, or steak entrées with all the side dishes people expect with a dinner.

DON'T TRIP
on your **SHOESTRINGS**

> With all this talk of per-head or per-person prices, it's easy to get lulled into thinking that's all you'll have to spend.
>
> Whenever a caterer or anyone else quotes you a per-person/head price, make sure you ask, "What does that price cover?" You want the number to be as all-inclusive as possible so you can get a realistic sense of how much you're going to spend on your reception. So if an off-premises caterer says he charges $15 a head but that covers food only, somewhere along the line you're going to have to add in the cost of everything else you'll need at your reception—drinks, linens, china, chairs, and more. On the other hand, on-premises caterers usually come with all the supplies needed, which is why on the face of it they may seem more expensive. But make sure you're comparing apples to apples when comparing caterers' prices—that these prices reflect the same services.

If you're looking to get the most bang out of your reception buck without having to cut your guest list, I strongly suggest you think about menu alternatives that might not have been on your radar—such as the Sunday brunch option.

But what about the notion of supplying your own food or having a potluck reception? If your family and friends are the potluck kind of people, this might make your wedding reception exceptionally affordable. Even if they're not, it's definitely a way to be able to feed a ton of people and not slash your guest list.

It's the option one couple I know went with, but only after they'd surveyed their friends and family about it. Because the couple works in the arts and the people close to them knew they didn't have a lot of money to spare, everyone was more than willing to chip in for their wedding. That included bringing a covered dish to share with the 200 other folks who would be there that day. In order to avoid duplications, the couple broke up the guest list by last name and assigned each group something different: A-F got appetizers; G-P got the main course; R-Z brought dessert. The couple did splurge on a real wedding cake and also picked up the tab for soft drinks, beer, and wine.

What added a special touch to the potluck nature of the reception was what many of the guests did—they brought their culinary contribution in a serving dish that doubled as the couple's gift. Given that the two had been living on hand-me-down serving utensils and cookware since college, they really appreciated the crock-pot, covered dish, pasta bowls, and other pieces that would go home with them and stock their kitchen cabinets.

How Liquor Can Inflate Your Bar Bill

Probably the easiest way to blow your reception budget is to offer an open bar that stocks a full range of drinks, including top-shelf liquor and premium brands. Everyone will drink to their heart's content, but you will have likely added a huge cost to your catering bill because of it.

There is no reason for you to take the financial hit so your guests can drink themselves senseless at your reception. That's not to say that you should go to the other extreme and have a dry reception (unless, of course, that's your preference). But you can find a way to offer your friends and family spirits and still end up in the black at the end of the night.

"The only drinks we offered at the wedding reception were water, lemonade, and unlimited champagne. No one seemed to mind."

—Maggie, Florida

Sensible Ways to Serve Alcohol

In this section, I'm going to help you figure out how to serve alcohol at your reception and still remain in the black. First, I'll make some broad suggestions. Then I'll provide worksheets and formulas so you can figure out just the right amount of alcohol to buy.

One of the first ways to keep your alcohol bill in check is to negotiate with your caterer to let you stock your own bar. This will help you avoid any unnecessary markups.

The second way is to limit the alcoholic selections at the reception. I would start with red and white wine as your basic drink offering. Why? Because wine works equally well as a cocktail and as a drink during dinner.

If you want to offer mixed drinks, again, limit the selections to keep your bar tab within reach. I recommend stocking gin and vodka so you could have gin and tonics, vodka tonics, and all the other combinations you can create with gin and vodka and mixers like tonic and club soda.

At my 150-person brunch wedding reception, we had negotiated ahead of time with our caterer to stock our own bar. She helped us brainstorm what to serve. We ended up buying white wine, champagne, gin, and vodka. We also had tonic, club soda, regular and diet soda, and orange and tomato juice available. That gave our guests the option of having soft drinks or juice. If they wanted something alcoholic, they could have mimosas, Bloody Marys, vodka tonics, gin and tonics, or straight champagne and wine. These were enough options that our guests didn't feel like they were being cheated, and we didn't spend more than a couple hundred dollars stocking the entire bar.

And the third way is to figure out ahead of time how much liquor you'll need to buy based on the number of guests you'll be entertaining.

"We limited alcohol at the reception to beer and wine only. Our one splurge was champagne to serve with the cake. However, since we bought it in bulk at a local winery, it was cheaper than anything we would have found at the liquor store."

—Cari, Michigan

Figuring out how much hard liquor, like gin and vodka, to buy is a bit trickier than with wine. On average (and remember this is just an average) a regular-size bottle of gin or vodka should yield about 27 mixed drinks. Most people who have mixed drinks have about two of them during a cocktail hour. With this number in mind, you can figure out how many bottles you'll need for your limited bar. However, if you're also offering wine during the cocktail hour and dinner, you may want to cut your liquor consumption expectations by a quarter or even a half, since more people drink wine with dinner than mixed drinks, and then up your wine purchase by about 25 percent.

Go Figure

Figuring out how much alcohol to buy for your wedding can be a tricky test of your arithmetic. Hopefully, the following worksheet will make your job a bit easier.

When it comes to wine, you should estimate one 750 ml bottle of wine will serve two people over a two-hour period. Or order one bottle for every two guests, for every two hours of your reception. For every hour over that two-hour period, increase your wine purchase by 50 percent.

Step 1: The number of guests you'll have at your reception   _____

Step 2: Based on a 2 to 1 ratio (2 guests per bottle of wine), the number of bottles of wine you need to buy   _____

Step 3: The number of hours you expect your reception to last   _____

Step 4: For a two-hour reception multiply Step 2 by 1. For a three-hour reception, multiply Step 2 by 1.5. For a four-hour reception, multiply Step 2 by 2 (and so on).   _____

Step 5: Final number of bottles of wine you need to purchase to serve your guests for the duration of your reception   _____

If you want to serve more than one kind of wine, divide Step 5 by the number of different kinds of wines you plan to serve. This will give you the number of bottles you need to buy for each variety of wine you will be serving.

If you do the math based on 150 guests, with each guest having two mixed drinks during the cocktail hour, you would need 12 bottles of gin and/or vodka to keep their whistles wet. If wine is on the menu and you don't plan to serve mixed drinks at dinner, you might be safe with eight bottles. However, you'll know best, based on the drinking habits of your friends and family, where you should up your liquor purchases and where you can hold back.

Finally, if you end up having someone else stock your bar, keep in mind that they may charge you an "uncorking" fee, meaning you pay for only the number of bottles of spirits opened during the affair. The only problem with this scenario is it's possible for a bartender to uncork more bottles that can be served during your affair. That means you'll end up paying for liquor no one got to enjoy. I would appoint someone to approach the bar about three-quarters of the way through your reception and ask them to stop opening new bottles of wine and liquor. At this point, cake and coffee are on the horizon, so it's a natural place to stop serving the alcoholic drinks that people enjoyed throughout dinner. If you must keep wine flowing, at least choose a dessert wine that pairs well with dessert. (You can speak to your caterer, bartender, or a clerk at a liquor store for recommendations for dessert wines.)

DON'T TRIP on your **SHOESTRINGS**

The best part about stocking your own bar at the reception is that you get to take home any leftovers. However, you won't be able to enjoy these leftovers if the person who is tending bar opens every bottle of wine at the start of the night—you know, to save time on getting the cork out. Explain clearly to the bartender that he or she is to open the wine one or two bottles at a time. Explain that you want to be able to take unused bottles home with you, not have to pour them (and your savings) down the drain at the end of the night.

Taking the Cake with Cake and Dessert Savings

At one of my first jobs out of college, I worked with a gal who dreamed of one day owning her own bakery. To get her feet wet in the pastry world, she baked wedding cakes on the side. Because her tiny apartment wouldn't allow for the oversize pans she needed for her cake-baking, she worked out a deal with a local pizza joint that she could use their enormous ovens after hours for her baking. She didn't charge much for her cakes—maybe a hundred dollars—but I know her customers were happy because they continued to recommend her to their friends and family members who were planning weddings.

The reason I'm offering this anecdote is because, until you've started talking with cake bakers, you probably have no idea how much wedding cakes cost. Forget the prices you've paid for a Carvel ice cream cake or a sheet cake in the supermarket: wedding cakes are a big and expensive deal. From the bakers I've spoken with, you can expect to pay anywhere from $3 to $10 per person for a cake. (Bakers price cakes this way to ensure they make a cake that can feed all of your guests.) If you're having a 100-person wedding, that means you can expect to pay $300 to $1,000 for your cake. Obviously, bigger weddings require bigger cakes. Also, the more intricate your cake becomes, with decorations, layers, and multiple flavors, the more you're going to pay.

"Since not everyone likes cake, we only ordered a cake that could feed half the people. We supplemented our dessert with chocolate-covered strawberries and cannoli."

—Nancy, Georgia

By any chance, do you know someone who bakes cakes on the side? If so, that person may be able to offer you the best deal on your dessert—and likely the freshest, most delicious cake you can find—without charging the $3 to $10 a person prices that traditional bakers do. Think about it this way: if she's a freelance baker and doesn't have to bake multiple cakes to put on display in some store, you know she will make your confection just for your event, which is how it should be. And, like my former colleague, she won't rip you off with over-the-top prices. Also, if this freelance cake baker is a good friend, she may just give you the cake as her wedding gift.

Want a designer-inspired cake? In your favorite bridal magazine, find pictures of the cake you'd love to serve at your wedding, and then ring up your local culinary school to see if any pastry whizzes there can do the job for peanuts. People who are studying to become chefs are just the kind of folks who know their way around marzipan and all that fancy confection that makes cakes look like works of art—but without the museum prices.

Another way to cut your cake costs is to have a cake that may not look like a wedding cake at all. I'm talking about a traditional sheet cake. I mean, who made the rule that wedding cakes have to have tiers? Serve your guests a flat (and cheaper) cake, and they'll never know the difference. Warehouse clubs like BJ's and Sam's have bakeries on-site that can cook up a fresh cake to serve your guests and won't charge you a bundle in the process. You can use fresh flowers to decorate a basic cake so it will look as delicious as it tastes.

Or do a combination of cakes. You can use a smaller, tiered cake for cutting and display. Then you can have a sheet cake that you'll use to feed your guests.

You also have another cake option that isn't a cake at all—cupcakes. I know, it's so *Sex and the City* to talk about cupcakes, but you know what? It's really affordable! I know a couple who bought 330 cupcakes to serve their 115 guests (they wanted people to be able to have seconds), and their cupcake bill added up to $330. At about $2 a person, this is a significant savings over a traditional wedding cake that starts at $3 a person. And remember: the folks at the cupcake wedding budgeted for two cupcakes per person so, really, the price was $1 per person, plus seconds.

If you're wedded to the notion of a traditional cake, but you love the idea of serving cupcakes, consider this—get a tiered cupcake serving stand and stack your cupcakes up to look like a cake. You can ask your friends and family to bake a batch of cupcakes to use at the reception as your wedding gift. Or you can visit a warehouse club like BJ's or Sam's to pick up a palette of 100-plus cupcakes, which you'll find in the bakery department.

Floral Centerpiece Savings

Much of the cost-saving advice for bouquets and boutonnières in the previous chapter applies to your centerpieces as well. That is, if you want fresh flowers and still want to keep your costs to a minimum, think about ordering flowers that are in season. Or go with dried or silk flowers as an economical—and long-lasting—option.

Another way to keep your costs down: keep your wedding colors minimal or to a more "normal" palette. Primary colors or those found easily in nature—yellow, purple, pink—will be cheaper for your florist to work with than more unusual or "unnatural" colors that he has to dye or special order.

Money in Your Pocket

When a bride I know was planning her wedding, she knew she was going to have 14 tables at her reception and she wanted a gorgeous centerpiece on each of those tables. However, when her florist told her it would cost $1,500 for the centerpieces, or about $100 per table, the bride said "No way."

Did she give up her idea on centerpieces altogether? Nope. And neither should you if you find out that someone wants to charge you way more than you want to pay for centerpieces. If you figure out how to get your supplies at a discount and maybe consider making your centerpieces yourself, you'll save a bundle.

Here's how this bride got $1,500 worth of centerpieces for only $215. For starters, she knew she wanted each table decoration to be a cluster of roses and wildflowers in a fishbowl-like vase. So she checked out a local crafts store and found her desired vases for about $1 each. After that she went online to see if there were any nearby flower wholesalers who sold to the public. There was one who specialized in roses, and through this outfit, she got seven dozen roses for $200. Finally, friends who own a farm opened up their garden to her, where she picked sunflowers and gerber daisies for free. She, together with these friends, spent the afternoon using the freshly picked flowers, the store-bought roses, and the vases to make her centerpieces.

Savings for you: $1,285   **Running total: $41,078**

Table Decorations That Don't Break the Bank

No rule says centerpieces have to be flowers only. Consider these other table decoration ideas that don't involve a florist. I'm confident any of these options will look as lovely as flowers but will be a heck of a lot cheaper:

- ✆ **Clusters of food.** A bowl of silver and gold Hershey kisses can look appetizing at the center of each table. So can fresh pears, apples, or other fruits and vegetables of the season. Having a fall wedding? Many people these days are, now that September is the number-one month for weddings. Why not have your table centerpieces reflect the bounty of the season? A cluster of gourds, pumpkins, and ornamental cabbage offer a colorful, unique centerpiece, and they won't cost much to buy at your local grocery store or Home Depot.

❧ **Topiaries.** A topiary created just for you by your florist might be one of a kind for your wedding but it will be an expensive centerpiece, to be sure. I've heard of florists charging $40 or more for each table's topiary. If you're a fan of topiaries but not of their price tags, why not visit a discount retailer that sells housewares and home decor, such as TJ Maxx or Marshall's, and see if you can't find enough artificial topiaries for all of your tables? They may not all match but as long as the topiaries complement one another, you can probably get away with spending about $12 or less for each of your centerpieces. Or sign up for a class at a craft store and learn how to make your own topiaries.

❧ **Candles.** One of the most inexpensive yet romantic ways to decorate your reception tables is to use a collection of candles. You can pick up candles for a song at a store like Target, or a craft store like AC Moore or The Rag Shop, or even Wal-Mart, which has a big crafts section. If you choose votive candles, you can put five or so of them together in the middle of the table and voilà, you have an inexpensive centerpiece. Prefer tea lights? Then get a shallow, clear bowl, fill it with water, float the tea lights in it, and you have an inexpensive yet effective centerpiece. Stick with these smaller kinds of candles, which tend to be less expensive than pillar-style or taper candles. I've seen packs of 20 tea lights at Target for less than $10, whereas a box of 6 taper candles cost more than $30.

> "We used non-floral centerpieces for our reception table decorations—candles, sparkling garland, mirrors, and clear glass cylinders. Each centerpiece cost about $10."
>
> —Jessica, Minnesota

❧ **Boxes of candy.** If you're getting married at a time of year when you can find an abundance of beautifully wrapped boxes of candy, why not go for a sweet centerpiece of boxed candy? For example, during spring months you might find pastel-wrapped boxes of candy that you can stack into a colorful tower in the middle of each reception table. Or you can visit a store that sells already-made towers of candy boxes, like Harry and David, and use them. Or check the clearance aisles for these goodies after big candy holidays, such as Christmas, Valentine's Day, and Easter, when you'll find great markdowns and lots of nicely wrapped boxes of confections. Bonus: if you buy enough candy for each guest at the table, you can give the candy/centerpiece away as your favors. (More on favors in Chapter 12.)

- ✆ **Freshly potted flowers and other greenery.** Yep, we're back to talking about flowers again, but with a twist. Instead of having your florist supply flowers, why not go to your local gardening center and get potted flowers for your centerpieces? If given enough notice, many gardening retailers will let you purchase pots, potting soil, and plants, and they'll put them all together for you for free. That's the option I used at my wedding reception. It was a cost-saving measure, but a memorable one—to this day, people still remark about the pots of petunias and pansies that adorned my reception tables. If you're getting married at a time of the year when flowers aren't in season, other kinds of potted greenery can easily stand in as a centerpiece. Pots of poinsettias, holly, or other evergreens would look great on a reception table at a winter wedding, for instance.

Don't go through the hassle of creating your own centerpieces—and spending money on them—if your reception locale will provide centerpieces as part of your package deal. For example, some spaces have silk flower arrangements, tiered towers of petit fours, or candelabras on hand for you to use. Ask up front and you might just save a ton by not having to rent or purchase centerpieces.

How Dancing at Your Wedding Affects Your Budget

Whether it's dancing in a circle to the Jewish classic "Hava Nagila" or doing a conga line to "Hot, Hot, Hot!" some of the most fun to be had at a wedding reception is out on the dance floor. Fun, that is, if you come from a family of dancers or if the two of you enjoy the notion of dancing. And you should keep this idea of "to dance or not to dance" in mind as you check out reception sites.

One bride I know admits fully to having the old two left feet problem and stressed out for months about how she was going to get through her first dance or the father-daughter dance. Then it dawned on her—she didn't have to have either dances if she didn't want to. It was her wedding and she'd dance if she wanted to. And guess what? She didn't want to after all.

This decision helped her psychologically, in that it eliminated her concerns about being the center of attention on the dance floor. It took the pressure off of her financially as well. How? Once she realized she didn't want dancing at her wedding, it dawned on her: she didn't need to rent a gigantic space, complete with dance floor, for her reception when no one was going to be dancing anyway. It just didn't make sense. What did make sense was to rent a private room, albeit a big private room, in a restaurant, where she could easily host the 150 guests she planned to have at her wedding.

Also, she didn't have to hire an elaborate band to entertain her guests if all they would be doing is eating and mingling. All she needed was a smaller musical group to provide background music. (More about your musical needs in Chapter 8.)

Why am I telling you all of this? Because if you're not interested in having dancing at your wedding, then make sure the space you choose for your reception doesn't have you paying for things you really don't need, like a place that's big enough to accommodate dancing.

Gift Table

I grew in the New York area where it's customary for people to give money as a gift. However, thanks to my experience writing wedding books, I realized that not everyone who would be coming to my wedding subscribed to the same way of thinking about gifts. That is, for some the proper thing to do is to arrive at a wedding bearing a wrapped gift. With this in mind, I made sure we had a designated gift table at our reception. Boy am I glad we did! By the end of the day, that table was overflowing with boxes.

So what does having a gift table have to do with your wedding plans and your budget? Well, two things. First, you should always plan to have a table or some other place set aside where people can put gifts. If you know a lot of people will be handing you envelopes with money in them, then provide a birdcage, basket, handbag, or some designated place where you can keep all the envelopes. (You can pick these kinds of money holders up at a craft store, or your reception location may even have one left over from another wedding that you can borrow for free.)

Second, designate a person or two to be in charge of getting the gifts from the reception to someone's home for safekeeping. Because if people give you money and you lose it, you hurt yourself financially, especially if you were counting on wedding money to pay your wedding bills.

Transportation to and from Your Reception

Like transportation to your ceremony (which I discussed in Chapter 3), you can save a bundle on transportation to and from your reception if you keep things simple. Here's a brief recap of advice, as it relates to your reception and saving money on transportation.

First, if you must hire a limousine or a fancy white car, don't do it from a company that specializes in weddings. Most have a two- or four-hour minimum, with hourly rates of at least $100, and they'll often jack up the price because they know that people tend to spend more on weddings. Just tell the car company that you need a car to take you from point A (your reception) to point B (the airport, a hotel, home, whatever). I'm pretty confident you'll spend hundreds of dollars less this way. Sure, the driver may be a bit surprised when you climb into the car in your wedding gown, but that's really none of his business.

Second, if you decide to forego the fancy car service, you can rent a car that feels special to you (whatever that kind of car is) and drive yourselves. For me, it would be a white VW bug convertible, but then again, I'm not planning a wedding anytime soon. Again, renting a car only—even for 24 hours—will be much cheaper than renting someone with a car to drive you around.

"We were staying the night in the same hotel where we had the ceremony and reception, so we never paid for any kind of transportation. We ended up taking the hotel's shuttle to the airport the next day instead of a cab, so our only cost ended up being the $10 tip we gave the driver."

—Amanda, Ohio

And speaking of driving you around, your third option could be to have a friend or family member drive you back from the reception, or at least loan you their car so your transportation costs will be practically nothing.

Finally, if you need to shuttle around a large wedding party, just rent a van, trolley, or bus and have everyone ride together. Keep in mind that to keep this kind of ride inexpensive, you need to forego the surround-sound system, mood lighting, and wet bar. As you would expect, these kinds of extras cost extra.

Dollar-Saving Do's and Don'ts

By now I hope you've figured out that you can have an awesome wedding reception without mortgaging your future. Here's a recap of some of the cost-saving ideas we covered in this chapter.

- ✆ Do shop around for caterers and reception sites to ensure you get the best deal possible.

- ✆ Do consider offbeat locations for a reception—they're often cheaper than traditional ones.

- ✆ Don't forget the costs of rentals (tables, chairs, linens, and more) when examining the per-head costs of your reception. If you need to bring all of this in, it's going to up your bill significantly.

- ✆ Do think about having your wedding at any time except a Saturday night or any months but June and September. For these most popular wedding times, you'll pay a premium.

- ✆ Don't let someone convince you that a wedding reception must always include a full meal. You can have just as elegant an affair when you're serving lunch, brunch, hors d'oeuvres, or cake only.

- ✆ Do think carefully about how you're going to handle alcohol at the reception. If left unchecked, a bar bill can really blow a budget.

- ✆ Do check out freelance bakers or culinary students for inexpensive yet yummy cakes.

❧ Don't think you have to serve only wedding cake. Plenty of brides supplement a traditional cake with fruit, pastries, or even cupcakes stacked up to look like a cake.

❧ Do keep the notion of in-season flowers in mind as a cost-saving option, if you must have fresh-flower centerpieces.

❧ Don't think you have to go overboard with your centerpieces. Tea lights floating in a clear bowl of water can be just as beautiful as an ornate candelabra, and they're probably way more affordable.

❧ Do tap into your inner Martha Stewart if you like to make things from scratch. A do-it-yourself centerpiece made in a class at a crafts store will probably be 10 times cheaper than one an expensive florist would make for you.

❧ Do consider objects other than flowers for your centerpieces. Candles, candy, and clusters of food can dress up a reception table just as nicely as flowers can.

❧ Don't pay for a space big enough for dancing if you won't be having any at your reception.

❧ Do designate a gift table at your reception—and someone who is responsible for collecting your bounty at the end of the night.

❧ Do think about your non-limousine options for transportation to and from your reception. Renting a regular car will be much cheaper in the long run, and you'll have use of that car for a longer period of time.

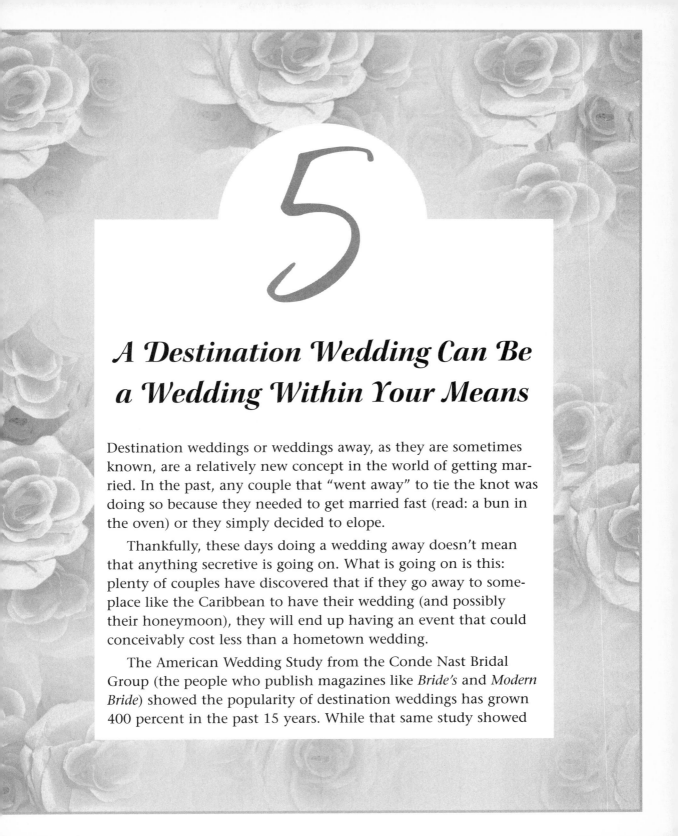

5

A Destination Wedding Can Be a Wedding Within Your Means

Destination weddings or weddings away, as they are sometimes known, are a relatively new concept in the world of getting married. In the past, any couple that "went away" to tie the knot was doing so because they needed to get married fast (read: a bun in the oven) or they simply decided to elope.

Thankfully, these days doing a wedding away doesn't mean that anything secretive is going on. What is going on is this: plenty of couples have discovered that if they go away to someplace like the Caribbean to have their wedding (and possibly their honeymoon), they will end up having an event that could conceivably cost less than a hometown wedding.

The American Wedding Study from the Conde Nast Bridal Group (the people who publish magazines like *Bride's* and *Modern Bride*) showed the popularity of destination weddings has grown 400 percent in the past 15 years. While that same study showed the average destination wedding costs about $25,000 and includes more than 60 guests, don't panic: I've uncovered ways to have the destination wedding of your dreams for a quarter of that price. And I'll help you figure out how to have a decent-size guest list join you. Now if you're looking to have your wedding away at a Four Seasons property somewhere in the Caribbean, I probably can't help you—that's going to be expensive no matter how you slice it. But if you take my advice in this chapter to heart and get creative about how to stretch your wedding dollar, you'll be able to pull off a destination wedding that doesn't deplete your bank account.

Why a Destination Wedding

What I love best about destination weddings, beyond the potential money-saving aspect, is that you can host your family and friends in a picturesque destination that will make for a memorable wedding in a way a cookie-cutter catering hall never could.

That's not to say that non-destination weddings aren't memorable. They can be. But for your budget's sake, a destination wedding is an option I strongly encourage you to investigate. Before you call your travel agent, though, check your calendar first. Why?

For one thing, you may be planning a wedding away during prime tourist season—normally the winter months. Things cost more during peak season, so if you want to find deals, if they exist, you're going to have to plan ahead. Even if you're planning a wedding during an off-peak time, the further in advance you plan things, the more likely you are to save money.

Also, many destinations discussed in this chapter need weeks, if not months, to process your marriage license request. So if you were hoping to skip off to the Caribbean next weekend to tie the knot, it's probably not going to happen. If you're desperate to become husband and wife that quickly, your local courthouse may be your best bet.

Money in Your Pocket

Just because the Conde Nast Bridal Group's American Wedding Survey says destination weddings cost on average $25,806, that doesn't mean you have to spend nearly that much on your destination wedding. In fact, if you plan things right, you can have many of your friends and family join you for your celebration and not end up in debt.

One bride I know was able to pull off a Mexican wedding, near Cancun, for $4,050. If you follow her lead, you should be able to do something similar. And let me point out that this $4,000 wedding included airfare, hosting 14 guests, and the honeymoon.

One of the ways her wedding became affordable is she booked it at an all-inclusive resort—the same resort where her guests stayed. That meant everyone's food and drink was included—even at the reception, which was held on the resort. They also had free karaoke entertainment at the reception. Thanks to the tropical location of the celebrations, she didn't need to spend anything on decorations. And finally, because friends and family pitched in by taking pictures, she didn't need to hire a photographer.

Savings for you: $21,756   **Running total: $62,834**

Location, Location, Location

Because the purpose of this book is to help you figure out how to have the wedding of your dreams—even the destination wedding of your dreams— without spending a lot of money in the process, I'll focus on wedding destinations in tropical locations that are closer to North America. These would include places like the Caribbean islands, including Bermuda and The Bahamas, which most people lump in with the Caribbean but which, technically, are in the Atlantic Ocean, and Central American countries like Belize. I'll also cover Mexico and Hawaii. I realize that plenty of people have destination weddings in the contiguous 48 states—the Florida beaches, the Vermont mountains—and information on that could fill an entire book. Because I don't have enough room to cover "local" destination weddings, I've chosen to spotlight only those areas mentioned above.

Go Figure

When you have a destination wedding in a foreign locale, much of your planning will center on making sure you fulfill all the requirements for a marriage license. While these requirements vary from place to place, using a worksheet might help keep a running tally of the paperwork you need to secure or tests you need to pay for before you can say "I Do" overseas.

Step 1: Check to see that your passport is valid and won't expire in the next 12 months. If necessary, set aside time to get a new one.

Step 2: If you need additional identification to apply for a marriage license, will you take originals or pay to have notarized copies done to take with you? These pieces of identification might include a birth certificate, a divorce decree from a previous marriage, or a "good citizen" letter from an attorney.

Step 3: Are any blood tests or health exams required? If so, how soon do you need them or for how long will they be valid? Make any necessary appointments for getting them and set aside funds to pay for them.

Step 4: Will you need to have any of your legal documentation translated into a foreign language? If so, contact the country's consulate to inquire about translation services—where to go for them, how much they cost, and how long they'll take.

Step 5: Do you need to "prove" your single status with a letter of good conduct from an attorney or proof of the dissolution of a previous marriage (either by death or divorce)? If so, arrange to have that paperwork ready to go.

Step 6: Will you need an on-site coordinator to walk your paperwork through the marriage license office in advance of your arrival or to arrange for you to have witnesses at your wedding? If so, ask your resort to refer you to someone in the business.

Step 7: Does one of you need to be "living" on the island or in the country for a set number of days before you can apply for a marriage license? If there are any such residency requirements, apply for time off from work and book your airfare and lodging as soon as you can.

Step 8: Is either of you younger than 21? If so, you will need written parental permission to marry. Make sure you don't overlook this detail.

Why should you consider the Caribbean region, Mexico, and Hawaii? First, they are most likely the easiest exotic locations for you and your guests to get to. Second, because they are physically located near the continental United States, they shouldn't be too expensive to fly to. And third, because the concept of destination weddings isn't brand new to many hotels and resorts in these three general locales, they know how to work with brides to plan affordable weddings away. Many hotels have packages available and incentives to offer that can cut your costs significantly.

Why a Caribbean Wedding Can Be an Affordable Wedding

Let me tell you about a couple I know and how they came to have a reasonably priced destination wedding. Really, the decision was pretty simple for this couple, Rebecca and Andrew, once their guest list hit the 400-person mark. When the Nashville couple realized they were talking about spending tens of thousands of dollars on what they thought would be a simple hometown wedding, they knew there had to be a better way.

Rebecca and Andrew had previously vacationed in the United States Virgin Islands (USVI) and knew how easy it was to get there from Tennessee. Just for fun, they started investigating how much it would cost to return to the USVI for their wedding. As soon as they realized the costs involved were so much less than a Nashville wedding, they booked a church on St. Thomas.

They tied the knot in an almost 400-year-old church in St. Thomas, and while they couldn't host all 400 of the original people on their guest list, they did have 30 friends and family members join them. Best of all, they pulled the whole thing off for about $4,000.

Believe it or not, that total included the couple's airfare and their lodging. Because they'd booked more than 10 rooms for their guests to stay in, their resort gave Rebecca and Andrew free lodging.

The $4,000 also included Rebecca's traditional wedding gown, Andrew's linen suit, the flowers at the ceremony (including her bouquet of bougainvillea, lilies, and hydrangea), and the steel band that provided the ceremony music. The minister at the wedding, their marriage license ($50), and the rental of the church were all part of the tab, too.

The tally doesn't end there, though. After the ceremony, the newlyweds, their four attendants, and their guests headed over to a nearby restaurant for brunch, with mimosas and wedding cake. The wedding party had the entire restaurant to themselves. And even the reception didn't blow their budget.

"I almost fell on the floor when we found out that all of the flowers for our wedding in Belize would cost $100. These were rain-forest flowers that were completely gorgeous and fresh from the property."

—Michelle, North Carolina

How did they get such a great deal? Well, they planned their wedding for mid-spring before peak tourist season—flights and hotels are often cheaper during spring. Speaking of flights, Rebecca knew enough to book all of her guests' airfare together so she could negotiate a discount, which she passed on to her friends and family who paid their own way. She also knew to ask about the free lodging offer for the four days they were spending at the resort, and to ask for a group rate for everyone else. They used that rate to secure all of the necessary guests' rooms, which ended up being $20 a night cheaper than any other rates Rebecca had seen.

What to Consider When Planning a Caribbean Wedding

The challenge with getting married in the Caribbean is that, in reality, you're looking at a region with nearly 30 different countries in it. Therefore, you're talking 30 different sets of rules and regulations that you have to navigate as you plan your wedding.

To make your planning a bit easier, use the following chart as a guide. It lists popular Caribbean region countries where you might want to have a destination wedding. I haven't included every single country simply because information about weddings in some isn't readily available.

The chart lists countries in alphabetical order, along with a website address for more information. I've included the cost for a marriage license in U.S. dollars (unless specified otherwise) and any waiting period you'll need to fulfill in order to say "I do" there. Finally, I've listed any requirements or regulations you'll need to know about in advance.

Keep in mind that although the paperwork and residency requirements may seem overwhelming at first, you don't have to do everything yourself. Nearly every couple I know who's had a destination wedding in recent years has hired a local wedding coordinator as an expediter to handle all of these behind-the-scenes details, including dealing with a country's red tape when it comes to marriage licenses. Many resorts will handle this paperwork on your behalf, for free, if you've booked a wedding with them.

I strongly suggest you investigate the services of a wedding coordinator—either on-staff at the resort where you'll be staying or someone in-country who has experience with destination weddings—and make sure you can find someone to do your legwork before finalizing your travel details.

Note: Nearly every country requires two pieces of picture identification to apply for a marriage license and/or proof of death of or divorce from any previous spouses, though some require more than that. The chart below assumes that having this identification is a given and lists only additional requirements or pieces of identification.

Also, information, including website addresses, was current as of publication but there is no guarantee that marriage license fees or residency requirements—or anything else, for that matter—hasn't changed by the time you pick up this book and read this chapter. So double-check this information on your own before you finalize your plans.

Finally, if you'd like to have a religious ceremony for your wedding, you may have to file additional paperwork and meet more requirements, which will vary from country to country, and religion to religion. Examples of what to expect might include proof of premarital counseling or a notarized letter from the religious leader at your home house of worship.

The following chart is a good starting point if you're considering planning a destination wedding in the Caribbean region.

Country	Website for More Information	Marriage License Fee	Waiting Period	Requirements*
Anguilla	anguilla-vacation.com	$284	Two business days	Two witnesses
Antigua & Barbuda	antigua-barbuda.org	$150	One day	Two witnesses; written parental permission if younger than 18
Aruba	aruba.com	varies	Submit all documentation 30 days ahead of time, first by fax, then via FedEx	Two witnesses; proof of single status; ceremony must take place on Wednesday, Thursday, or Friday only
The Bahamas	bahamas.com	$100	One day	Evidence showing the date of arrival in The Bahamas
Barbados	visitbarbados.org or barbados.org	$150 plus $25 in postage stamps	None	Return tickets home; statement from person who will officiate at wedding
Belize	travelbelize.org	$100	In country three days to apply, then must wait one week to be married	Two witnesses
Bermuda	bermudatourism.com	$200	Mail completed marriage application, with check, at least two weeks in advance of your wedding. Will be valid for three months.	You must pay and fill out additional paperwork for civil or religious ceremony before arriving on the island
Bonaire	infobonaire.com	$150	Six weeks or longer for all processing of paperwork, then four working days on island	One person must establish temporary residence status; passport must not expire within six months of wedding
Cayman Islands	caymanislands.ky	$200	None	Two witnesses; proof of entry into the country
Curacao	curacao.com	$167	Three days, though wedding planner must deliver documentation two months before wedding	Request in writing to be married, including two possible wedding dates; proof of single status

*Beyond passport and driver's license with picture, and death certificate or divorce decree, if necessary

Country	Website for More Information	Marriage License Fee	Waiting Period	Requirements*
Dominica	dominica.dm	$300	Two days	Additional paperwork stating each person is available to be married—a $5 fee applies to each of these forms
Dominican Republic	dominicana.com/do	$20	24 hours	You must write to the American Consulate for permission; single-status paperwork translated into Spanish; two witnesses (if not island citizens, they need to bring their passports)
Grenada	grenadagrenadines.com	$15	Three days on island before applying for license, then two days for license to be processed	If either person is under 21, he or she needs written parental permission notarized or generated by an attorney
Guadeloupe	consulfrance-newyork.org	Free	One month residency required	Residency card; medical certificate, including blood test; certificate of "good conduct"; all documents translated into French
Jamaica	visitjamaica.com	$75 to $80 (depending on exchange rate)	24 hours, if you've made arrangements ahead of time to get your marriage license	Written parental consent if under age 18
Martinique	martinique.org	Free	One month residency required, plus allow 15 days between application and ceremony	Residency card; medical certificate, including blood test; certificate of "good conduct"; all documents translated into French
Montserrat	visitmontserrat.com	$200 in Montserrat stamps	Three business days	Written parental consent if under 18

Beyond passport and driver's license with picture, and death certificate or divorce decree, if necessary

continues

continued

Country	Website for More Information	Marriage License Fee	Waiting Period	Requirements*
Nevis	nevisisland.com	$80; however, if your stay on Nevis will last longer than 15 days, the fee is only $20	Two business days	Declaration of single status
Puerto Rico	gotopuertorico.com	$30 (in stamps)	None	Blood test report from a federally certified lab, in Puerto Rico or U.S. Test must have been done within 10 days of the wedding date; doctor must sign and verify the blood test results and the marriage license
St. Barthelemy	consulfrance-newyork.org	Free	One month residency required	Residency card; medical certificate, including blood test; certificate of "good conduct"; all documents translated into French
St. Kitts	www.stkittstourism.kn	$200 (Eastern Caribbean dollars)	Two working days	Affidavit of your single status, if never before married
St. Lucia	stlucia.org	$335 if on island more than seven days before the wedding; $540 if on island fewer than seven days. (Fees are in Eastern Caribbean dollars.)	Four days	Notarized parental permission if under 18; passport must not expire within six months of the wedding; if the bride is changing her name, she may be required to file additional paperwork called a "deed poll."
St. Maarten	st-maarten.com	$285.90	Submit request 14 days before ceremony	Original birth certificate; six witnesses; written proof of bride and groom's employment

Beyond passport and driver's license with picture, and death certificate or divorce decree, if necessary

Country	Website for More Information	Marriage License Fee	Waiting Period	Requirements*
St. Martin	st-martin.org or consulfrance-newyork.org	Free	One month residency required	Residency card; medical certificate, including blood test; certificate of "good conduct"; all documents translated into French
St. Vincent and the Grenadines	svgtourism.com	$185, plus $8 in stamps	One day	None
Trinidad and Tobago	visittnt.com	$47	3 days	Airline tickets for return flight
Turks and Caicos	turksandcaicostourism.com	$50	48 hours on island to apply for a marriage license, which you'll receive two to three days later	Written parental permission if under 21; declaration of single status and that the bride and groom are not related to each other; letter stating couple's occupation, age, current address, and each father's full name
U.S. Virgin Islands	usvitourism.vi	$50	At least eight days (your application for a marriage license must be posted in public for this time period, though you can apply for an exemption if you cannot be on the island for eight days prior to the ceremony)	Do not wear shorts or "slippers" when applying for your marriage license or you will be turned away; you must specify up front if you're going to have a civil or religious wedding

Beyond passport and driver's license with picture, and death certificate or divorce decree, if necessary

Getting Married in Mexico or Hawaii

Planning their recent wedding, Aimee and Adam had visions of exchanging vows on the beach near their California home. When they discovered how much their dream wedding would cost in California, they adjusted their vision to include a beach wedding somewhere else. However, that somewhere else couldn't be too far away, such as the Caribbean, because all their guests would be traveling from the West Coast and the couple didn't want to inconvenience them by having them travel long distances. That's why Aimee and Adam decided to marry in Mexico.

It's easy to think you can have a destination wedding for peanuts when you look at package prices that resorts promote, but I beg you to read the fine print. Many of the really inexpensive wedding packages are for a ceremony with only the bride and groom, plus witnesses in attendance. The price does not include food, drink, or any guests. It also doesn't include your lodging or airfare. If you're planning to have your family and friends join you at your destination wedding, ask what the per-head cost will be and how much having them along will add to this package price. Once you have this information, you can figure out if this affordable destination wedding is really so affordable.

Not only was the wedding cheap—the whole shebang, including travel, cost about $6,000—but it was personal as well. Instead of a champagne toast, they did tequila shots. Instead of steak or chicken at the reception, they fed their guests fish tacos. Instead of having their reception in a hall somewhere, they held it on the beach. "There's no way we could have had such a unique wedding, with this menu and at these prices, back home," says Aimee. The couple did indulge in one thing, though. The resort where they had their wedding was able to arrange for a private fireworks show to culminate their big day. It cost a whopping $1,000. But for the couple, it was a worthwhile expense.

If you're a West Coast couple looking to tie the knot somewhere exotic, your two best bets that don't require too much travel are either Mexico or Hawaii. Like the countries in the Caribbean region, both destinations have certain requirements for couples looking to marry there, which you'll need to keep in mind as you make your plans.

Mexico

When most people think of Mexico, they consider only its well-known places—Cancun, Tijuana, or Puerto Vallarta, for instance. In reality Mexico is a country comprised of 32 states. It's also quite large, stretching from the U.S. border in the North to the Guatemala/Belize border in the south, the Gulf of Mexico in the East, and the Pacific Ocean in the West. What does this mean for the couple planning a wedding here? Your location options can be as big as the country itself.

No matter where in Mexico you choose to get married, keep these important facts in mind about marrying there. This information comes from the Consulate General of Mexico:

- ✆ Foreigners must have a civil marriage first, if they want it to be legally binding. A religious ceremony alone is not considered legal. However, you can have a civil wedding ceremony to fulfill the legal requirements, followed by a religious one.

- ✆ Because of the civil marriage requirement, only an employee of the Civil Registry can perform your ceremony. You have to apply in writing ahead of time to arrange this. (A wedding coordinator at a resort can handle all of these details for you.)

- ✆ A Mexican doctor must certify, in writing, that you're both in good health and free of diseases. (This requires a blood test and x-rays done in Mexico no earlier than two weeks before your wedding, so you need to plan your time accordingly.)

- ✆ There is no residency requirement, but you must present proof of your citizenship—passport, birth certificate—and any proof of previous marriages no longer existing in order to apply for a marriage license. You must have all documentation (except for the passport) translated into Spanish.

- ✆ If you are divorced, you can't marry in Mexico until at least one year after your divorce was finalized.

✂ While a civil registry ceremony is free, the accompanying marriage certificate is not. Each Mexican state charges different fees.

✂ For up-to-date details on marrying in Mexico, visit the website of the Consulate General of Mexico in New York at consulmexny.org. (Note: When I checked out this website, here's how I got to the wedding information. First, I had to click on the "other nationalities" link in the menu. Then, when I got to the next page, I had to search for the "Marrying in Mexico" section.)

✂ For information on traveling to Mexico, visit the Mexico Tourism's website at visitmexico.com.

"Having our wedding in Tulum, Mexico, was the best decision we'd ever made. We had our ceremony and reception at the same resort where we honeymooned. While our guests complained at first about having to travel that far for our wedding, everyone ended up having a wonderful three-day holiday. Best of all my husband and I bought our first house this past winter, and we definitely would not have been able to afford it if we were still paying off the $20,000-plus wedding we would have had here in Atlanta!"

—Melissa, Georgia

Hawaii

Hawaii is an archipelago in the southern Pacific Ocean, nearly 2,400 miles off the coast of the United States. Its six main islands are (the big island of) Hawaii, Kauai, Lanai, Maui, Molokai, and Oahu. When it comes to geography, topography, and location, Hawaii is miles away from the rest of the United States. No wonder so many couples choose to get married—or as they say on Maui, "mauied"—here! It's the United States' own tropical paradise, with rainforests, volcanoes, and all.

Restrictions and regulations are a lot less stringent in Hawaii for U.S. citizens hoping to have a wedding there. For example, there is no waiting period, and you don't have to be a Hawaiian resident to marry in Hawaii.

Also, the rules of the state cover all of the islands, so you needn't worry about jurisdiction differences from island to island. However, you still need to keep some things in mind when marrying in Hawaii, such as the following:

- ℰ If either of you are 19 or younger, you must bring your birth certificate with you when you apply for your marriage license. A passport isn't enough.

- ℰ You are required to have a photo ID, even with a birth certificate.

- ℰ You can use your marriage license to marry anywhere in Hawaii, but you must do so within 30 days, or the license becomes null and void.

You can get all your paperwork ducks in a row before leaving for Hawaii by visiting the Hawaii Department of Health's website at hawaii.org/doh. There you can download your marriage license application and have it filled out before you even board the plane. For general travel information about Hawaii, visit gohawaii.com. This latter website includes an entire section devoted to wedding information.

The Time of Year Can Affect Your Wedding Plans

The time of year you choose to tie the knot in the Caribbean region, Mexico, and Hawaii can affect your plans in ways you never expected. The weather and prices can work in your favor—or against you.

One thing to keep in mind is hurricane season, which officially begins on June 1st and ends on November 1st. Though hurricanes have occurred before and after these dates, this five-month stretch is when most hurricanes hit land. And what land do they normally hit? Anywhere in the Caribbean (South Florida down to South America, from the Eastern-most Caribbean islands west to Mexico) and up the East Coast. The West Coast of Mexico and Hawaii aren't immune to hurricanes during this time period, either.

So what does this mean for your destination wedding plans? You need to accept the reality that having your destination wedding during the United States' high wedding season (June through September) means that you're also having your wedding during prime hurricane season. But this hurricane season connection can work to your advantage as far as prices go.

High season for weddings doesn't match up with high season for tropical-destination resorts, which usually occurs in the winter months when more people want to escape the cold. Summer months, while busy, aren't as in demand in the Caribbean, which means you'll likely be able to get better deals for your destination wedding at the same time The Weather Channel is watching tropical depressions form off the African coast.

If you wait to marry in the Caribbean during winter, you won't find as many deals. There's another drawback to weddings away during winter: it's possible that snowstorms in areas that experience winter weather could delay your travel plans. Just something to keep in mind.

DON'T TRIP
on your **SHOESTRINGS**

> Just because you're trying to spend as little as possible on your destination wedding doesn't mean you should be so cheap that you put yourself in a potentially bad situation. Case in point: don't skimp on travel insurance, especially if you're planning to wed in a hurricane-prone place. Insurance will help you recoup your costs if you decide to postpone your wedding due to the weather before the big day gets here. Speak to your preferred insurance agent about your travel insurance options.

Planning a Traditional Reception

Not every couple who ties the knot in the Caribbean wants to toast their guests with a glass of champagne and a slice of cake, which is what the typical, basic destination wedding package includes. Like Andrew and Rebecca, who took their guests out to brunch, you may want to plan a more traditional reception to celebrate your big day. And the good news is this—even a reception at a destination wedding could be cheaper than one back home.

For example, Sandals Resorts, which has properties all over the Caribbean, offers a WeddingMoon program—a combination wedding and honeymoon. Normally, these are small affairs with the aforementioned cake and champagne for a reception. But Sandals is smart and recognizes that people may want more to their reception than that. Want to offer your guests hot and cold hors d'oeuvres, wedding cake, and an open bar? You can do so for only $25 a person. What about adding on a sit-down dinner, with an open bar? That will cost $50. (Note: These prices were current when I was writing this book.) Try getting a per-head rate like that, with an open bar, back on the mainland. You may be able to do it, but I'll bet it won't be easy. Heck, try getting that kind of rate at another resort in the Caribbean. The ones I've checked out start their fees at $150 a head—similar to the expensive rates I've seen back in the States!

Another reception cost-savings comes into play when you're having your wedding at an all-inclusive resort where all of you are staying. There's a chance that if you book your reception at one of the resort's restaurants, you won't have to pay extra for the celebration. Remember: it's an all-inclusive.

That's what happened with Melissa and Dan, who had their wedding at an all-inclusive in Mexico. Because all their guests were staying there, too, they just took over a portion of the restaurant and ate and drank to their hearts' delight—without shelling out a dime. That's because food and drinks were included in their resort package. How cool—and cheaply smart—was that of them? A wedding reception that's practically free!

Finally, if you'd like, you can have the wedding coordinator at your resort arrange for you to have all the extras you'd expect to find at a traditional wedding—again probably for a lot cheaper than what it would cost to hire a band or deejay or photographer for a wedding back home. The coordinator may also help you select favors, which I would recommend you make symbolic of your wedding destination and purchase locally. I'm thinking things like fresh flower leis for the guests at your Hawaiian wedding. However, check first with your wedding coordinator about how much you think these favors might set you back. If having her get items locally for you won't save any money, then do your favor shopping before you leave and bring them with you.

"Because we both travel a lot for business, we had a ton of frequent flier miles saved up. We ended up using them to get to and from our Caribbean wedding, meaning we spent nothing on airfare."

—Mindy, Housto

How to Pay for as Little of Your Wedding as Possible

While destination weddings offer great deals on ceremonies and receptions, you can also find plenty of financial incentives that can help to cut your wedding costs. Take the notion of the bride and groom staying for free when you book your guests' lodging, like Rebecca and Andrew did. That's a common enticement resorts use to fill their rooms, so make sure you ask any resort you contact if they do something like this.

Also, some resorts will throw in a free wedding ceremony when you book a bunch of rooms together. Unfortunately, most resorts won't give you a free room and a free wedding—you'll have to choose one or the other. In my opinion it's a no-brainer to go with the offer that saves the most.

Here's how these incentives play out in the real world with an example from one location.

The Elegant Hotels Group in Barbados offers destination-wedding packages along with incentives for couples and their guests who stay on-property. One package, which normally costs about $850, includes the ceremony site, marriage license, official for the ceremony, transportation to and from the ceremony, flowers for the bride and groom, wedding cake, champagne, and dinner. However, if you book three rooms (the happy couple's reservation counts as one of the three rooms) for five nights, the wedding is free. This is a fantastic program if you plan to honeymoon in the same place you hold your destination wedding. Besides the package deal, you'll make out like a bandit for another reason: by honeymooning where you tie the knot, you save paying for another set of travel expenses to get to and from your honeymoon—you're already there.

Weddings at Sea

As I mentioned earlier, one of the greatest things about planning a destination wedding is that not only will your family and friends be along to celebrate with you, but also chances are they'll be picking up the tab for their airfare and lodging to do so—meaning it's one less thing to add to your destination wedding tab. The same is true if you're planning a wedding at sea on board a cruise ship. You and your future husband will cover the cost of your stateroom, which usually includes your meals, and so will your guests. Then, like the all-inclusive resorts, where food is already paid for, you can plan your wedding reception on board without incurring too many extra costs.

According to Cruises Only, a Boston-based travel agency that specializes in cruise packages, you can find affordable wedding packages on Carnival and Royal Caribbean Cruise Lines. Sure, the other lines offer them, too, but Cruises Only found them difficult to understand, and they included too many nickel-and-dime add-ons to fit the book's $5,000 criteria.

For example, a wedding on board a Carnival Cruise ship sailing from Port Canaveral to the Bahamas in August costs $800. This price includes the ceremony, which will occur while in port in the state of Florida, plus flowers, champagne and keepsake flutes, wedding cake, music, and photography. The cheapest stateroom for this kind of cruise is about $400 per person. (In October, when prime cruising season is over, the price drops to $350 per person.) Now say you want to give your attendants the gift of sailing with you, instead of loading them down with trinkets. You could pick up the tab for eight of you, all together, with the wedding ceremony, for about $4,500.

Royal Caribbean Cruise Lines has similar prices for staterooms, but the wedding packages cost a bit more. With this cruise line, you can choose between an onboard, onshore, or on-the-beach wedding ceremony in four of its ports—Fort Lauderdale, Miami, Port Canaveral, or Tampa. Prices for these offerings start at $1,095, but Cruises Only recommends the slightly upgraded $1,295 Harmony Onboard package, because it offers more flexibility if you're going to have a larger group of attendants and guests. In other words, it doesn't limit how many guests can attend your ceremony. Here's what that package includes:

- Ceremony with officiant and music
- Bridal bouquet and groom's boutonnière

- Wedding coordinator

- Wedding cake and cake-cutting ceremony

- Champagne toast

- Photographer for ceremony, cake cutting, and champagne toast

- Photo album, plus additional 5×7 and 8×10 photographs

- Priority boarding and check-in for the couple and their sailing guests

Keep in mind that these prices were current when I was writing the book. Please visit cruisesonly.com or the website of each individual cruise line to see if comparable deals still exist.

Dollar-Saving Do's and Don'ts

Here's a recap of some of the money-saving notions discussed in this chapter regarding destination weddings:

- Don't automatically think you can't afford a destination wedding somewhere tropical. These kinds of weddings often can be cheaper than hometown celebrations.

- Do look carefully at the residency and other requirements that various destinations require when people want to marry there. If a country requires one of you be on-island for 30 days before your wedding, that's going to blow your budget.

- Don't be stingy about hiring a wedding coordinator to handle the paperwork and details of your wedding.

- Do consider having your wedding at an all-inclusive resort—and have your guests stay there, too—so that when you have your reception, everyone's food and drinks will already be covered in their lodging.

- Do invest in travel insurance so you don't end up losing your hard-earned dollars if you have to cancel your destination wedding.

- Don't assume you can't a have an affordable destination wedding at sea.

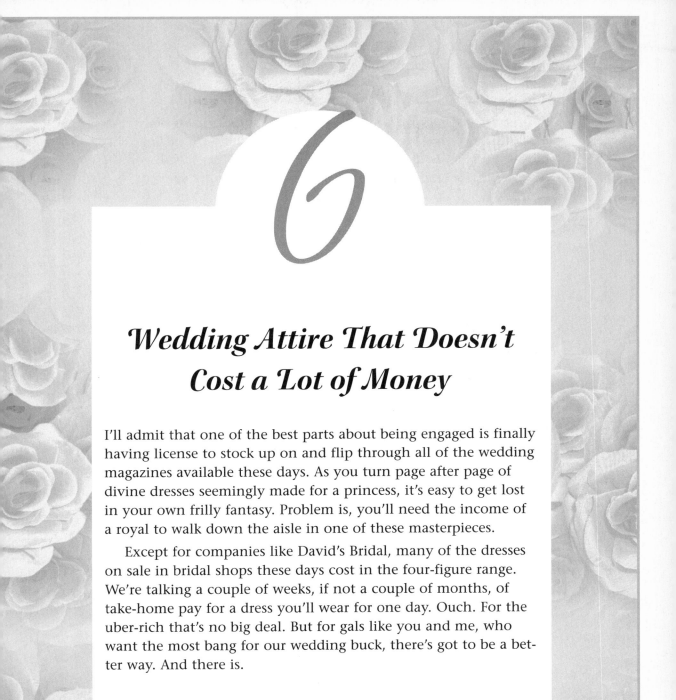

6

Wedding Attire That Doesn't Cost a Lot of Money

I'll admit that one of the best parts about being engaged is finally having license to stock up on and flip through all of the wedding magazines available these days. As you turn page after page of divine dresses seemingly made for a princess, it's easy to get lost in your own frilly fantasy. Problem is, you'll need the income of a royal to walk down the aisle in one of these masterpieces.

Except for companies like David's Bridal, many of the dresses on sale in bridal shops these days cost in the four-figure range. We're talking a couple of weeks, if not a couple of months, of take-home pay for a dress you'll wear for one day. Ouch. For the uber-rich that's no big deal. But for gals like you and me, who want the most bang for our wedding buck, there's got to be a better way. And there is.

In this chapter, I'll give you lots of ideas on how you can find the dress of your dreams, plus the accessories to go with it, for a car payment or less. Better yet, I'll tell you about real-life brides who did just this so you'll know I'm not pulling your garter or offering ideas in a wedding vacuum.

Go Figure

When you get dressed on your wedding day, you're going to end up wearing much more than a wedding gown. A number of elements go into a complete bridal ensemble, and I've outlined all of them below.

This worksheet will help you decide what you need to buy for your bridal outfit and how much you expect to spend on each of these items. Also, one of the big trends in bridal attire these days is for a bride to wear one gown to her ceremony and another, simpler dress to the reception. If you plan to do something like this, then you'll probably need to buy two sets of attire and accessories.

Step 1: Wedding dress(es) you like   _____

Step 2: Special undergarments (bra, corset, crinoline)   _____

Step 3: Hosiery and how many pair   _____

Step 4: Headpiece and/or veil   _____

Step 5: Gloves   _____

Step 6: Handbag   _____

Step 7: Shawl or coat   _____

Step 8: Jewelry (necklace, earrings, bracelet)   _____

Step 9: Final cost estimate for attire-related items
        from Step 1–8   _____

Also, I'll provide similar tips for securing clothing at a great price for the rest of the people in your wedding. You'll want to read these sections on choosing the groom's attire, dressing your attendants, and finding clothing for your family members—especially if you'll be footing the bill for these expenditures. And even if you're not, the folks in your wedding will appreciate your taking the time to investigate the best deals possible for their wedding-day attire.

Best Bets on Your Bridal Gown

When my friend Carol got engaged, she was so excited to go shopping for her bridal gown. She planned an entire day around the event and even invited some friends along for moral support. Boy, did Carol need that support once she started trying on gowns. Not only was she disappointed that she couldn't fit into any of the gowns—the store stocked one size only for try-ons—but she also had no idea how frustrating buying a wedding gown would be.

First, it's hard to get a sense of what your gown will look like on you. Because shops stock a sample size (usually a size 6 or size 8), if you don't wear a size 6 or 8, you're out of luck. Then you have to resort to slipping the dress on the hanger over your neck and imagining what you'd look like in it. Or you could try to squeeze your hips into the dress and have someone hold up the back, even though you can't zip it. That's what Carol ended up having to do.

Next, Carol discovered that once she ordered this dress, she had to wait weeks if not months for it to come in. Then she had to schedule an array of fittings and pay for the alterations. Only in the days before her actual wedding would Carol be able to get a glimpse of what she would look like as a bride, in all of her regalia.

"I fell in love with a crystal-beaded dress but couldn't love the price—$1,250. However, quite by accident I found out that if I waited until the New Year to order the dress, it would be considered last year's design and sell for much cheaper. So I took the risk of waiting until January to place my order and sure enough, the price had dropped to $750."

—Kim, Connecticut

Keep in mind that while many brides find the dress of their dreams on their first shopping trip, many do not. Don't put pressure on yourself to find it your first time out. And definitely don't let a salesperson pressure you into a decision you're not ready to make. This is especially true if the dress just seems too expensive for your budget.

The final straw for Carol was the price tag involved in all of this. One of the gowns she liked cost $2,500. Research says that, on average, a bride will pay about $1,500 for her gown, so this dress was a bit above the average. It shouldn't have surprised Carol, though. She told me that before her shopping trip, she'd been flipping through a recent issue of a national wedding magazine and saw dresses priced at $350, $900, and $2,700. If you average those out, you end up at about $1,500. However, Carol was hoping she'd find the dress to wear at her wedding more in the $350 range. Keep in mind that the cost of alterations usually adds a couple hundred extra dollars to your final tally.

So what did Carol do? She surely didn't plan to go to her wedding in sweats. No, Carol got creative. She knew there must be a way to find a brand-new wedding gown that looked great on her and that looked even better in her budget.

Finding Great Deals in Bridal Salons

Once Carol got herself together, she asked the bridal salon's proprietor if there were any gowns a bit less costly and which she might actually be able to try on. The proprietor sighed a bit but then led Carol to an out-of-the-way section of the store. There she pointed out a rack of dresses, with the following sign above it: "Clearance dresses. Priced as is." At first Carol wasn't sure what to make of this, since she assumed the store had samples only, and the only way to get a dress was to special order it. So she asked.

"These dresses are here for a number of reasons," the owner explained. "They could be sample dresses from last season that I took out of circulation because they're not making them anymore. They could be dresses that a bride ordered but, for one reason or another, the wrong size got delivered. Or these could be dresses that a bride never picked up or, heaven forbid, didn't end up needing because she called off her wedding." Then she leaned toward Carol and whispered, "Some of these dresses are actually bridesmaid or mother-of-the-bride dresses. But because they're a light shade, I figured a bride might want to wear one of them." Returning to her normal voice, she added, "I'll let you look around a bit. Let me know if you have any questions."

Carol couldn't believe what she was seeing! As she began looking through the racks, she found dress after dress, all in perfect condition, for a tenth of the price of the new gown she'd just been looking at. Not only did she find traditional wedding gowns at a great price, but she also discovered cocktail dresses for less than $100. Best of all, many of these garments were in her size—size 12. She found many dresses she wanted to try on, and by the time she returned to the dressing room, her left arm was buried in dresses. About an hour later she found the dress she would wear for her march down the aisle—and it cost $300.

You can employ similar tactics to get a great deal on a bridal gown, without leaving a high-priced salon. Don't be afraid to ask if the store has a clearance or "off the rack" rack or if any dresses are on sale. Additionally, some bridal salons stock dresses that are called "designer inspired"—that's "knock-off" to you and me—and if you say the code phrase, you might be surprised at the additional options you'll find. Jessica, a bride in Minnesota, used that code phrase on one of her shopping trips. "I asked if they had any 'designer-inspired gowns'," she recalls, "and next thing I knew I was trying on dresses that looked like the expensive ones I'd seen in magazines. But they weren't expensive at all."

Finally, trunk sales and sample sales can be a treasure trove for a bride on a budget. Usually you have to live in a big city to take advantage of these, but a Google search using the phrase "bridal sample sales" turns up a ton of possibilities. However, if you do live near a big city, then I recommend checking city magazines, like *New York* magazine, or the website www.dailycandy.com for a heads up on these kinds of sales.

You shouldn't feel bad about wanting to save money on your wedding dress. If someone at a bridal salon treats you less than respectfully for inquiring about these less-expensive options, then I respectfully suggest that you take your business elsewhere.

"I ordered a white cocktail dress for $300 from NeimanMarcus.com, bought my shoes on eBay for $88, got a handbag at a sample sale for $25, and then wore my grandmother's vintage coat for free (we were married in February)."

—Kate, New York

Money in Your Pocket

How many brides do you know who spent thousands of dollars on their wedding dress—a dress that they wore for one day only? Sure, a wedding dress can have terrific sentimental value, but when you're looking for values for your wedding, practicality has got to win out over sentimentality when you're thinking about your dress. The Conde Nast Bridal Group's American Wedding Survey shows that the average bride spends about $1,000 on her dress. But that's on her dress only. Add in the various accessories you'll need for your big day, and you'll see that "average" number creep up. Headpiece and veil? Add $165. Shoes, gloves, purse, and jewelry? Another $165. So in reality, many brides spend $1,330 or more just to get dressed on their wedding day.

You can still look like a princess bride when you spend like a pauper, and you don't have to skimp on the fancy gown or headpiece. Here's how one bride I know spent wisely on her wedding-day attire—and how you can, too.

For starters she visited a traditional bridal salon, but instead of choosing Amsale or Vera Wang, two amazing designers that are typically quite pricey, she ordered a dress from a lower-end designer. It cost $248, plus $50 for alterations. The dress didn't need a crinoline or any fancy lingerie; all she needed was a strapless bra, which she got at Victoria's Secret for $25. Because she was getting married in the summer, she had no need for gloves or a shawl. She purchased her shoes at Payless for $19.99. "No one is going to see them under my dress, so who cares where they came from," she told me. She made her own veil for $20, and her mother loaned her jewelry and a handbag.

If you saw pictures of this bride on her big day, you never would have guessed she'd spent only $362.99. She looked like she'd stepped right out of a bridal magazine.

Sure, it's fun to fantasize about wearing the designer dresses you see celebrities wearing in your favorite gossip magazine, but if you want to avoid having buyer's remorse as a bride, don't blow thousands of dollars on your wedding attire. As this story shows you, it's possible to look like a fabulous bride when, in fact, you're a frugal bride.

Savings for you: $967.01   **Running total: $63,801.01**

Affordable Dress Options at "Regular" Stores

When I got married, I knew immediately I didn't want to go the traditional bridal gown route. This high-maintenance way of buying a dress didn't fit with my no-nonsense personality, and I knew the costs involved definitely didn't fit my budget. However, I never expected to find the dress I'd wear on my big day in a big department store.

But one day on my lunch hour, I found it there, waiting for me on a mannequin that looked like the angel I knew I'd be if I wore it on my wedding day. Okay, maybe I was just feeling woozy and lightheaded about the dress because I was hungry and had low blood sugar. But it was a pretty dress (still is!), and it was a great deal. I took a couple of different sizes with me into the dressing room, and if it weren't for the piped-in Muzak coming from the ceiling, I could have sworn angels were singing when I tried on the size 10 and it fit beautifully. It hugged my curves in all the right places and hid my flaws as well, and it didn't even need to be altered. I plunked down my plastic, signed the bill for $175, and took the dress, in a garment bag, home with me that night.

I'm not the first person to find her wedding dress in a regular store—it's what Susanna of Colorado did after she got engaged. "I went to the evening section of Lord & Taylor and found my dress for $225," she says. She describes the dress as a vintage-looking, 1920s-style tea-length dress, made of ivory fabric with a beaded bodice. Savvy brides like Susanna know you can find great deals in stores like these.

> "Originally, I'd budgeted to spend about $500 on my dress. But because the dress I eventually chose was technically a bridesmaid dress, it cost only $250."
>
> —Jill, Florida

That's why I'm recommending that if you hadn't considered doing so, you may want to plan a shopping trip to your local "better" chain boutique (think Talbot's, Ann Taylor, or J.Crew, for example) to see what your options are.

If you'd like to find a more formal-looking dress without buying an actual wedding gown, I recommend starting your search in a department store's evening wear section. You may just find a white or beige garment designed to be a cocktail dress but that can easily work as a wedding dress, much like Susanna's dress did.

> Just because you're getting married doesn't mean that every garment of clothing you buy has to be made specifically for a wedding. In fact, sometimes something that is designated as a wedding (fill in the blank) has been marked up significantly. This is because shop owners know brides come shopping with a fantasy in mind and often spend way more on their wedding attire than they'd planned to. Don't let this happen to you.

To show you that Susanna's and my dress-shopping experience aren't isolated cases, I'd like you to consider this. Recently at Nordstrom, what some consider to be an expensive department store, I saw great deals on dresses in the "occasions" area. There I found a white slip dress for about $200. I saw a comparable slip dress in a wedding magazine that cost $2,600. Why the difference in price? Well, it couldn't have been the fabric—both were made of white silk. And it couldn't have been the silhouette—both had spaghetti-strap tops and floor-length skirts. My guess is the difference was simply this— one dress was sold as a special occasion dress but not necessarily a wedding dress in a department store, and the other was offered exclusively as a wedding dress in a traditional bridal boutique.

Checking Out Outlet Stores

Have you been to an outlet mall lately? Then you know that the kinds of stores and the quality of clothing you can find at these shopping areas are often as good as (if not better than) your local mall. I happen to live in an area with two gigantic outlet malls nearby. One is home to the outlets of Neiman Marcus and Saks Fifth Avenue. The other has top brands like Brooks Brothers, Anne Klein, and Coach. Other outlets I'm familiar with include JCPenney (which has a bridal division), Bridal USA (which is a big prom store but carries wedding gowns, too), and bridal designers Alfred Angelo and Jessica McClintock.

There are four companies that run most of the outlet malls in the United States, so I recommend starting your shopping by checking them out. You can get information on locations and stores on each company's website, listed here:

- ⚭ Chelsea Premium Outlets   www.premiumoutlets.com
- ⚭ The Mills Corporation   www.themills.com
- ⚭ Prime Retail Outlets   www.primeoutlets.com
- ⚭ Tanger Factory Outlet Centers   www.tangeroutlets.com

When shopping for bridal attire, I would definitely take some time to see if any outlet store is a viable option.

Looking Online for Bargains in Bridal Attire

It's entirely possible that you could find and purchase your wedding gown without ever leaving the comfort of home. That's because the online world offers many options for wedding gown shopping.

First, you have traditional online shopping sites. These include the virtual version of a brick-and-mortar store, such as Nordstrom.com. There's also e-tailers like Overstock.com, which may not sell wedding garb, per se, but which often has evening wear that could easily pass for wedding attire.

Next, you can find online communities and bulletin boards that have a "for sale" element to them. I'm thinking of Craigslist, which as of this writing has "locations" in more than 150 U.S. cities, plus Canada and other countries. Under the "clothing and accessories" portion of the "for sale" section, you could easily come across a great deal on a wedding gown, as I just did in the Philadelphia Craigslist. There, I found a brand-new designer wedding gown being offered for $350.

"I went online to research where designer Jessica McClintock has her outlet stores and then visited the one nearest to me. I headed straight to the clearance rack and get this—I found a wedding gown that fit me and it cost $15."

—Shawna, Pennsylvania

Another online community is Freecycle, which most people equate with furniture giveaways and recycled goods. But it's possible that someone, somewhere may be giving away a wedding gown, so I wouldn't write off Freecycle as a shopping option.

Finally, there are online auction sites. In my opinion these may just be the best friends a bride on a shoestring budget can have. But before I begin to wax poetic about online auctions, let me get one thing straight for you. You don't have to slum when you buy items through an online auction. Not all of the items you could possibly buy on eBay, Amazon Auctions, Yahoo Auctions, or elsewhere are worn or used. Here's what I mean.

Believe it or not, many bridal salons and other boutiques use online auctions as their online clearance rack. That means that you can find never-been-worn (but probably tried-on) dresses for a great price on these online auction sites. Additionally, brides who cancel their weddings or change their plans often attempt to recoup their investment by selling their brand-new dress online. Yes, you may stumble across a wedding dress that someone dragged out of granny's attic, but most of the time you're going to be bidding on dresses in perfect condition.

Another thing to keep in mind: because you can get such a great deal on a dress online, it isn't unheard of for brides to bid on and buy more than one dress. That's what my friend Leigh did. When she saw she could buy three dresses in three separate auctions and spend only $150, she figured it was worth the risk of two of those dresses not working out. Also, because Leigh is petite, she has to have all her clothes altered. Since she would likely have to have any dress she bought altered, she figured if she could get a dress for a lot less online and have to pay for alterations, she would still come out ahead financially. And she did. One of the eBay dresses worked out for her, just as she planned. Best of all, she was able to put the other two dresses back up for sale on eBay and ended up making back about half of the $150 she'd spent up front.

Considering Consignment and Resale Shops for Savings

Another bride I know used the used-clothing route to find a fabulous deal on her wedding gown. "Because I collect vintage clothes, I enlisted my friends to help me find a vintage wedding dress on eBay or through estate sales," says Jackie, a recent bride from New York. "I didn't want to spend more than $500, and at first I wasn't sure if that was possible. But a few days after I'd asked my girlfriends for help, one of them called me from a garage sale; she'd found an off-white, organza-and-beaded gown and wanted to know if I was interested. Was I—the dress was only $25! After I got it home, it needed some alternations and a cleaning, but all of that cost only $100." So all told Jackie spent $125 for a vintage gown, exactly what she wanted to wear to her wedding.

Does the idea of trolling garage sales sound like a viable option for your dress shopping? What about checking out consignment shops? A friend of mine spent just a couple of hundred dollars on a wedding gown she found in a consignment shop. Another got a great deal on a dress in a resale store. How is that possible? Each of these stores was in a relatively upscale part of a city or a neighborhood, where the elite live. The wealthy here would wear a dress or gown once, and then either consign their "castoffs" or give them away to the resale store.

If you have access to such a store near where you live, definitely check it out. This isn't like a church thrift store. These are retail establishments with inventory that could rival some of the finest department stores. Remember, they're more Saks Fifth Avenue than Salvation Army.

Embracing the Past Can Save You a Pretty Penny

In years gone by it was pretty traditional for daughters to wear their mothers' wedding gowns. I'm not sure when that tradition became less popular, but I'm hearing now that many brides are returning to the nest to pick up Mom's gown. Perhaps it has something to do with sentimentality. Or, more likely, it could be the sticker shock so many women get when shopping for a gown.

I think it would be awesome for you to consider wearing your mom's gown or another relative's gown, if they offer it to you. This is a great option for a number of reasons. First, it gives your gown more meaning. Second, it takes care of that whole "old" and "borrowed" thing in the "old, new, borrowed, and blue" tradition brides try to follow. And third, it won't adversely affect your wedding budget. That's great news if you're trying to plan this whole thing on a shoestring.

DON'T TRIP on your **SHOESTRINGS**

> Unless your daily life includes showing up in the fashion pages, there is no reason to think you must have this season's dress for your wedding. You can often save big bucks by buying a dress from a couple of seasons ago—mainly because the bridal salons want to get them out of stock to make room for new (and more expensive) dresses. In the grand scheme of things, who is going to know if your dress is a couple of seasons old?

Making Your Budget Work by Having Your Dress Made for You

Plenty of women choose to have their dresses custom-made for their wedding and, surprisingly, not all of them pay through the nose for it.

Take Becky in Michigan. Years ago her mother majored in home economics in college and became quite adept at making clothing. Becky recalls that when times were tight in her childhood, Mom would take the kids to the fabric store, stock up on patterns and material, and take out her trusty Singer sewing machine to make her family a whole season's worth of new clothes.

"I saved $1,200 on my dress by having a dressmaker recreate something I'd found in a pricey boutique."

—Catherine, Washington

When Becky got engaged, her mother offered to make her dress. Like old times, they went to the fabric store together and $100—and a few weeks—later Becky had her gown. "I never wanted to spend thousands on a gown," she recalls, "but I didn't think I'd get something custom-made for so little."

Other brides have hired seamstresses not related to them to make custom gowns as well. While they didn't get off as cheaply as Becky did, some spent only about $500.

The best part about going the custom-made route is it removes the need for alterations. This dress has been cut to fit your body, not some mannequin's shape, so it should be a perfect fit once it's done.

Savvy Shopping for Shoes and Other Accessories

Just as a traditional bridal salon would have you think you must spend thousands on your dress, the same is likely true for the accessories that go along with the dress. I'm sure any salon you'll visit will have shelves filled with shoes, crinolines, shawls, tiaras, veils, handbags, and jewelry. And I'll bet the prices of these items will make you feel as faint as the dress prices did.

Many of the tricks for getting a great deal on a dress would work for accessories as well. I know plenty of brides who got their crinoline or veil on eBay for a steal, and other women who were proud to say that they purchased their shoes at Payless for less than $30. (Heck, some of Payless's wedding-type shoes cost $15!) You can get inexpensive handbags at Payless, too.

As far as shawls, veils, and tiaras go, you can find them, too, on eBay. And if you're the do-it-yourself type, you can easily buy materials at a craft store and make them yourself. Hand-me-downs also qualify for accessories.

Then there's the possibility of asking your crafty friends or relatives to make your veil and headpiece. See if they'll do so as a gift to you.

Getting Great Deals on the Groom's Attire

When it comes to wedding clothes, guys really do have it so much easier than the gals. They wear a tux, or they wear a suit. They don't have to go for elaborate fittings, and they surely don't have to spend the kind of money that manufacturers expect women will spend on their wedding-day clothing—unless, of course, their taste runs with the Saville Row, expensive-suit crowd.

When it comes to weddings and tuxedoes, you'll want one if you're having a late-afternoon formal wedding or a ceremony held in a more formal setting. Of course, it would be ideal if the guy owned his own tuxedo, thus tapping into the logic used above. But I realize not everyone these days has a tuxedo ready and waiting in his closet.

So, then, how do you get a tuxedo on the cheap? Simple. Arrange to have your groomsmen (who will pay their own way) rent their tuxedoes from a store that offers some sort of deal on the groom's tux.

Many rental operations give the groom's tuxedo for free if you rent four or more tuxedoes at a time. I recently saw a special at the Men's Wearhouse just like this, which said the groom's tuxedo rental would be free if four or more of his groomsmen rented their tuxes from the store as well. And the groom wouldn't just get the jacket and pants for free. The deal included his shoes, shirt, vest or cummerbund, tie, and any cufflinks he needed.

Probably the easiest way to keep your shoestring budget on track, in regard to the groom's attire, is to not plan to have him wear anything fancy at all. Most men look exceedingly dapper in a blue blazer, button-down shirt with a tie, khaki pants, and simple shoes. I've been to many weddings where this is exactly what the groom wore (as did his attendants, but more about them later), and not only was it a stylish choice, but it also was a prudent choice.

My husband, for example, wore the above-described uniform to our wedding. The only cost he incurred for his outfit was the new tie he splurged on—and then he'd splurged at discount store Marshall's, where that new tie set him back only $20. Because he already owned the blue blazer, button-down shirt, khaki pants, and shoes, his clothing added only $20 to our total wedding budget.

Sometimes, though, the time of day or the setting for your wedding warrants something a bit fancier for the groom. Perhaps you're having your wedding after dark, and khakis and a blue blazer simply won't cut it. Well, would a

"My husband bought his seersucker suit at J.Crew; the boys' ties came from J.Crew, too, and I got the bridesmaid dresses at Ann Taylor. I got my wedding dress there, too—though it wasn't marked as a wedding dress—and it was $375."

—Mandy, Massachusetts

dark suit do? That's what David, a groom in Florida, decided would work well for his evening wedding. "There was no reason for anyone to spend money on tuxes," he says. "Dark suits were a great idea."

Does your future husband already own such a suit? Chances are if he works in the corporate world or in an industry that requires him to dress up from time to time, he does. There's no reason that, for the sake of saving money, he can't wear that suit to your wedding. Like my husband did, though, he may want to give the suit a newer feel by getting a new tie or even a new shirt. But by shopping shrewdly, he should be able to get a few new duds without busting your budget.

Affordable Attire for Attendants and Others

While the easiest way to keep your attendants' attire affordable is to make them pay for it or to not have any attendants at all, I realize that these aren't options for everyone. Some couples choose to pick up the tab for these folks' frocks as their gift to their attendants. If you decide to do this, you may be wondering: how do you dress everyone and dress them well without depleting your savings account?

"I mail-ordered my bridesmaid dresses from Chadwick's. They were affordable and the ladies could wear them again—for real!"

—Dana, Colorado

Much of the same advice that applies to the bride's and the groom's attire applies here as well. That is:

- ✆ Look for deals in bridal salons and tuxedo shops, especially on the clearance rack.

- ✆ Check out "regular" retailers, chains, and department stores for everyday clothing that would work well for a wedding.

- ✆ Spend some time in the aisles of discount retailers looking for deals.

- ✆ Log on to see if you can find great prices online.

- ✆ Ask your seamstress sister or someone you know who knows her way around a sewing machine if she'll consider making these garments as her gift to you.

In addition, your attendants and your family will have an easier time finding clothing—and so will you—if you're flexible about your expectations. In other words, if you've decided to have sky blue be your wedding color, make the color your only requirement for their clothing. Letting people pick out a favorite outfit or matching tie in that color, as opposed to limiting them to one style of clothing only, will be a lot easier on their outlook and their pocketbook. Of course, before anyone buys anything, you should probably approve their version of "sky blue" because one person may see that as aqua and another may see it as robin's egg blue. At the same time, make sure that you've described a dress style that fits the formality (or informality) of your occasion. You want to give your attendants some freedom but, at the same time, you don't want them to clash or look out of place with the dress they're wearing.

As far as accessories go, keep this anecdote in mind. Last year I visited a well-known salon on the request of my girlfriend who was getting married. She'd asked each of us five bridesmaids to buy certain dresses (price wasn't too bad) and then a specific set of jewelry to go with the dress—the same set she'd be wearing. Sure, the fake-pearl, teardrop earrings, and the matching necklace were pretty, but when the cashier rang the set up at $110, I nearly spit out the coffee I'd been gulping to keep me awake through the dress-shopping ordeal. For that kind of money, I'd want jewelry from Tiffany on New York City's Fifth Avenue, not some chain store in the mall. But what was I going to do? My friend had asked me to get these items, and since I'd agreed to be in her wedding, I had to oblige.

Please don't choose pricey items that your attendants must wear for your wedding. I know, if they're buying it, what's the big deal? Well, you're right, it doesn't affect your bottom line; but it's not very nice.

But let's say that you've decided, after the fact, to pick up the tab for your maids' jewelry or other accessories and give it to them as your thank-you gift for being in the wedding. Do you really want to be shelling out over $550 for five pairs of earrings and five necklaces—which is what my friend would have had to do if she'd gone the gift route? I think not.

Just as you can find great deals on dresses and other clothing in regular, discount, and department stores, the same is true for the accessories your attendants will need. eBay and other online venues are also a good bet.

Here's another option to consider: get your bridesmaids together one weekend day for a craft afternoon at a store like JoAnn Fabrics or AC Moore. Book a private room for an afternoon with your girlfriends to make the earrings you'll wear at the wedding or any of the other accessories you'll need. Bead stores have separate work areas, too. Everyone collects her supplies, pays for them, and then meets around a big table to begin working on her projects.

Places like JoAnn Fabrics often have sewing machines available for use, so you can all sew your own shawls. Not only will you and your friends get to spend quality time together before the wedding, but you'll also be saving money and getting the accessories you need for the big day.

As long as you keep these options and ideas in mind as you begin shopping for clothing and accessories for everyone in the wedding, you're sure to find great deals.

Dollar-Savings Do's and Don'ts

Here's a recap of some of the money-saving notions we've talked about in this chapter:

- Don't settle for spending thousands on your wedding gown.

- Don't be afraid to ask if the bridal salon has anything in stock that's more affordable than the gowns costing thousands.

- Do look at any off-the-rack dresses or dresses on the clearance rack, which may come in your size and cost a lot less than the made-to-order dresses.

- Do check out the wares at low-cost bridal chains like David's Bridal, which prides itself on fashion-forward dresses at rock-bottom prices.

- Don't be afraid to ask if a shop stocks "designer-inspired" dresses (the fancy way of describing knockoffs).

෫ Do spend time looking at the evening section of your local department store for wedding dress and even bridesmaid dress options.

෫ Do consider regular stores like Talbot's, J.Crew, Ann Taylor, and others when shopping for a dress—including the dress your attendants will wear.

෫ Do investigate outlet malls and bridal sample sales as options for finding an affordable gown.

෫ Don't be afraid to try your hand at online auctions, where you'll often find never-worn wedding gowns and other accessories you'll need at "get-out-of-town" prices.

෫ Don't think there's anything wrong with wearing hand-me-down wedding attire.

෫ Do take a friend or relative up on her offer to loan you a garment or make you something from scratch.

෫ Do include a shopping stop at bargain shops like Marshall's, TJ Maxx, and Payless for shoes and other accessories.

෫ Don't forget to look inside your future husband's closet to find the outfit he'll wear at the wedding; if he already owns it, you won't have to buy it.

෫ Don't be shy about negotiating a deal on your groomsmen's tuxes so that the groom can get his free.

෫ Do think about using classes at your local craft store as a way to make accessories that you and your attendants can wear on your big day.

෫ Do make it easier on your attendants by identifying a color for their garb—and not a specific dress—and then letting them find the outfit that fits their budget.

7

Finding Economical Entertainment for Your Ceremony and Reception

As you begin to plan and budget for the entertainment you'll have at your ceremony and reception, I want you to think outside the box for your options—and I'm going to help you do that as we make our way through this chapter.

Taking the out-of-the-box approach can greatly help your bottom line. According to the Conde Nast Bridal Group's American Wedding Survey, the average couple spends more than $1,000 on ceremony and reception entertainment, about $230 for the ceremony and $850 for the reception. If you want to keep your entire wedding budget around $5,000, you can't really afford to blow 20 percent of that on music alone, can you?

Also, I want you to realize that you don't have to follow everyone else when hiring musicians, especially if everyone else has a budget ten times the size of yours. You can hire a band or a deejay to play at your reception, or you can go with prerecorded music instead and still figure out a way to fit this into your budget. You can hire a pro or you can hire students. Your options are endless, and as long as you keep these options in mind, you're sure to uncover creative ways to find wedding entertainment you can afford.

Ceremony Music

Everyone knows the traditional music people expect to hear at a wedding ceremony—the "Wedding March" when the bride walks down the aisle and then the "Recessional" when the couple leaves together. However, have you given any thought to what kind of musician you want playing this music at your ceremony?

Most couples choose to go with live musicians for their ceremony. If you decide to go this route, the good news is you have a number of options that should work well with a limited budget.

Start by asking any musical friends and family members if they'll honor you with their talent by singing or playing an instrument during certain parts of your ceremony. You can make a similar inquiry at your house of worship. Maybe you can bring in an organ player, choir, or other musical group. Many such folks will sing for free or for a small donation made to the church or synagogue on their behalf. One bride was a member of her church's choir, and their gift to her was to perform at her wedding. The church's musical director played acoustic guitar during the ceremony—for free as well.

Next, see if any of the members of the band you've hired for your reception (assuming you've hired a band) can play at your ceremony. Oftentimes a guitarist or strings players are available to do so, and this extra playing can be part of how you negotiate their fee.

In fact, this is the very deal one bride I know arranged for at her wedding. She tapped into the talents of her reception entertainment in this way: "We had the keyboardist and saxophone player perform at the ceremony. Then, they added a bass player and did jazz combos during the cocktail hour," she recalls. "Finally, they all got together to play during the reception." Instead of having to hire three separate groups, she got a three-for-one deal.

Go Figure

Before you hire entertainers for your ceremony and reception, you need to consider a few things. First, decide what kind of music you'd like played at both the ceremony and reception. Second, establish how many people you'll need—whether you're using musicians for your ceremony and/or reception or going with a deejay. And third, decide for how long you'll need these people, since some entertainers charge by the hour. This worksheet should help you determine your anticipated needs—and costs—for hiring entertainers.

Step 1: Number of musicians for ceremony   _____

Step 2: Per musician cost or hourly rate   _____

Step 3: Multiply Step 1 and Step 2 to get a subtotal for ceremony music   _____

Step 4: Hourly rate of deejay for reception   _____
   or
Step 5: Price per musician per hour for reception   _____

Step 6: Number of musicians to hire   _____

Step 7: Hours of reception/how long you'll need music   _____

Step 8: Multiply Step 4 and Step 7 for subtotal   _____
   or
Step 9: Multiply Step 5, Step 6, and Step 7 for subtotal   _____

Step 10: Add subtotals from Step 3 and Step 8 or Step 3 and Step 9 for total anticipated cost of ceremony and reception entertainment   _____

What about musicians from a local college or university? If there is a school with a stellar music program nearby, check to see if students or faculty there freelance. It's not unheard of for students or staff to play at special events—both on campus and off. This is an awesome way for students to get real-life performance experience and a great way for any musician to earn money. Many of them will probably have played weddings before and, even if they haven't, I'm sure they'll be eager to learn the music for a ceremony.

Best of all, they probably won't charge a great fee—probably a couple hundred dollars, if that.

Finally, you can go the prerecorded music route for your ceremony. However, if you do, make sure you have someone with technical knowledge manning the CD player, iPod, or boom box. I would hate to have a skip in the music mess up your procession, simply because you wanted to save money on your ceremony music.

Reception Entertainment

Back in Chapter 4 we discussed how having dancing or not affects your reception site choice, so it's not surprising the same "am I having dancing at my reception" idea applies to your entertainment choices as well.

DON'T TRIP
on your **SHOESTRINGS**

> Sometimes you can find out about bands and deejays through your reception site, which may refer to these companies as "preferred providers" or something like that. Sometimes that terminology can be a red flag for "more expensive than other folks," though that's not always true. Many reputable hotels have a preferred list—and suggest that couples use them—because, as one catering manager told me, "We prefer to work with these vendors because we know that they'll show up on time and won't be dragging instruments through your cocktail hour." This prescreening of vendors is great for your peace of mind but it isn't always ideal for your pocketbook: vendors often have a set price when working with certain venues. Again, this isn't always true but I find you have less wiggle room with negotiation when a vendor comes "preferred." Definitely check out these recommended vendors nonetheless. If you want other options, though, find out if there is any flexibility in bringing in your own people. If they say "No," then you have to decide if this reception locale is providing enough of a savings that you can afford to use their vendors.

Before you decide which entertainment company to hire for your reception, determine what kind of entertainment you'd like to have. If your vision for your wedding reception is all of your guests up and cutting a rug most of the evening, then you'll definitely want to bring in a group that won't disappoint those dancing feet. What if you're more interested in background music for the meal with dancing later on? Again, this will affect the kind of music you bring in and how much you should expect to pay for this kind of entertainment. We'll talk more about that in a bit.

If you have no dancing expectations whatsoever, you can probably get away with a miniscule entertainment expenditure, if any at all. Again, just because bridal books and wedding magazines talk about a band or deejay at a reception as being the status quo, this isn't a rule that's set in stone. And if it doesn't make sense for your wedding plans or your budget, then don't do it.

Finally, keep in mind how the time of year can work in your favor when negotiating with your entertainment. Like other wedding vendors, musicians, bands, and deejays are busiest during wedding season—primarily June and September but also the warm-weather months surrounding them. That means they book up early and are less likely to negotiate their prices. Chances are someone is going to book them for a wedding, so why should they settle for a lower fee during this time of year? However, if the entertainer wants to work during late fall, all of winter, and early spring, when fewer couples marry, he'll probably be more willing to negotiate on your terms, or the rates he offers right out of the gates will be significantly lower. The one caveat to this off-season suggestion is any weekends with popular holidays in them, like Valentine's Day. Then rates might be higher.

A couple I know discovered this when they moved their wedding up a month from April to March. "I was shocked at how much less the vendors were charging just one month earlier," the bride recalls. "I mean, my deejay would have cost double if we'd kept our original wedding date in April." It's amazing what a difference a month can make when you're planning a wedding.

Of course, if you do decide to have your wedding during a less popular time of the year, I don't recommend totally low-balling a bandleader or a deejay—or any vendor for that matter—because that's simply not fair. However, if a deejay normally charges $800 and you ask him to do your wedding for $500, that's not an unreasonable request. Who knows? It may still be worth his time to work your wedding at this reduced rate, especially if he doesn't have any other business booked. Basically, if you never ask, you'll never know.

Money in Your Pocket

Wedding entertainment isn't cheap. The average couple spends about $230 for ceremony musicians and about $845 for entertainment at the reception. Altogether that's $1,075. Given that many of the couples I've interviewed in the years I've been writing wedding books tell me about deejays charging this much and bands charging three times as much, this figure doesn't seem too outrageous. Then again, with the average wedding costing close to $30,000 these days, a thousand bucks isn't that much. But that's irrelevant for our purposes. Because our goal is to keep your wedding costs to the $5,000 level, having 20 percent of your budget go to music may be just a bit too extravagant.

Let me tell you how one bride in Michigan hired entertainers for her wedding for a lot less than what the average couple pays. She knew she wanted a string trio to play at her ceremony and cocktail hour. Professional groups were quoting her fees between $450 and $750 for the two-hour span of the ceremony and cocktail hour. So she called the local Youth Symphony Orchestra to see if they had any young musicians who would do the job. They did, and she ended up with a lovely string trio that charged $20 an hour per musician or $120 for the ceremony and cocktail hour.

This bride was similarly creative with her reception entertainment. She was having an exceptionally long reception and needed someone on hand for eight hours. Every deejay she called suggested fees in the $1,000 range. No way, she thought. Someone great should be available to do it for cheaper than that. With persistence she found a fun deejay who charged only $500. Not only was she pleased with his fee, but also with his services—he provided nonstop, enjoyable entertainment throughout the night.

If you were to find similar great deals for your ceremony music and your reception entertainment, compared with national averages, you'd save a bundle, too.

Savings for you: $455   **Running total: $64,256.01**

Hiring a Band When You're Budget-Conscious

Besides referrals and recommendations, the best way to be sure the band you hire will deliver is to see them in action. Since you can't crash other people's weddings where the band is playing, ask to see video or a DVD of recent performances.

Another important idea to consider when hiring a band is to think about the kinds of music you want played at your reception. This is key for a number of reasons.

If you are into musicians like the Dixie Chicks or Rascal Flatts, don't waste your time looking at bands that specialize in swing or 1970s disco classics. It's true that most professional bands are versatile enough to play anything you put on their playlist, but you want the best band possible for the kinds of music you hope to hear at your reception. Also, to make your entertainment dollars go the farthest, have a clear picture of your music choices ahead of time so you can pick the most appropriate entertainer for your event.

Knowing this is also important because it could affect not only the number of musicians you need in a band but also the instruments those musicians play. If you aren't interested in a big band, then don't let a bandleader convince you that you need an extensive horn section. Do you know that a 5-piece band can sound just as good as a 10-piece one if you choose your instruments and musical selections wisely?

If you look at some of your favorite bands from the radio, many have, on average, four to five members. And within these quartets or quintets, musicians usually play two or three instruments. I suggest you look for similarly versatile musicians in the bands you interview for your reception. A band with a guy who can play the piano, guitar, and, say, the accordion will be a better investment than a band that needs separate people to play each of those instruments.

"We really wanted to have a band at our reception, but every band we checked out cost $4,000 or more. We were going to just go with a deejay when we happened to find a nearby band on Craigslist. We struck up a conversation with the leader via e-mail, and before we knew it, we'd negotiated to have him play with his full band at our reception and to have him play classical guitar at our ceremony—all for $1,800. Since music is so important to us, we felt like this was a great deal."

—Mandy, Massachusetts

Finally, advice for hiring inexpensive ceremony musicians can apply to your reception music needs as well. Don't shy away from calling the music department of a local college or university to see if any of the students or staff freelances for weddings.

One bride I interviewed was able to secure a college-based jazz combo for the ceremony and reception and paid only $50 per musician for the night.

One last thing on the cost of hiring musicians: because you are expected to feed your musicians, and the other vendors you use, if you hire a big band, you'll have more mouths to feed. Usually, though, you can work something out with your caterer where he'll make a separate (and cheap) entrée for vendors so you won't be adding too much to your bill in providing your vendors with a meal.

DON'T TRIP on your **SHOESTRINGS**

No rule of wedding planning says you must hire an entertainer who plays weddings for a living. Sometimes you find the best talent—and the most affordable person—when he has a day job. This person isn't jaded about weddings because he doesn't do them all the time. And because he has another job to pay his bills and insurance, he can usually afford to work with people who have somewhat limited funds. So don't automatically assume that a freelance bandleader or deejay isn't worth checking out. He might just be your best budget bet.

Deejays at a Discount

One constant in wedding entertainment is that a deejay is typically cheaper than a band. And we're talking significantly cheaper! One bride I know interviewed bands that were charging $2,000 to $3,000 for a four-hour affair, whereas deejays were charging $300 to $400.

Ambiance also comes into play as you weigh the pros and cons of a band versus a deejay. If you're not interested in what a live band can bring to your wedding atmosphere, then go right to the deejay option. This is also a good idea if you're hoping to have a range of music at your wedding—something not every band can promise. And if you want this music to sound true to the original artist, well, it has to because he'll be spinning the actual tunes.

Despite the economical aspect of a deejay, his prices can quickly ratchet up as well. If you want him to give out goodies to your guests or bring in a special effects machine, that's going to cost extra. It also costs extra if he brings in additional people to help him out. I'm not saying the deejay is going to slip in four of his buddies as his assistants and then charge you without telling you, but it's important to find out exactly what the deejay will offer for what price. And find out how extras are going to affect his price if you want to add things on or if he does, for example, need an extra hand.

Probably the best way to keep a deejay's price within your budget is to know someone in the business who can give you a break or, better yet, give you his services as a gift. Since iPods have revolutionized how people mix music, you just might be surprised to learn that your college-age cousin deejays on weekends at a club and could easily act as the (free) deejay at your wedding.

One bride hired a colleague from the radio station where she worked to be her deejay. He quoted a great rate—about $150 for the evening—but when she went to pay him, he refused her money. "He said it was his wedding gift to us," the bride recalls.

I realize that not everyone works at a radio station or rubs shoulders with deejays every day of the week like this bride does, but it doesn't mean that her anecdote doesn't apply to you. Just because *you* don't work in entertainment doesn't mean that *someone* you or a friend or family member knows can't help you out. To borrow a cliché, it really is a small world, so don't read these anecdotes and think, "Oh, that bride was so lucky. I could never get such a great deal." Yes, you can, if you try. I mention in another part of the book that in order to find people in the business who can give you a great deal on wedding services, you need to do some serious networking, like you would for your career. This is another example of how asking people to put you in touch with someone in the business could pay off for you.

DON'T TRIP
on your **SHOESTRINGS**

To ensure you end up paying exactly what you'd planned to pay for entertainment, get everything in writing. No reputable musician or deejay should shy away from signing a contract that spells out not only the agreed-upon fee but also the time period and any selections you expect to hear at the wedding. If a vendor balks at having a contract, walk.

Let me give you an example, based on my life in suburbia. Through a girlfriend, I know a local family that owns a wedding photography and videography company. If I was planning a wedding and needed to hire photography and videography pros, you can bet that the first person I'd call is this local family. After seeing what kind of deal they might be able to offer me, I'd ask if they could recommend a caterer, florist, makeup artist, and musicians. Ideally, they could and, in telling these other vendors that the video person referred me, they might offer me a deal. Of course, there's no guarantee that each and every vendor you network with is going to give you a good deal, but if you don't even make the effort to investigate how knowing someone in the business can help you financially, then you might not have as much luck planning a wedding for less.

Have You Considered Prerecorded Music?

In Chapter 4, we discussed the notion of dancing at your wedding reception and how the need for a dance floor could affect the kind of space you settled on for this portion of your wedding celebration. And, as I mentioned earlier in this chapter, if you want traditional dancing, then you'll likely be looking at the band or deejay options. However, prerecorded music may be an affordable option for other kinds of receptions.

"Instead of spending $500 on a deejay, we danced to pre-burned CDs. As part of our RSVP card, we asked people for their favorite dance tunes. Then, based on their responses we burned the pre-mixed CDs. Everyone loved the music and that we kept the volume low enough that people could talk. I loved that when my cousin asked for rap, I could say, 'Sorry we don't have any'—and it was the truth."

—Christie, Ontario

My husband and I chose this option for our reception, which, to us, was more about mingling with friends and sharing delicious food than cutting a rug or doing the "Chicken Dance." At that time our sound system of choice was a multi-CD player, which we brought with us to the reception. We hooked it up to a sound system and snaked speakers through the place. Then, we put in five of our favorite CDs, which we thought would work well at a wedding reception. These CDs ranged from jazz classics to pop music. By keeping the CD player on shuffle the entire time, we were guaranteed four hours of ever-changing music, which created the perfect musical background for our wedding.

You may want to consider this option or a more modern one—creating a digital jukebox of your favorite music with an iPod or other kind of MP3 player. You can download (legally, of course) your favorite music from a site like iTunes ($.99 per song—what a great deal) or upload your favorite CDs to it. Then hook it up to a sound system connected with speakers and, voilà, you've got a digital deejay. And the cost to you is? Not much—just a couple of downloaded songs and maybe the rental of a sound system, which your reception space should be able to provide. In some reception locations, you may not have to pay extra to have them hook up a sound system for you, but always ask ahead of time. In fact, a bride I know used the iPod option and saved $800 in the process—the price deejays wanted to charge.

Dollar-Saving Do's and Don'ts

There's no reason to spend an arm and a leg to get great entertainment for your ceremony and reception. Let's recap some money-saving ideas about music from this chapter:

- Don't be afraid to ask any musically inclined friends or family members if they would perform at your wedding ceremony.

- Do inquire at your house of worship about a choir or other musicians who can sing or play instruments at the ceremony for free or a reduced price.

- Don't disregard college musicians or the faculty and students at music colleges as a resource for wedding musicians.

- Do keep your desire for dancing (or no dancing) in mind as you consider your reception entertainment options. There's no reason to hire an orchestra if you're not planning on having a dance floor at your reception site.

- Do be wary of the reception site's "preferred vendor" status on entertainment companies. Just because the reception place prefers them doesn't mean you can afford them.

- Do ask if your reception site will let you bring in your own entertainment.

- Don't be afraid to ask about any discounts a bandleader or deejay might be willing to offer you if you book them for your wedding during an off-season time.

- Do make sure you see a band or deejay in action before hiring that company for your wedding. A video or DVD of recent performances should show you exactly how this person performs and whether this performance is up to your standards.

- Don't think you have to hire a 10-piece band, just because the bandleader tells you so. Many music companies work with bands of all different sizes, which charge different amounts. Find the one that works for your budget and your musical needs.

- Don't think it's unreasonable to "borrow" musicians from your reception band to play at your ceremony. People do this all the time.

- Don't forget you have to feed your vendors, including musicians. Negotiate with your caterer to provide them with a meal, albeit a less expensive one.

- Do look to your local youth orchestra or symphony for younger musicians who play like pros but don't charge like them.

- Do understand that the more extras you ask your deejay to bring to your wedding—prizes, special effects—the more your reception will end up costing.

- Do get everything in writing, in a contract, with any vendor you hire, including your band or deejay. You need to spell out the time period when you need them, what they'll provide, and what price you've all agreed upon.

- Don't think that prerecorded music won't work for a wedding. Sometimes it's the easiest and cheapest way to have music.

- Do think about tapping into today's technology, namely an iPod, to create a free digital deejay.

8

Getting Your Invitations and Other Printed Materials for a Great Price

You'll need to do a lot of communicating with your family and friends before, during, and after your wedding—and I'm not talking about chit-chatting on the telephone. Weddings require a staggering amount of printed materials.

What kinds of printed materials will you need? Well, it all starts with save-the-date cards, which tell your guests in advance when your wedding is going to be. Then you have the actual invitation and everything that goes into it. At your ceremony you may want to have a program and a guest book. At the reception you may want to print menus and cards for all kinds of reasons—to tell people where to sit, to label the tables so your guests can find the table where you've just told them they're sitting, to explain the favors, to encourage the guests to use the disposable cameras on the table, or to present anything else you want to tell your guests. Finally, after the wedding you'll need to send thank-you notes.

In this chapter, I'll help you figure out how to get everything you need in black and white (or whichever color ink you choose) for a great price. That way you won't end up all red with anger because the information you had to get on paper ended up costing so much.

Save-the-Date Cards

With the average engagement lasting about a year, save-the-date cards have become de rigueur for out-of-town or destination weddings. Or if you're planning your wedding on a holiday weekend when cheap airfares and hotel rooms might get snapped up long before your guests get your wedding invitation, it's a good idea to send save-the-date cards. These cards are important because they give your guests a heads up on your upcoming wedding and allow them to pencil-in the date on the calendars and make any necessary travel arrangements.

Despite their importance for the aforementioned wedding categories, don't go the top with your save-the-date cards if you decide to have them. A simple postcard or folded card is all that's necessary, and it's easy to make this using your computer and a word processing program, like Microsoft Word, which offers invitation-like templates. Just make sure to include the important stuff—who is getting married, where the wedding will take place, and the date when it will occur. If you'd like, you can also include when you expect to mail the wedding invitations.

A new trend in save-the-date cards is to have them printed on magnets. The thinking here is this: many people slap things up on their refrigerator as a reminder, so having a save-the-date card that "sticks" on its own would be especially convenient for your friends and family. Online retailers that specialize in printing, like VistaPrint.com and iPrint, are also in the business of doing magnets.

Inviting Ways to Make Your Invitations Affordable

Typically, a wedding invitation is sent out about 8 weeks before the big day—and 12 weeks in advance if you're having a destination wedding. This gives your guests enough time to check their calendar and make plans to attend—assuming they RSVP "yes." You, too, should give yourself enough time to get your invitations ready, especially if you want to save money on them. Why? If you wait until the last minute to place your order, you may incur costly rush charges.

As with most things in a wedding, the more complicated, intricate, or fancy you want your invitations to be, the more expensive they're going to be. The average couple spends about $425 on invitations, so says the Conde Nast Bridal Group's American Wedding Survey, but I want you to spend way less than that—and I know you can.

For starters, check out various online options for your invitations. Two such online companies that I've used for printing purposes and which have decent deals are VistaPrint.com and iPrint.com. Recently, on iPrint.com you could get 100 invitations for $49. That's great! Have you ordered business cards or holiday greetings from an online site? Did they treat you well as a customer and give you a fair price? If so, you should investigate if they do wedding invitations on the cheap, too.

I'm also hearing from more and more brides about the great deals to be found on eBay or Craigslist. As always, check references or, if it's an online company, see about a money-back guarantee. While I love finding bargains online, I hate getting ripped off—so references or return policies are a must.

"We ordered our wedding invitations online. They were a plain white card and not expensive at all, but they looked great. I mean, no one even notices if you do real engraving anymore, so why spend the money!"

—Maggie, Florida

Go Figure

If you've got a guest list of 200, that doesn't mean that you need to buy 200 invitations. Instead, break out your guest list by address and use that information to determine how many invitations you'll need to purchase.

Keep in mind that in addition to ordering the actual invitation, you'll need to order the RSVP card and envelope, and a reception card if you want to enclose a separate one. Some people just include reception information on the bottom of the invitation. You may want to go with the "bottom of the invitation" options, simply as a means of saving money.

Also, purchase about 10 percent more inner and outer envelopes that come with wedding invitations. This helps to compensate for any mistakes when addressing the inner envelope (writing the names of the actual invited people) and the outer envelope (for mailing the invitation set). By buying more up front, you'll more likely qualify for a volume discount.

Use the following worksheet to help you get your numbers in line so you can get moving on your invitations.

Step 1: Number of addresses to send to   _____

Step 2: Multiply Step 1 by .10   _____

Step 3: Multiply Step 1 by the number 2   _____

Step 4: Add Step 1 and Step 3 for total envelopes
         (inner and outer) to order   _____

Another way to keep your invitation costs in check is to make them. Do you have a computer and a laser printer? That's all you'll need to get the job done. Sure, you'll have to invest some time into doing the printing, but this option will be a huge benefit to your bottom line. Note: Before printing all of your envelopes, do a test run, especially if you'll be using a laser printer. Because these printers use heat to make the print adhere to the paper, the heat may seal your envelopes during printing. If that occurs, you may have to use an inkjet printer instead, which doesn't have a heat-transfer process during printing.

You can find all kinds of places from which to buy wedding invitation stock. Office supply chains and craft stores usually have at least one aisle devoted to specialty papers and blank card stock. You may also want to check out companies like Paper Direct (though it can be pricey if you don't buy in bulk).

To give you an example of what you might find, here's a comparison of invitation kits available at three national stores. Each kit includes supplies for 50 invitations, envelopes, response cards, and response envelopes:

AC Moore: $23.99

Bed Bath & Beyond: $24.99

Office Depot: $29.99

Not a bad deal, right? It would cost you about 50 cents per invitation set, not including the cost of ink for your printer or your time. But if you're looking to save some serious dough, you should give this DIY invitation idea some serious consideration.

One bride purchased her invitation stock at Staples for about $50. She printed everything using her laser printer and then sent the invitations out to a calligrapher to address the 60 envelopes. She said having a professional calligrapher add the final touch to the invitation set made her homemade and computer-generated invitations look much more expensive than they really were. In fact, she got lots of compliments and questions about where she had them done.

To save even more money, skip the calligrapher and check out the wedding-inspired or calligraphy-like fonts available through a word processing program like Microsoft Word. Some examples would be Apple Chancery, Bradley Hand, and Mona Lisa.

If you're having an unusual or offbeat wedding, you might be able to get away with sending unusual or offbeat invitations as Jill, a bride in Philadelphia, did. She was holding her ceremony and reception at the Jersey Shore, in a town known for its tourist attractions. Jill decided that she and

> "Instead of a traditional RSVP card with an envelope, we had our RSVP card printed on a postcard. That saved us on postage—postcard rate versus first class—and no one had to worry about losing the reply envelope."
>
> —Cari, Michigan

her future husband could really set the mood for their upcoming whimsical wedding by using postcards of the beach town as their invitations.

To avoid writing each postcard/invitation by hand, they printed up a clear label on the computer and stuck them on the postcard. This label saved time and ensured that each guest received the same information. Also, because the invitation was going out as a postcard (with postcard postage, thank you very much), there was no way to include an RSVP card. So they offered a phone number and e-mail address for responses. Total cost for sending 50 invitations was $28.50, for postcards, labels, and postage.

Wedding Invitation Basics

As you plan your invitation purchase, keep this in mind: a wedding invitation is more than just a card inviting people to your wedding. In addition to the actual invitation, you'll need to order the following as part of your invitation set:

- Reception card (if ceremony and reception are in different places)
- RSVP card and envelope
- Inner envelope to put the invitation package into and on which you write the names of the people you've invited
- Outer envelope, which is big enough to contain the inner envelope. You use this envelope for the actual mailing of your invitation.

Other elements to an invitation can affect how much (or how little) you spend on them. For example, choosing an oversize card with matching envelope will likely double your postage costs. Currently, the U.S. Postal Service considers that any envelope bigger than $11\frac{1}{2}$ inches long and $6\frac{1}{8}$ inches tall needs additional postage. Also, an envelope shaped like a square needs extra postage, regardless of size.

If you have someone else print your invitations, the printing process they use can affect price as well. Thermography, which uses a heating process to put ink on paper, is the cheapest. Letterpress, whereby the letters of your text are literally pressed into the paper, and engraving (engraves text onto paper) are more complicated printing processes that require metal plates and machinery. Not surprisingly, they're more expensive.

Speaking of professional printing, if you choose to have more than one font placed on your invitation, that will cost more, too.

So as you begin your bargain-shopping for invitations, don't just go looking for invitation card stock. You'll need to consider these additional elements as well—and whether they are a must have or do-without for your invitations.

Considering Ceremony Programs

Couples usually decide to have programs at their wedding ceremony for two reasons—to acknowledge the important people involved (either directly or indirectly) or to explain what will happen at the ceremony.

The former reason can be sentimental and a cost savings for your total wedding budget. That is, couples who choose to keep their bridal parties small don't want folks who were not asked to be in their wedding to feel left out. A wonderful way to give a nod to these special people is to mention or thank them in the program. This nod ends up being so much cheaper than having a larger bridal party, for whom you would need to buy bouquets and all of the other extras that come with being in a wedding party. (Read more about saving money by having a small bridal party in Chapter 3.)

First let me tell you why a program is a good idea at a wedding. Then I'll tell you how to save money on yours.

You can use your program to list all the people who will be standing up with you or contributing to your wedding in one way or another—doing a reading, singing a song, or manning the guest book. Also, it's a wonderful place to recognize your parents.

The latter reason turns your ceremony program into something akin to a playbill at the theater. It not only tells who will be playing which part in the ceremony but also what will occur in what order. In addition, if your ceremony will include certain rituals that people may not understand or that you would like to explain further, the program is the place to enlighten everyone.

A bride I know in Colorado used her ceremony program for all of the above reasons, especially to mention special people at the wedding and to give her guests a heads up on what was to occur at the ceremony. One of the reasons she decided to create a program as her ceremony guide was because she was having a Catholic Mass but a large number of her invited guests were not Catholic. "I wanted to list every single line of the Mass, including the three songs we would sing, so everyone could participate," she recalls. She even pointed out when people would be kneeling. Everyone at her wedding mentioned afterward how much a part of the ceremony they felt.

Money in Your Pocket

Just because you have a ton of things to get printed for your wedding, that doesn't mean you have to spend a ton of money doing so. On average, couples spend $560 getting everything into black and white. According to the Conde Nast Bridal Group's American Wedding Survey, that number breaks out this way—$426 for invitations, $101 for thank-you notes, and $33 for personalized printed matter like napkins and matches.

Luckily, there are inexpensive ways to get everything on paper. A bride in Colorado found out that Party City (you know, the chain party supply store) had fantastic deals on invitations, thank-you notes, and more. "They had books filled with all of the same kinds of invitations you would find at high-end stationery stores," she recalls, "but they offered a 30 percent discount off the list price, just for ordering with them." Well, this deal was simply too good to pass up. She ordered 110 invitation sets, which included the printed invitation, an inner envelope, a sheet of tissue to place inside with the invitation, a printed RSVP card with envelope, and the outer envelope. Her total bill? $165.

At the same time she ordered her invitations, she also ordered thank-you notes. She had her and her husband's name printed on them, and she ordered a larger quantity than she knew she'd need in order to get a better price. Also, she knew she'd be able to use leftovers for holidays and other times when the two of them would be sending thank-you notes. The total cost for 250 thank-you notes was $54.

The last part of her Party City order was for the reception escort cards and the table cards. For all of these she spent $18.

Her need for printed materials didn't end there, and so she turned to other methods to get the job done. She created an eight-page ceremony program on her PC and had it printed, collated, and stapled at Kinko's for $134. At Kinko's she made 220 copies ($12) of maps to the ceremony and reception locations so she could insert those in the invitations.

She didn't bother with any personalized napkins or matchbooks. She reasoned that with fewer people smoking these days, there was no justification in investing in custom-printed matchbooks. She felt the same way about printed napkins or the little ribbons to put on her favors. Since most people just toss these anyway—she sheepishly admitted that she'd done just this after attending friends' weddings—she couldn't see spending her hard-earned dollars on these unnecessary items.

By the time the wedding day arrived, this bride had managed to spend only $383 on everything she'd needed to get printed. You, too, could easily follow her lead and save as much as she did.

Saving for you: $137   **Running total: $64,393.01**

As far as saving money on a program, the easiest way to do that is to create your program at home. Once you've designed it, I would recommend taking it to a copy shop, where you can get it reproduced for pennies.

Guest Book

Technically, the guest book, which people sign at your ceremony, isn't a printed item, but since it's made of paper, it's something to add to your tally sheet for the topics covered in this chapter. That said, who says a guest book has to say "guest book" anyway? If you troll stationery stores right after school ends, you might find some great deals on autograph books—what some kids use to get school-year memories in lieu of yearbooks. Also, blank-paged journals or other kinds of blank books can serve as a guest book for your ceremony.

If you'd like to go with a traditional guestbook, I recommend going online to check out eBay for deals. A friend of mine found a fabulous guest book this way; with shipping it was only $16. Also, you can often find guest books on sale after wedding season (June through September) at party supply stores. Another idea is to buy a fabric-covered journal or blank-paged book at a bookstore and call it your guest book. You can get these for between $5 and $10.

Speaking of going online, with so many couples setting up wedding websites, have you considered creating a digital guest book on your website? In this way you'll be able to read your friends' and family members' good wishes before the wedding and after as well. If you're so touched by what they post online, later on you can print these messages and put them in a scrapbook. By using this online version of a guest book, your only costs will be the design and hosting of your website, which you would have paid for anyway by having the website, and then the paper you'd use if you decide to print the messages out at a later date.

If you're not a sentimental person and you suspect that you won't even look at your guest book in the future, then probably the best way to keep the costs on your guest book down is to not have a traditional one at all. Also, think about the timeline for your ceremony. Do you think your guests will have enough time to sign or will there be space to set up a guest book-signing area before the ceremony? Every wedding I've been to lately has featured so much pre-ceremony hubbub—people mingling in the lobby, or reconnecting with old friends—that if there was a guest book we were supposed to sign, I never saw it and no one ever pointed it out. If you have any hesitancy at all about whether you need a guest book, I suggest you just skip it altogether.

All the Printed Items for Your Reception

If you're having assigned table seating at your reception (as opposed to open seating, where guests can pick and choose where they're going to settle in), you'll need to guide your guests to the tables where you've seated them. That's why you need escort cards available for them to pick up at the start of your reception. These cards are designed to "escort" each guest to his table. Similarly, you're going to need table cards to designate each of the reception tables, so guests can put two and two together and find the table where you'd like them to sit.

It's easy to make your own escort cards and table cards. Chances are if you did the DIY invitation thing, you can find paper stock at the same place where you purchased your invitation supplies. Also, nearly every computer these days has some sort of template available in its word processing program that will allow you to make text boxes big or small enough for these cards.

You may also want to print up favor cards, especially if you're foregoing the traditional favor and making a charitable donation instead. You can place a card on each table, saying something like "In lieu of favors we have made a donation to the American Cancer Society." (More about favors in Chapter 11.)

Also, if you're stocking your reception tables with disposable cameras, a card that instructs your guests to play shutterbug would be helpful as well. That card could say, "Please feel free to be a photographer for us, and use this camera to capture fun shots you see at the wedding. Pass the camera around the table so everyone gets a turn. At the end of the evening, just leave the camera on the table. Thanks!"

Another item to add to your "to print" list might be a menu of what you'll be serving at your reception. This isn't a must, but if you've done something creative with your food choices and want to make sure your guests are aware of these special selections, then creating a menu is a good idea. Don't go crazy printing one for each guest. Having one or two framed at each reception table should be sufficient.

If you're not interested in making any of this printed stuff yourself, there's no need to worry. You may just discover that it's cheaper and easier to go someplace like a Party City to place your printing order or to do the same through one of the discount online printing companies I mentioned earlier.

It seems like every time you turn around, the U.S. Postal Service is raising the postage rate. If there's a chance this could happen before you send out your invitations, don't stock up on stamps bearing the wrong postage before it's time to mail your invitations. Also, regarding postage, take a complete invitation set to a post office and have the clerk weigh it before you drop all of them into the mail. This is the best way to know for sure how much it will cost to mail your invitations. It's best not to "guesstimate" postage. Also, if your invitation set, when placed in the envelope, is "bumpy," it might get caught in the postal sorting machines and be shredded to smithereens. To avoid this, it's best to take the envelopes to the post office to be hand-cancelled. When it comes to your invitations, you don't want to send them all out, only to have them come back "return to sender" because they lacked the proper postage, or returned in pieces, in plastic bags, because they were damaged in transit.

Thank-You Notes

Many brides find that it makes sense to order their thank-you notes when they order their invitations, especially if they are having those notes printed on the same paper stock as the invitations. This makes a lot of sense because paper dye lots can change from one ream of paper to another. Also, it's usually cheaper to have a printer do your entire job in one fell swoop than to go back later and add things on. The bigger the job or the larger the quantities, usually the greater the potential discount.

That said, there is no reason you must order matching thank-you notes, especially if you're trying to keep your printing and paper budget in check. If there's one area of your wedding where you can get away with something not being cookie cutter, it's your thank-you notes. Sure, it's nice to have both of your names printed on cards, but is it really necessary?

I'm a big fan of stocking up on note cards that say "thank you" on the cover flap whenever I see them on sale in stores. By constantly being on the lookout for these deals, I don't have to run out at the last minute and purchase expensive boxes of thank-you notes when I need to thank someone for something. Places to look for these kinds of ongoing deals on notes is the clearance aisle of an office-supply chain like Staples or the "end caps" at Target, where you'll usually find all kinds of stuff marked down. (End caps, by the way, are literally the ends of a store aisle.)

Another option for thank-you notes is using blank notes. Just as having your names printed on your notes isn't necessary, when you think about it, neither is having a thank-you note that actually says "thank you" on it. As long as you share your sentiment inside, that's all that counts, right? You can take a similar stocking-up approach on blank note cards in the weeks and months leading up to your wedding. Again, no one is going to care if the card stock you use to thank your grandmother is green while the stock for someone else's note is purple.

Finally, who says that a thank-you note has to be a traditional card at all? Plenty of couples I know have used the downtime during their honeymoon to tackle their thank-you notes. Instead of sending note cards, they pick up postcards from where they're honeymooning and send their appreciation that way. Considering how cheap postcards (and postcard postage) are, this is a terrific way to add novelty to your thank-you notes without spending a ton of money.

Dollar-Saving Do's and Don'ts

Here's a recap of how to get everything printed for your wedding without having to declare bankruptcy:

- ✆ Don't worry about sending save-the-date cards unless you're having a destination wedding or having your wedding on a holiday weekend.

- ✆ Do check out online printing websites for deals on wedding invitations and everything else you might need printed for your wedding.

- ✆ Do look to find deals on printing in brick-and-mortar stores. Places like Party City print premium invitations at a discount.

- ✆ Do keep in mind that when you order invitations, you're also ordering the RSVP card, reception card, and envelopes, so compare prices accordingly.

✆ Do place your printing order all at once to qualify for a volume discount.

✆ Don't forget to purchase 10 percent extra envelopes to account for addressing mistakes and to avoid last-minute (and expensive) supply purchases.

✆ Do consider taking a DIY approach to your invitations and other printed materials.

✆ Do look in office-supply and craft stores for great deals on paper stock.

✆ Do consider taking an offbeat approach to some of your printed materials, such as using a postcard for your RSVP card, which will save on buying envelopes and paying for postage.

✆ Do take one invitation set to the post office before you mail all your invitations. Be sure to budget for and purchase the correct amount of postage.

✆ Don't go crazy having a professionally printed ceremony program. You can print off pages from your computer and have them copied and stapled at a place like Kinko's.

✆ Don't purchase a guest book if your guests won't have time to sign it and you're never going to refer to it.

✆ Do consider stocking up on generic thank-you notes instead of ordering personalized ones, which will cost more.

Low-Cost Ways to Capture Memories on Film and Video

If you want physical memories of your big day, you'll probably want to arrange to have someone capture it on film and/or video. Keep in mind, though, there are no set rules when it comes to photographers and videographers, and that can help to spare your budget.

The wedding police won't show up if you hire a photographer but not a videographer, or vice versa. You also won't get arrested if you don't even use a professional to capture your wedding. Plenty of couples find talented individuals who know their way around a camera and who'll photograph or videotape their wedding for a peanuts price. Also, there's nothing wrong with finding a traditional photographer in an untraditional way. Couples are turning to Craigslist and eBay to uncover nearby photographers and videographers that come cheap. Perhaps, though, the best way to find a photographer or videographer is through referrals from friends or other wedding pros you've hired.

Of course, as with most things you spend money on, it's buyer beware: sometimes you really do get what you pay for. A dirt-cheap photographer might muck up your pictures or a cut-rate videographer could wreck your video. That's why it's critical to do two things when interviewing photographers and videographers.

First, ask to see their portfolio—and not just a best-of compilation of all the weddings they've ever shot. You want to see at least one couple's wedding, from start to finish, so you can see that, 90 percent of the time, they got great shots—or 90 percent of the time, the photographer's finger was in front of the lens. If you don't like what you see, which will never happen in a "highlights" or "best of" album, find another photographer.

And second, check their references. Ask them to put you in touch with two or three couples who married in the past six months or so and used their services. Ask the couple not only if they were happy with the resulting images but also what the photographer or videographer was like to work with. Did he inconspicuously capture terrific images—the couple forgot he was even around—or was he a total diva to work with, from start to finish? Personality is just as important to consider as quality of work when you hire your photographer or videographer. This person (or persons) is going to be with you for most of the day, and if this person rubs you the wrong way, then you're not going to want to have him or her around. Hire someone you won't mind spending time with, or you're going to end up having that person ruin your big day.

Finally, figure out up front exactly what you want a photographer or videographer to accomplish at your wedding. Ask yourself these questions before you start asking around for names and numbers of people to call:

♲ Do I want photo albums for my family and myself and, if so, how many?

♲ Are formally posed shots important to me?

♾ Do I want a more traditionally photographed wedding or would a journalistic or artistic approach make me happier?

♾ Do I want pictures in black and white, color, or both?

♾ Am I willing to do some of the behind-the-scenes work to save money, such as getting film developed myself?

In the following pages, I'll get into more specifics on how you can find a fabulous photographer and videographer who won't leave you in the poorhouse.

Young Photographers Can be Affordable and Fantastic

You'll never hear a professional photographer admit this, but the truth is sometimes the younger the photographer, the better the photographer is to work with. When I say a "young" photographer, I'm not talking about a high school shutterbug. Rather, a junior photographer who has apprenticed with a more experienced photographer and is either just starting out on his own or is on-staff at a studio.

Here's why I like the notion of a "younger" photographer: not only will he charge less, but also he won't have developed any habits or long-standing demands that will render him inflexible. My sense is he will allow you to have more control over how he shoots your wedding. (Of course, keep the portfolio and reference ideas in mind.)

It doesn't surprise me to hear that professional photography outlets promote their junior staffers as a way for couples to save money. Kim, a bride in Ohio, discovered this option after meeting with a photography company she loved and nearly passing out when she saw how much they charged. Luckily, the company wanted to do business with her and offered her the junior photographer option. "We still were able to book two photographers for unlimited hours and locations," recalls Kim, who was thrilled with the end result—fantastic photos of her special day. Best of all, Kim had spent $1,200 for all of her photography needs, including albums for herself and their parents. "We did not want to skimp on the photographer," she adds, noting that photography ended up being one of the biggest budget items (about 40 percent). Still, in the end Kim felt like she got a great deal and great photos, too.

Other young photographers you might consider are those at a college or university. I know at my college, which had a journalism and film department, many students studying photography photographed special events as a way to get experience, build a portfolio, and earn extra cash. If you haven't checked out these academic options, I strongly suggest you do.

Speaking of academia, students aren't the only ones who might do weddings. Plenty of faculty and staff freelance as wedding photographers and videographers. One bride hired a photographer who spends her days teaching photography at New York City's School of Visual Arts. The bride found this professor-to-wedding photographer incredibly professional to work with and not at all intrusive at the ceremony or reception. While her demeanor was great, her prices were even better—only $325 to shoot an entire wedding.

Point-and-Shoot Photographers Offer Great Deals

Professional wedding photographers usually fall into two categories. First, you have the traditional photographer who shoots your wedding and provides you with a leather-bound album and individual pictures for framing. He takes care of all of the behind-the-scenes details, and for this, you pay him handsomely.

The other kind of photographer, which I'll call a point-and-shoot photographer, takes pictures at your wedding but leaves the after-the-fact stuff up to you. A few days after the wedding he might send you a disk of all of the digital shots from the day, or upload them to a website. His approach to weddings is as professional as any other wedding photographer, but he understands that savvy couples on a budget may want to handle the after-market part of a wedding—developing film, printing photos, or making albums. It's not unreasonable of you to inquire about this possibility.

Money in Your Pocket

When you hire a traditional photographer for a wedding, usually a lot of extras are assumed. That is, wedding photographers tend to have pretty standard packages from which you have to choose. These packages include not only the photography services for the entire wedding day but also any proofs, albums, or prints you may want. For some couples this is the preferred way to go, despite the price tag. No wonder the average couple spends about $2,000 on wedding-day photography.

If you take a page from the following couple's story, you can spend significantly less on your photographer yet still get the images you want to remember your wedding day by.

So what did this couple do? They went with a traditional wedding photographer but tweaked how things were going to work. Instead of a full-blown package, they negotiated what they would describe as a "mini package." They had the photographer on hand to shoot the ceremony and the posed pictures afterward with family and friends. But when it came to the reception, the couple realized there was no reason to have the photographer on the clock from the start of the cocktail hour to the end of the night. They figured all the action they wanted the photographer to capture was going to occur from the first dance to the cake cutting. Once that was over, they sent the photographer home. They still ended up with hundreds of photographs to choose from but only paid $750 for everything the photographer did for them.

Savings for you: $1,250   **Running total: $65,643.01**

In my experience, the latter kind of wedding photographer will offer you the best deals. Some of the biggest fees from a wedding photographer get generated after the wedding. That is, the photographer marks up the price of printing the digital images and charges quite a bit for albums. That's not to say that all of this work isn't worth the money, but if you're approaching your photography with the idea of spending as little as possible, then the point-and-shoot photographer is probably the way you want to go.

Don't worry about going with this kind of photographer—they take as good, if not better, photos than traditional photographers. In fact, I find that point-and-shoot photographers end up taking more pictures at a wedding for less money. That's because a traditional photographer usually shoots with a photo album—and a prenegotiated number of images he's agreed to shoot—in mind. Once he's captured the shots he expects he'll need, he may slow down his picture taking. On the other hand, the point-and-shoot photographer is being paid for her time and her skills and that's it. She, too, will be shooting with an album in mind (if you've asked her to do so), but she will likely continue to look for good pictures to take throughout the affair. She won't be working on a "quota" system like the traditional photographer might be.

One of the best places to track down an affordable point-and-shoot photographer is at your local newspaper, especially if staffers do weddings on the side. These people work every day as photojournalists and know how to capture important moments on film—and capture them well. Who knows? Many media photographers have a freelance business doing weddings, for which they are sure to offer you a rate that's competitive with other photographers you've interviewed. As always, references and a portfolio are key.

Another benefit to the point-and-shoot photographer is that you can turn the pictures into prints at your leisure. You won't have the pressure on you to get proofs or order albums (though your parents may bug you about it), and you'll have the time to search around for the best deals possible.

A Photographer Doesn't Have to Be in the Picture the Whole Day

A terrific cost-saving option most couples aren't even aware is available to them is having a wedding photographer for only part of the day. One couple I know brought in a professional photographer for the ceremony only. After the ceremony, the photographer stuck around to get posed shots of the bride and groom along with the special people in their lives. Then he left. The couple relied on friends and family to take pictures at the reception.

Another couple used this part-time photographer approach but in a slightly different manner—and for different reasons. It turns out that the bride is terrified of having her picture taken. She knew she'd be enough of a nervous wreck at the ceremony, and didn't want anyone standing by taking her picture and pushing her to the edge of a panic attack. Instead, she asked her family and friends to take candids, and then she brought in a pro to photograph the reception. This allowed her to feel relaxed while taking her vows yet feel confident that she would have some photographic memories of her big day.

What's so smart about this approach to a wedding photographer is you end up paying for what you want from the photographer, not what the photographer's package says you have to take. In fact, in both of these situations, the couples were able to negotiate with the photographer to pay on an hourly basis, which ended up being cheaper in the long run. They also chose to handle picture printing—another move that allowed them to control their photography costs.

Very Good Deals on Videography

When it comes to wedding videography, finding the right vendor is a lot like hiring a wedding photographer. For starters, I would ask everyone you know if she can recommend a gifted videographer with a great price. Also, as with still photography and wedding musicians (mentioned in Chapter 7), you may find that your local college or university can be a treasure trove of photographic talent. It's possible that students or staff in a film department film weddings on the side and charge way less than a professional outlet does but still deliver great results.

Regardless of who you hire, give your videographer your budget up front and then ask how he can work within those financial parameters. This is important, since the Conde Nast Bridal Group's American Wedding Survey says that the average couple spends $600 on videography. Will that work for your budget? Perhaps not.

That's why you want to talk with him about cost-cutting measures. For example, having a multi-camera setup at a wedding ceremony and reception means he can film the same action from varying angles, which gives him more to choose from when editing. If you're having a small wedding without dancing, there's no reason to buy into a sales pitch for a three-camera setup. In fact, one expert I talked to told me in confidence what a videographer might not tell you: if you're having fewer than 100 people at your wedding, there's no reason to have more than one camera running. One camera can capture it all.

However, different size weddings may require different video setups. Let's say you're having a large, traditional Jewish wedding, where there will be a huge dance floor packed with people hoisting you and your family members on chairs and then dancing a hora. You're going to be talking about a lot of people moving in a lot of different directions. In order to film this well, it probably makes sense to have more than one camera capturing the action from different vantage points.

Videographers do more than shoot wedding video, of course. After the wedding, they edit the footage into your own personal movie. With editing comes special effects and other add-ons—music, montages of baby pictures, etc. With each of these add-ons, you can expect to pay more. That's why it's critical to find out ahead of time what kind of package a videographer might offer and what it includes.

Now, having a wedding video isn't for everyone, so let me ask you this— when was the last time a friend had you over to watch her wedding video? Has anyone you know even watched a wedding video more than once? Do you even like to watch TV?

I'm asking you these questions because, I'll admit, I'm a skeptic when it comes to wedding videography. I think it's one of those unnecessary things that has grown popular with weddings, simply because so many people think they need to do it. But if you can't envision yourself ever sitting down with a bowl of popcorn and reliving your wedding day on video, you've just got to wonder if it's worth the expense.

Do-It-Yourself Photography and Videography

One of the biggest wedding trends to come out of the last century is the notion of arming wedding guests with disposable cameras so they can shoot their version of the wedding. Truthfully, years ago you would never have gone to a wedding reception and expected to see disposal cameras on the table. Nowadays, you come to assume that the cameras will be there, and some guests even plan ahead for the kinds of pictures they'll take.

Considering the average couple spends close to $2,000 on photography (not including videography), you simply can't afford to be that extravagant with your photography expenses if you want to keep your wedding in the $5,000 range. And if having formally posed and photographed pictures for your entire wedding day isn't high on your priority list, you may be able to get away with a modified photography plan. For example, you could hire a professional for the ceremony only (as mentioned earlier in the chapter), and then take the do-it-yourself route for the reception by providing your guests with disposable cameras. (By the way, you can find these cameras at warehouse clubs like Sam's and Costco for about $3 each.)

"We wanted cameras on each reception table, but didn't want to spend the $5.99 to $7.99 each for the wedding-motif cameras that are out there. Instead, we bought regular old disposable cameras on sale for $2.99. No one noticed the difference, and the photos still came out great."

—Aimee, Colorado

Go Figure

When you decide to arm your wedding guests with disposable cameras at the reception, it's important to have enough cameras to go around—but not to overestimate your needs. Most guests at an 8- to 10-person table will just about get through one 24-image disposable camera. If friends and family members are confirmed shutterbugs, you may want to have two cameras per table. Nonetheless, a good rule of thumb is one camera for every 10 guests, or at least one per table. Use this worksheet to figure out how many cameras you should buy.

Step 1: Number of guests at reception _____

Step 2: Divide Step 1 by 10 for number of cameras to buy _____

Step 3: Number of tables at reception _____

Step 4: Divide Step 2 by Step 3 for number of cameras per table _____

To ensure your guests put the disposable cameras to good use, I would include a card on the table that explains that you and your spouse hope your guests will share in the joy and fun of the day by acting as your de facto photographers. Ask them to feel free to shoot anything and everything they see at the wedding, and perhaps even include a list of "suggested" shots or moments. By giving them this tipoff, such as your first dance or a picture of your sorority sisters together, you'll have a better chance of getting the pictures you'd hoped for but didn't want to shell out big bucks to have a stranger, er, professional photographer take. In fact, one bride took this approach of sharing the idea of "suggested shots" with her guests. When she developed those disposable cameras, she was pleasantly surprised to discover that her guests had taken so many wonderful shots that she was able to fill two photo albums with the pictures.

In addition to supplying disposable cameras, why not ask your shutterbug family and friends to bring along their cameras to capture various aspects of the day? Again, this is a way to get great pictures of your big day without paying big bucks. Plus, you'll be able to see your wedding from a variety of vantages and points of view—perhaps in ways that a professional photographer, who doesn't know you as well as your guests do, could never capture.

Also in the DIY vein, you can use computer software to turn your photographs into prints and albums. Programs like Apple's iPhoto or, if you work in graphic design, PhotoShop can make anyone's amateur pictures look like a professional took them.

Or you can check out online companies like Shutterfly and PhotoWorks that make hard- or soft-cover, bound photo albums. You upload your pictures to their site, and they create a fancy photo album for you—often for about $20. No one would ever know that you ordered one of these deluxe-looking photo albums through a website—and paid less for them than to fill your car's gas tank!

Finally, is there anyone in your family who has experience shooting or editing video or DVDs? With today's editing software readily available on computers—the iBook I'm writing this book on came with the Apple iMovie program, which allows me to upload video and edit it—perhaps the cheapest way to get your wedding video done is to have someone you know shoot it and then edit it yourself when you've got the time.

Dollar-Saving Do's and Don'ts

While a photographer and videographer can capture your wedding images forever, it shouldn't take you forever to pay off their bills. Here's a recap of some ways to get the great shots you want at your wedding without going into debt:

- Do figure out ahead of time exactly what you want from a photographer or videographer so you'll be able to hire someone who fits the bill—and doesn't bill you too much.

- Don't be afraid to ask a professional photographer if he has any junior photographers on staff. If so, they're often cheaper than the more senior people.

- Don't write off amateur, freelance, or student photographers, or people who teach photography, when thinking about wedding photographers. All of them may be the best way to get great shots of your wedding without paying a lot.

- Do ask if a photographer charges hourly or by the day. If hourly, you can save big bucks by using the photographer for only a portion of your wedding.

- Do find out if the photographer will be printing the pictures himself, because this add-on service can add on to your photography bill.

- Don't assume your photographer has to be with you—and on the clock—every minute of your wedding day. If you limit how much time she spends shooting, you can save money on her fee.

- Don't shy away from printing your own photos. Today's technology lets amateurs create professional-looking photos.

✆ Do call your local newspaper to see if any staff photographers do weddings. Do the same with a local TV station for your videography needs.

✆ Don't let a videographer convince you that you need two or more
cameras at your wedding, especially if you're having a smaller event.
One camera can easily capture all that goes on at an affair of 100 people or fewer.

✆ Do save money on disposable cameras by going with the generic kind.
The ones made for weddings have the same film and technology as the
generic ones, but because they're marketed for weddings, cost significantly more.

✆ Don't think you can't get great wedding shots with your family and
friends as your ad hoc photographers. If you arm them with enough
disposable or digital cameras and give them a list of things to look for,
you're going to end up with fabulous pictures that didn't cost a lot.

✆ Do consider taking a DIY approach to all of your photography and videography needs by taking advantage of software programs like iPhoto
or iMovie on personal computers. You don't have to be too terribly
tech-savvy to edit your own wedding video or put together your wedding album.

✆ Do ask a tech-savvy friend to edit your video for you as a wedding gift.
It will save you money, and it will mean more because a friend did it
for you.

10

Beauty on a Budget for the Bride and Everyone Else

If you're a fan of celebrity wedding magazines—or just celebrity magazines in general—then you know that the stars never go anywhere without first consulting a makeup artist or a professional stylist. Well, since I'm guessing that you don't earn a celebrity's big bucks, it probably isn't a good idea to blow your budget on an overpriced makeup artist and hairstylist for your wedding. Now that's not to say you can't hire someone to make you and your maids look gorgeous; you just have to approach the task with your bottom line in mind.

In this chapter, I'll give you tips on how you and your wedding party can look gorgeous even if you don't have a lot of money to spend on a professional makeup artist or hairstylist. I'll help you figure out how to bring someone affordable in to do hair and makeup and also talk about how you can do both on your own. I'll offer similar ideas for nails and any other part of your body you want to primp before the big day. Finally, I'll help you put together toiletries kits so if you or your guests have any beauty emergencies at the ceremony or reception, you'll have the tools you need on hand to fix them.

How to Hire a Makeup Artist Who Isn't High-Priced

Probably the best place to start when looking for an affordable makeup artist is the makeup counter of your local department store or a store that sells makeup—a la MAC or Sephora. The women (and men) who work there spend their days making over people, and many of them are quite good at it. Chances are many of them do freelance makeup jobs on the side. If you know a makeup person whose work you're always happy with, quietly ask if she would consider doing your wedding. Know ahead of time how much you can afford, and see if your budget fits in with her fees.

DON'T TRIP
on your SHOESTRINGS

> Just because I've mentioned hair stylists and makeup artists in separate sections doesn't mean you can't find one person to do both jobs. In fact, it would be in your financial best interest to find one person who can do both hair and makeup for your wedding. For example, at my salon they charge $110 for an updo. A local makeup artist I know charges $45 per person for a full application. If I needed both my hair and makeup done—and hired each person individually—I'd be spending $155 for their services. It's not unreasonable, then, to want to spend significantly less and to find someone who can do both your hair and makeup for something in your price range.

Another place to find a makeup artist is through your wedding photographer. Many photographers who shoot weddings also take portraits and actors' headshots. These photographers usually work in collaboration with hair and makeup artists. So see if your photographer can recommend someone you can call about your wedding-day makeup and/or hair.

Money in Your Pocket

According to the Conde Nast Bridal Group's American Wedding Survey, the average bride will spend about $370 on wedding-day beauty for herself and her maids. Jane, a bride I know, found this out fast when she started looking into hiring someone for her bridal beauty. "There was no way I could spend that kind of money," she says. By chance she happened to mention her dilemma to her wedding photographer, who gave her the phone number of a hair and makeup artist he regularly worked with.

When Jane called this makeup artist, she quoted a fee of $150 an hour. Jane was speechless because she thought the makeup artist would take a couple of hours to do five people—the bride, her mother, and her three attendants. But before Jane could interject, the makeup artist promised she would work quickly and do everyone in about an hour. Because of that promise, she would charge a flat fee of $150. Jane booked her, and as promised, she got everyone done in that hour, and everyone looked fabulous. To Jane this $150 was money well spent.

If you can find a hair and makeup artist who can quote you a flat fee like this artist did, you'll surely be ahead of the financial eight ball when it comes to your wedding beauty costs.

Savings for you: $220   **Running total: $65,863.01**

Finally, don't overlook beauty schools and academies, or technical high schools with cosmetology departments. Soon-to-be-graduates will have had plenty of on-their-feet training and should be able to offer you incredibly low prices for hair and makeup services.

Do-It-Yourself Makeup Is Often a Good Idea

Just as I suggested you visit your local makeup counter to find a freelance makeup artist, that same makeup counter can help you if you want to save money by doing your makeup yourself. If you plan to purchase new makeup for your wedding anyway, ask the salesperson to give you an impromptu makeup lesson. These folks are usually more than happy to try products out on you (to get you to buy more, naturally), so say straight out that you're getting married, want to do your own makeup, and would appreciate some tips on doing the job well. At the same time, be firm that you only want to buy makeup basics and that you're not interested in purchasing an entire skincare line. Also, be sure to state your preferred budget. Ideally, this information will help the person at the makeup counter hold back from her hard sell and keep your spending in line.

Another way to get a similar lesson is to host a makeup party at your house. One bride arranged to have her May Kay Cosmetics consultant come over one evening for what ended up being a spa bachelorette party with her bridesmaids. Not only did the women learn tips and tricks for applying their makeup, but they also left with a bunch of new makeup they would have bought either way. Best of all for the bride, her bridesmaids purchased so much product that she ended up with a "credit" for an entire makeup bag full of lipstick, nail polish, and other beauty products. (With these kinds of at-home parties, the hostess usually earns free stuff based on how much her guests spend.) So in the end she got to spend a fun night with her bridesmaids; they all learned how to do their makeup; and they all went home with new makeup to boot.

Finally, have you heard about the latest trend in learning makeup tricks? Women get together at one person's home, for dinner and drinks, with a special guest in attendance: a makeup artist who is there to teach the latest techniques using makeup that the women already own. She isn't looking to sell any products, just share her knowledge. Price to the host? About $50 for an hour's time.

No matter which way you choose to purchase your makeup or learn the tricks you'll need to know to do your own makeup, remember one thing—always do a practice run-through a few days ahead of time. That way, if a color of blush or eye shadow that you thought worked suddenly doesn't, you'll have time to go get a different one—cheaply, of course. Also, this run-through gives you the opportunity to pack everything into a cosmetics case, which will help cut down on the chances of forgetting something and having to run out at the last minute to buy new products.

Avoiding Hair-Raising Prices in Getting Your Hair Done

Who can blame a gal for wanting to have her hair look fabulous on her big day? At the same time, who can blame a gal on a budget for balking at the notion of spending hundreds of dollars to get her hair done? And who can blame a gal for wanting to pull her hair out in frustration because hairdressers can be so outrageously expensive?

Well, you can find a happy medium in this hair-raising topic with these ideas on how to keep your hair-related costs within budget and, at the same time, avoid having a bad hair day on your big day.

First, find out if someone you're close with is smart with hair design. A good friend of mine went to cosmetology school but never got around to putting that degree to good use. So while she may not have a stylist's chair, she's still a darn good wizard with a round brush and hair dryer. And if I needed to get my hair looking fabulous for a special event, she'd be the first person I would call. Also, because she doesn't have a stylist's chair or any overhead, I know her prices are far below what I would pay in a traditional salon. If you know someone like this, definitely tap into her expertise.

Next, is it possible you could barter hairdressing services for your big day? As I mentioned in Chapter 1, bartering is a fantastic way of getting services you may not be able to afford when you have a talent to offer in return. A few years ago the salon where I get my hair done was planning a special event for which they needed public relations done. In exchange for my pitching the story of their event to the local media, they gave me a gift certificate worth three visits to the salon. That was a brilliant barter, in my mind, and one you might be able to pull off if you can figure out a way to trade your talent.

If bartering is out of the question, do you know someone who knows her way around a head of hair—and could do your styling for free, perhaps even as her wedding gift to you? You'll never know if you don't ask.

Go Figure

One piece of advice I offered earlier in the book was to limit the size of your wedding party to keep your costs down. Makeup and hair is one of those areas where you're really going to pay (literally) if you have a lot of maids who need to get made up and where having a smaller wedding party will really pay off in the long run. To get a sense of how much you could potentially spend to get hair and makeup done, use the following worksheet:

Step 1: Number of female attendants, plus bride _____

Step 2: Cost per person for hair services _____

Step 3: Multiply Step 1 and Step 2 for hair costs _____

Step 4: Cost per person for makeup services _____

Step 5: Multiply Step 1 and Step 4 for makeup costs _____

Step 6: Add Step 3 and Step 5 for total beauty costs _____

Final total: _____

Would you consider getting your hair done before you get on the plane to your wedding location? One bride I know lives in a less expensive area of the country than where she was having her wedding—Southern California. "Rather than fly my hairdresser out or something crazy like that, which I could never afford, I got my hair blown out the day I was flying to California," says the curly-haired bride. "Then when I got there all I needed was a touch-up. The only embellishments I made to my hairstyle were hair ornaments I'd gotten for a steal on eBay."

If you're getting married outside of a city, you might find that hairdressers there will charge way less for hair services. One bride found that if she booked the salon where her mom gets her hair done, they could do her French twist for $35, including tip. Definitely investigate this option, especially if you have your heart set on having your hair done professionally but don't want to spend a lot of money in the process.

Finally, who says you have to get an elaborate hairdo for your big day? A simple hairstyle can be an elegant one. If you keep your hairstyle expectations simple, then you likely won't end up spending a ton on hairdressing services. Look at all the bridal magazines that show the models with long, straight-down hair. Have you considered wearing yours like this? If so, then you won't have to sit through an updo or having your hair put into a bun (with all those bobby pins!), and you won't have to pay for those services either.

DON'T TRIP
on your **SHOESTRINGS**

Decide how you want to wear your hair before you buy your headpiece, so you can pick something that works well with your style. I'd hate to see you do things the other way around—buy your headpiece first, only to discover it won't work with the way you want to wear your hair. You'll have wasted money on the first headpiece, and now you've got to go buy something new.

Getting the Celeb Smile When You Don't Earn Their Salary

Probably one of the biggest trends in beauty these days is the white smile. And when you're going to be wearing wash-me-out white on your big day, you don't want your smile to look yellow by comparison.

I'll admit I've had my teeth whitened, and I paid handsomely for it— $400 for the honor of sitting in my dentist's chair for two hours, a torture contraption holding my lips apart and a bright blue light shining in my face. But that was five years ago, and with only two at-home touch-ups in between, I still get compliments on my white teeth.

Can you afford to sneak in a visit to your dentist for a whitening? Is there any chance you could ask for it as a gift from someone? Maybe you could barter a teeth whitening for something else with your dentist? If none of these options will work or you simply can't justify this kind of expense (understandable, of course, given the small budget I've suggested you use for your wedding), you can take comfort in knowing that you can still get a bright white smile before your big day without spending big bucks.

For starters, schedule a tooth-cleaning visit with your dentist in the weeks before your wedding. You know you should be going to the dentist every six months anyway—you do go, right?—and if you've got dental insurance, you won't have a big out-of-pocket outlay for this visit. Sometimes an in-office teeth cleaning is all you need to get your smile shiny again.

If it's not shiny enough for you, consider this. The last time I was in my dentist's chair, she told me a little secret: if you use an over-the-counter whitening system right after you've had your teeth cleaned, you'll get better results because your teeth are the cleanest they can be. So after your dentist visit, get a package of Crest White Strips (they're a steal at places like Costco or Drugstore.com) or the other kinds of at-home whitening products you can buy these days, and start using them right away. These will only cost about $25 or $30.

There are other ways to keep your pearly whites bright without spending a dime—whether you whiten them or not. Here are a few ways:

- Drink your coffee, tea, or soda through a straw. This will help you avoid having your teeth soak in these stain-causing liquids.

- Switch from red wine to white wine temporarily. Red wine is a known teeth-stainer—along with a stainer of clothes, rugs, and tablecloths, should you spill it.

- Stop smoking. You know you should do this anyway to protect your health and to save money, but did you know that smoking makes your teeth yellow, too? If you want your teeth to be whiter for your wedding, you need to stop the root cause of the yellow—that cigarette in your hand. I can't promise they'll get back to their original color in time for your nuptials, but if you quit smoking now, at least they won't be getting any more yellow over time.

- Brush with a whitening toothpaste. Okay, so this is the claim the toothpaste companies make, that their toothpaste can make your teeth whiter, but since you've got to brush your teeth anyway, why not add this kind of toothpaste to your oral hygiene regimen? (Note: As one person with tooth sensitivity to another, be careful when switching to a whitening toothpaste. It can make your already-sensitive teeth even more sensitive.)

Making Manicures and Pedicures Affordable

How can I delicately say this? Well, here goes—I find that the best deals these days in manicures and pedicures can be found in the storefront nail salons that Asians run. I'm sure you know the kind I'm talking about—the ones with prices that are too good to be true. Not all of them can give you spa-quality services, but many of them can. Recently, I visited one such salon in New York City, where for $30 I received a spa pedicure and manicure. I couldn't believe it didn't cost more. Better yet, my nails looked fantastic for a full two weeks after I'd had them done. You can find similar deals if you live in a college town or have a beauty school nearby.

The most important thing to remember when getting your nails done at such a place—or any place for that matter—is your health, so consider the cleanliness of the salon. According to experts, you can take some precautions to make sure you leave a nail salon looking gorgeous and without getting a bacterial or fungal infection, which is going to add medical treatment costs to your bridal bill:

- ☼ Never shave your legs a few days before or the day of your pedicure. Not that this happens often, but it is possible for bacteria in the foot spa water to enter your body through microscopic cuts in your skin.

- ☼ Query the salon owner on how they disinfect the foot spa and the instruments the technicians use, and how frequently they change the foot-spa filter.

- ☼ Don't go to technicians who use razors to shave the soles of your feet. A pumice stone can do just as good a job.

- ☼ No matter which tool the technician uses to exfoliate your feet, make sure she uses a new one for each customer.

✆ While you shouldn't cut your cuticles, anyone who's had a manicure or pedicure knows that you look neater if you let the technician do this. If she does, make sure she's sterilized her instruments beforehand in a liquid sterilizer—look for the kinds of jars you see hairstylists putting their combs in, and make sure the liquid inside is a strong alcohol solution to kill germs. Better yet, bring your own instruments.

Besides giving yourself a manicure and pedicure at home, you can easily recreate another nail service for free. It is the paraffin wax wrap. You can add one of these paraffin dip machines to your wedding registry—and then hope that someone buys it for your bridal shower. Or you can get similar results at home without using any paraffin wax at all. Before bed simply slather your hands and feet with petroleum jelly or a thick moisturizer, and then put socks over your feet and hands. Between the warmth of your body heat and the emollient nature of the creams you've applied, you'll wake up with really soft skin.

Other Pre-Wedding Pampering to Add to Your List

Other ways you may want to prepare yourself to look beautiful on your big day might include having your eyebrows shaped or your legs waxed. What are the chances that someone gave you a spa gift certificate for your engagement, bridal shower, or even a recent birthday? If they did, now is the time to cash it in. And if they didn't, say something! People love to give gifts they know others have asked for and will use, so make someone (and yourself) happy by telling them you'd love a spa gift certificate! This will allow you to get these beautifying services without laying out any money (save for the tip you'll need to give each person who provides a service).

If you're not lucky enough to have a gift certificate burning a hole in your pocket, then I recommend you get a crash course in the services you'd like to have done and do them yourself. Pick up a copy of any beauty magazine, especially any "makeup" issue, and you're sure to find tips on how to get your eyebrows perfect for your face. Here's a warning to the new eyebrow pluckers, though: strive to pluck fewer rather than too many eyebrow hairs your first time. You don't want to end up looking like some 1960s freak, with barely a brow to speak of, because you went a little crazy with the tweezers. Just clean up the stray strands under the brow, stay true to your natural arch, and you should be okay.

Now let's say you'd like to get your legs waxed. Would you consider doing it yourself? Plenty of professional-quality waxing kits are available in drugstores these days that work as well as the waxing kits spas and salons use. I'm particularly fond of the Sally Hansen "ouchless" wax, which costs about $15—a waxing in a salon is about $50. Now, it takes a tough soul to wax your own legs, and you must follow directions carefully to avoid burning yourself. However, if you don't have a high threshold for a short amount of pain, then I recommend sticking with your shaving routine or whatever way you get rid of hair on your legs.

Note to newbie waxers: don't try to wax anything but your legs. If you must wax your arms, underarms, bikini line, facial hair, or eyebrows, hire a professional. I would never recommend doing this yourself.

Affordable Toiletries Kits for Your Ceremony and Reception

One of the nicest things you can do for your wedding party is to have an emergency toiletries kit on hand for any mishaps. You should also make up a similar kit for the ladies' room at the ceremony and reception. (Have one of your friends be responsible for transporting this kit from one location to another, if your ceremony and reception will be in separate places.) I can't tell you how many times I've been to a wedding and had a run in my stockings or needed a spritz of hairspray. Thanks to that bathroom kit, I could put on a dab of clear nail polish to stop the run in its tracks or get my hair to hold its shape for a little longer when all it wanted to do was lie flat.

In addition to the aforementioned clear nail polish and hairspray, you should include in your kit hand tissues, breath mints, sewing kit, tampons and sanitary pads, pain reliever, emery board, comb, bobby pins, and Band-Aids. If there's anything else that you think your guests might appreciate having at their disposal, like contact lens solution, then add that to your kit as well.

Now that you know what to stock, how do you do it affordably? First, you don't have to go out and buy everything. I'd start by looking under your bathroom sink to see how many of these items you already own. (I'm talking never-been-used items, of course.) You may have enough extra tampons, sanitary pads, and Band-Aids for your needs, and I'll bet you've got a bottle of clear nail polish somewhere that you can add to the kit.

Whatever you can't find under the sink, you'll need to buy. Do you have any coupons from the Sunday paper you can use? These may help shave some cents off your purchases. I know that drugstores like CVS regularly give their customers money-off coupons right on their receipts. These could help you stock up for less.

Don't automatically buy the travel-size version of everything you need. Sometimes when you add up the prices of these smaller items, they're considerably more expensive than if you'd purchased the full-size bottle or box. So do the math before loading up your shopping cart. If you do end up buying full-size items, you can have one of your maids take any leftovers home for your use.

Dollar-Saving Do's and Don'ts

There are plenty of ways to keep your makeup and hair costs in check. Here's a recap of some of the tips discussed in this chapter:

- Do figure out ahead of time how much it's going to cost to get hair and makeup done for everyone in your wedding party. If you've kept your wedding party small, bringing someone in may not be so expensive after all.

- Don't think you have to hire a separate person to do your hair and your makeup. You'll get the most bang for your buck if you can find a pro who can do both.

- Do visit your local makeup counter to see if a makeup artist there freelances for weddings.

✿ Do ask your photographer if he can recommend an affordable makeup artist for your wedding-day beauty.

✿ Don't be shy about pre-negotiating an affordable hourly or flat fee for the makeup artist's services.

✿ Don't feel bad about doing your own makeup on the big day. It's a great way to save money.

✿ Do get a free lesson at a department store makeup counter if you're doing your own makeup, and learn professional tips and tricks for looking your best.

✿ Do think about hosting a Mary Kay or other kind of makeup party as a way of getting free makeup, since hostesses often earn free products based on how much their guests buy.

✿ Do inquire if any of your friends who are well versed in hair design would be willing to do your hair for a reduced fee or, better yet, for free.

✿ Do look into bartering for hair and makeup services if you believe you've got a service you can offer in return.

✿ Do pursue having your hair done before you arrive at your wedding destination if it would be cheaper to use your local stylist.

✿ Don't think that you can't find great hairdressers in a small town, if you happen to be getting married in one. You may just find a truly talented and affordable person to do everyone's hair.

✿ Don't assume that a wedding equals an elaborate hairdo. A simple style you can do yourself may look just as elegant as one a professional would do but will be way cheaper.

✿ Don't buy your headpiece before you know how you want to wear your hair. If your headpiece and hairstyle are incompatible, you may have to buy a new headpiece.

✿ Do consider asking for the gift of teeth whitening if you'd like a brighter smile.

- ⚭ Do look into at-home whitening kits, which cost hundreds less than an in-office whitening at the dentist.

- ⚭ Do check out inexpensive storefront salons for a cheap pre-wedding manicure and pedicure.

- ⚭ Do think about giving yourself a manicure and pedicure at home, as the ultimate money saver.

- ⚭ Do consider doing other spa-related services at home as well, including eyebrow shaping and leg waxing.

- ⚭ Do put together a toiletries kit for the big day, so you can stop panty-hose runs and deal with any beauty emergencies of the day.

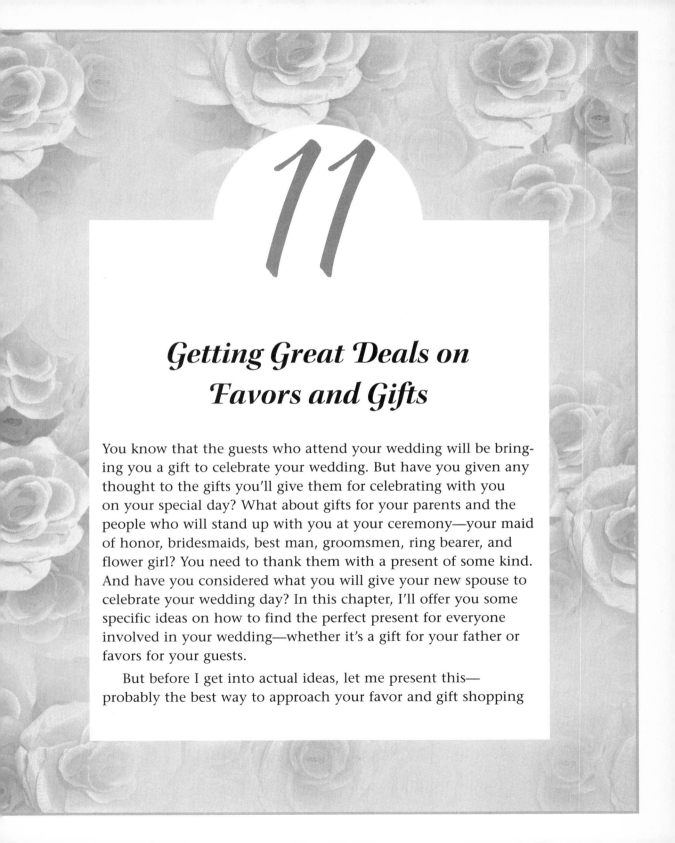

11

Getting Great Deals on Favors and Gifts

You know that the guests who attend your wedding will be bringing you a gift to celebrate your wedding. But have you given any thought to the gifts you'll give them for celebrating with you on your special day? What about gifts for your parents and the people who will stand up with you at your ceremony—your maid of honor, bridesmaids, best man, groomsmen, ring bearer, and flower girl? You need to thank them with a present of some kind. And have you considered what you will give your new spouse to celebrate your wedding day? In this chapter, I'll offer you some specific ideas on how to find the perfect present for everyone involved in your wedding—whether it's a gift for your father or favors for your guests.

But before I get into actual ideas, let me present this— probably the best way to approach your favor and gift shopping

8

is with practicality in mind. It's the same logic you use when buying some- one a birthday or holiday gift. You want to find something the person really wants and will actually use. Of course, what that "something" is will vary from person to person, but if you keep common sense in mind as you plan your shopping, you'll do a better job of buying a great gift.

What's also important is not blowing your budget in the process. This is key since studies show that brides and grooms tend to go overboard when buying favors and gifts. The Conde Nast Bridal Group's American Wedding Study showed these staggering figures: on average, couples spend about $500 on their attendants' gifts, $280 on gifts for parents, and about $285 on favors. If you're trying to keep your wedding budget in the $5,000 range, you simply can't afford to spend about 20 percent of your budget on these gifts. This chapter will show you how not to do that and, at the same time, how to find great favors and gifts everyone will appreciate and love.

Frugal Favors for Your Guests

My favorite way to be frugal about wedding favors is to figure out something that does double duty. Perhaps you feel the same way. In case you don't, let me explain exactly what I mean. In this case you would choose a little gift your guests can take home but which serves another purpose during the wed- ding reception.

Case in point: last year my husband and I attended a friend's wedding. Outside the tent where the reception was to be held was a table lined with mason jars, each with a tag that stated the guest's name and the table where he or she was sitting. Inside each mason jar was a candle, which looked like some sort of freshly canned fruit and was reflective of the season—fall. That is, the candles were all in fall's color palette of gold, red, brown, and orange. They created a lovely scene. We used the tag on the mason jar to figure out where we were sitting, and at the end of the night we took the mason jar candle home with us as our favor.

This mason jar candle/seating arrangement notification was practical from a seating and a schlep standpoint. The candle was small enough to fit in a purse, and now we use it to decorate our dining room. Back at the wedding, the colorful collection of mason jar candles added extra color to the reception tables.

I know of brides and grooms who've done similar double-duty kinds of things with their favors—including picture frames that hold your seating place card and which you can take home. Think about other ways you can do this with your favors.

You could cluster small potted plants in the center of the table as your centerpiece decoration. Have enough plants for every person at the table, so each guest gets to take one home at the end of the evening. You can do the same with clusters of candy boxes and candles. Just include a note of some sort that lets people know these are for the taking. Otherwise, everyone will go home empty-handed.

Another popular favor idea is a CD of the bride-and-groom's favorite songs. (Please download and burn responsibly to avoid breaking copyright laws.) You can make this favor a double-duty one—actually triple-duty—by having the names of the people in the wedding party on one side (no need for programs, right?). Then handwrite on the outside your guest's name and where he or she is sitting at the reception. If you give these out at the ceremony, you'll save the cost of paying for an additional table for escort cards at the reception, and, at the end of the event, people can take these CDs home as their favors. Best of all, you can do all of the printing on your home computer, and all you'll need to invest in is a box of burnable CDs in jewel cases—you can find these at any office supply store for about a dollar apiece.

"My husband decided that it was important for our favors to be something personal and something useful. Because he is an architect and a contractor, he's always using a tape measure. Because of this we decided to get mini tape measures for our guests. They cost $1.50 each."

—Aimee, Colorado

When shopping for your favors, don't just start stocking up on cute items that could potentially be your favors, and paying full price for them all along. You may end up with a favor you don't find at all favorable, and then you'll have wasted money along the way. Start out by identifying what you want to buy your guests. Next, find a place where you can buy them in bulk. Oftentimes stores will give you a volume discount when you buy a large quantity of something, and how each store defines a "large quantity" varies from establishment to establishment. However, you may be surprised to find that in buying bulk, you can save 30 percent or more on your overall purchase.

How Food Can Make a Fantastic Favor

Sometimes something sweet and unexpected makes the best wedding favor. One bride I know put out trays of caramel apples for her guests to nosh on after the wedding was over. The favors were perfect because they evoked childhood memories for many (caramel apples happened to have been the bride's favorite fall snack when she was younger), and once they were eaten, they were gone. Of course, they were a bit messy, which is why the couple also handed out individual packets of wet wipes. Best of all, between the cost of the apples, caramel, sticks, and the wet wipes (purchased in bulk at Sam's Club), the favors cost less than $100 for more than 100 guests.

Another bride took the food—and inexpensive route—by combining her dessert, centerpieces, and favors. It just so happened that the women in both the bride's and the groom's family loved to bake cookies, and both of them grew up eating fresh-out-of-the-oven cookies at every family event. It's no wonder, then, that they decided to have a cookie dessert table at the wedding. The couple asked their relatives to do the baking as their gift to them. All agreed. However, the cookie theme ended up being about more than just dessert.

Because the couple decided to use cookies for their table centerpieces as well, they purchased gigantic cookie jars, with removable lids, to place on each table. Each jar would feature one relative's sweets, whether it was grandmother's Italian wedding cookies or the bride's mother's peanut butter cookies. In addition, there would be similar jars of one relative's cookies on the dessert tables. Each jar featured a label explaining its content.

At the end of the evening, when they rolled out the cookie tables, the guests received pink vellum bags to place their selected cookies in. These bags featured clear labels with the bride and groom's names and their wedding date. "They could eat the cookies throughout the night or take them home as their favor," the bride recalls. And the bride was delighted to discover how much her cookie craftiness had saved her—she ended up spending $97 for dessert, centerpieces, and favors for 300 guests. Now that's sweet.

Go Figure

Here's how the bride who served cookies for dessert and her favors figured out what supplies she needed to buy so her 300 guests could go home happy with yummy cookies. If you decide to adopt a similar plan for your favors, use this worksheet to figure everything out.

Step 1: Number of guests at reception _____

Step 2: Use Step 1 to determine how many bags and labels to buy _____

Step 3: Number of cookies per guest _____

Step 4: Multiply Step 1 and Step 3 for number of cookies for favors _____

How Charitable Donations Can Make Sense for Your Favors

I mentioned earlier that the average couple spends close to $300 on favors for their guests. While it's a lovely gesture to give your guests a little something to thank them for attending your wedding, don't you sometimes wonder if your money would be better spent somewhere or somehow else? Truth is, since you're on a budget, it is important for you to find a better way to spend money on favors, if you can't find affordable, traditional favors. One way is to make a charitable donation in lieu of the expected wedding favors, a trend that continues to grow more popular as weddings have become such expensive events.

Couples usually decide to make a donation instead of handing out favors for several reasons. One of them is having a cause that's near and dear to their hearts and therefore wanting to use their wedding to support that cause. Another is to avoid going through the hassle of shopping for favors when they think their guests might just toss them anyway. Finally, writing a check to a charity can be cheaper financially than buying favors, but richer emotionally and spiritually in the long run.

Money in Your Pocket

Despite what the statistics tell you, you don't have to spend $280 on wedding favors. There are plenty of ways to use your hard-earned dollars creatively so that you can recognize your wedding guests with some sort of favor that doesn't leave you broke.

Probably the easiest way to make your favors affordable is to not give them at all and make a donation to charity instead. This way you can control how much you spend and feel confident that you've spent your money wisely. Also, and check with your accountant first, this donation may be considered a tax write-off.

Recently, bride and groom Kim and Aaron went the charitable donation favor route because it made sense for their budget and was a way to support a cause they cared about—THON, a student-run philanthropy that they'd both become involved with while undergraduates at Penn State. By giving $2 per guest for their 100-person wedding, they donated $200 to charity and still spent under the national average for favors. If you were to adopt the same strategy of giving an amount per guest or a similar strategy of giving a lump sum for your donation, you can do what Kim and Aaron did: support a good cause and keep your favors budget in check.

Savings for you: $80   **Running total: $65,943.01**

Regarding causes near and dear to the couple's heart, here's how that played out with one couple I know. The year before they became engaged, the bride's father was diagnosed with cancer. He was a practicing physician who, once he went into remission, began working with other doctors to start a cancer research foundation. "Given my dad's situation, it made sense to have our wedding help this foundation somehow," the bride recalls. Already not sold on the notion of favors, the couple decided to make a donation to the foundation and then tell the guests about it via cards made on their computer and placed on the reception tables. "Probably 80 percent of our guests commented on how nice it was that instead of a favor we made a donation. Better yet, by telling our 145 guests about my dad's foundation, we were able to raise awareness of the work they were doing." And as far as her budget was concerned, the money spent on donations was way less than what they had budgeted to spend on trinkets. (Interesting side note: the guests at this couple's wedding were so moved by the gesture that many ended up making donations on their own after the big day. All told, this wedding helped to raise $5,000 for this good cause.)

Any couple can do something like this for their favors—find a cause they support, make a donation, and then print up cards to notify their guests of their gesture. But what if you don't know which cause to support? Or you're not sure how much to donate? Or you're not interested in having to print out hundreds of cards to place on your reception table? The good news is that a relatively new organization can help couples make their wedding benefit a good cause without breaking a sweat. It's called the I Do Foundation, and part of what they do is help couples find charitable organizations to which they can make donations in lieu of favors.

When you visit www.idofoundation.com, you'll see on the homepage that one of your options is "wedding favors for charity." Once you click through that link, you'll discover the step-by-step process of registering with the I Do Foundation, plus the different philanthropies you might want to help out with your donations. Their good causes generally fall into these categories: children, youth, families; community development; education; environment; health; social justice. And they include everything from well-known charities to obscure good causes.

Not only does this organization help you figure out which charity to support, but it also does all of the behind-the-scenes work for you—including making up those place cards you can put out at the reception. Finally, the organization handles the actual donations, too. And if on your list you don't see a charity that tugs at your heartstrings, you can suggest a new charity to I Do. If the charity meets their criteria—it has to be a registered tax-exempt organization with the IRS, for example—they'll set everything up for you and your favors so that you can work with the I Do Foundation to have your favor donations support this good cause.

Great Gifts to Give Each Other

There is no end to the kinds of gifts you can give each other to celebrate your wedding day. Watches and jewelry or something sentimental, like a time capsule of your first date together, are popular selections. Since you're planning your wedding on a shoestring, I would strongly recommend you not do something frivolous when buying each other a wedding gift— especially since the average couple spends about $370 on gifts for each other. Instead, lean toward gifts of practicality and simplicity.

For example, is there something you need for your home that you couldn't register for? Are there things you both enjoy or need that won't cost a lot of money but from which you could get great mileage as a wedding gift? One couple I know didn't spend a lot on each other's gifts, but they meant a tremendous amount to each other. He bought her a couple of gift certificates to the local car wash, since he knew his new wife preferred to have her car spotless most of the time. And she bought him tickets to see his favorite minor league baseball team. Neither spent more than $50, but because there was so much meaning behind each gift, it was worth millions.

Another way to handle each other's gifts is to buy something for the wedding. One bride collects Hummels, so her husband's wedding gift to her (given before the ceremony), was a Hummel cake topper. It was personal, sentimental, and useful.

You can also take the austere approach to each other's gifts by not buying anything outright. This is a good idea if the two of you are paying for your own wedding and are going to be on a tight budget because of everything you're paying for in making the wedding a reality. Couldn't you consider this personally planned wedding your gift to each other? Or could you promise to buy each other something amazing for your first anniversary? By the time your first anniversary rolls around, the sting of paying for your wedding will likely have long worn off, and perhaps you will be in a better place financially to spend a bit more on each other.

A Little Something to Thank Your Attendants

The best way to approach your attendants' gifts is to keep things simple. I don't want to see you blowing your budget on what's supposed to be something small. I mean, the average bride spends more than $300 on her attendants' gifts, and the groom spends close to $220. That's more than $500, and with our $5,000 goal in mind, spending 10 percent of that on attendants' gifts is out of the question.

Probably the best gift you could give the people in your wedding is something that they're going to need for the wedding anyway—something you probably told them they should buy but expected them to pay for to be in your wedding. This may not work with every budget, but I do know brides who picked out bridesmaid dresses, then found them for a great price at an outlet and bought them for everyone. That was their gift to their attendants. You can do the same for the jewelry you want your maids to wear or the handbags you hope they'll carry to match their outfit. On a similar note, the groomsmen could benefit from a new set of cufflinks if the groom has asked them to wear shirts with French cuffs and its likely the men don't already own a pair of cufflinks.

One bride in Minnesota made her attendants' gifts practical. She suspected that there would be a nip in the air on the night of her September wedding. And even though Mother Nature wasn't going to cooperate with a warm fall day, it was too late to change what the bridesmaids would be wearing—strapless gowns. "So I gave my bridesmaids a gift they could use to keep warm—pashmina wraps, which I purchased from a street vendor for only $5," the bride recalls. "Sure they may not have been the real pashmina deal, but they were lovely, and I knew my attendants appreciated them when the mercury dipped that night." In fact, the shawls, in the same complementary colors as each bridesmaid's gown, added a lovely touch to the wedding photos.

Something else to consider when thinking about attendants' gifts is to search out gifts that will remind your attendants of your wedding day—either the time of year or the location of the wedding. For example, if you plan to be married on a beach, could you give each gal a large conch shell? This would help bring back memories of your wedding each time she looks at it or holds it up to her ear to hear the sea. Do you plan to marry at Christmas? Could you give your attendants Christmas ornaments that somehow speak to your December wedding? What about choosing a framed print or painting from an artist who is local to where your wedding is held—and is affordable, too? One bride did just this, and then attached a handwritten, heartfelt note to the back of each attendant's painting to add a truly personal touch to the gift.

"We planned ahead when buying gifts for our attendants, and hit the stores right after Christmas. We got great deals that way."

—Aimee, Colorado

Speaking of frames, sometimes the simplest gift is the one that evokes the most emotion. If you and your attendants are planning to get together before the wedding, have someone take a picture of all of you together. Then, you can make your gift to them a framed picture from that day. It will be simple; it will be affordable; and I'm sure it will mean a lot to the recipients.

Showering Your Parents with Something Special

Perhaps the best gift you could give your respective parents is the gift of paying for your wedding yourselves. Since you're reading this book and planning a wedding on a shoestring, chances are that gift is doable. Even if you can't cover 100 percent of your wedding costs, it would be wonderful if you can spare Mom and Dad the pain of having to dip into their IRA to pay for your wedding. That in and of itself would be a gift they'll appreciate many years into their retirement.

Let's say, though, you'd like to give them a gift that's a bit more tangible—you know, something they could display on a shelf or show off when people come to visit. I think the first thing that would fall into this realm is their own photo album from your wedding. It doesn't have to be anything fancy, like the leather-bound, gilded-edge albums most wedding photographers offer and charge an arm and a leg for. Rather, I'm suggesting you gather personal photographs from the big day and make your parents an album. And do you want to add an even more personal touch? Find pictures from your childhood or other momentous events in your life and intersperse those pictures with the ones from the wedding. Those will surely give your gift individual flair.

If you'd like to give your parents something engraved, such as a picture frame or a keychain, stores like Things Remembered can offer really affordable options. Along the lines of personalization, have fun and make a "wedding" t-shirt that features a picture of you and your parents that you have transferred onto the shirt. You can buy t-shirt transfer kits at office supply stores and superstores like Target or Wal-Mart to make this shirt at home, using a color printer and your iron. Or you can upload your photos to websites like Yahoo Photos, Snapfish.com, CafePress.com, and others like them to have someone else do the printing. Finally, you can give Mom and Dad a gift that doesn't cost too much but plays into their hobbies and favorite pastimes, such as a bottle of wine, tickets to see a play, or reservations at their favorite restaurant.

Dollar-Saving Do's and Don'ts

Here's a recap of how to make favors and gifts affordable:

- ⚭ Do think about choosing favors that can do double duty, such as picture frames that hold seating cards or centerpieces that can be dismantled to become individual favors.

- ⚭ Do keep in mind that food can make a truly memorable—and frugal—favor for your wedding guests to take home with them.

- ⚭ Do create a card on each reception table that explains your favor choice, if it needs explaining.

⚭ Don't write off the notion of making charitable donations in lieu of traditional favors. Your wedding guests may appreciate not having to take anything home, and the good causes you choose to support will surely appreciate your contribution. Also, this philanthropic option can be cheaper in the long run.

⚭ Do keep gifts to each other on the simple side, especially if you're spending all your extra cash on the wedding.

⚭ Don't think there's anything wrong with not buying each other a wedding gift. Getting married to each other can be a gift in and of itself.

⚭ Do stay on the side of practicality when buying your attendants gifts. It would be awesome if you could afford to pick up the tab for any jewelry, clothing, or other accessories you've requested they wear at your wedding.

⚭ Do look for gifts that will remind your attendants of your wedding but won't cost too much to buy.

⚭ Don't write off the powerful emotional punch of a picture frame or a photo album as a gift, especially for your parents or your attendants. Pictures are a wonderful way to remember your special day and shouldn't cost too much to get.

⚭ Do think about giving your parents the best gift possible—the gift of picking up the tab for your own wedding.

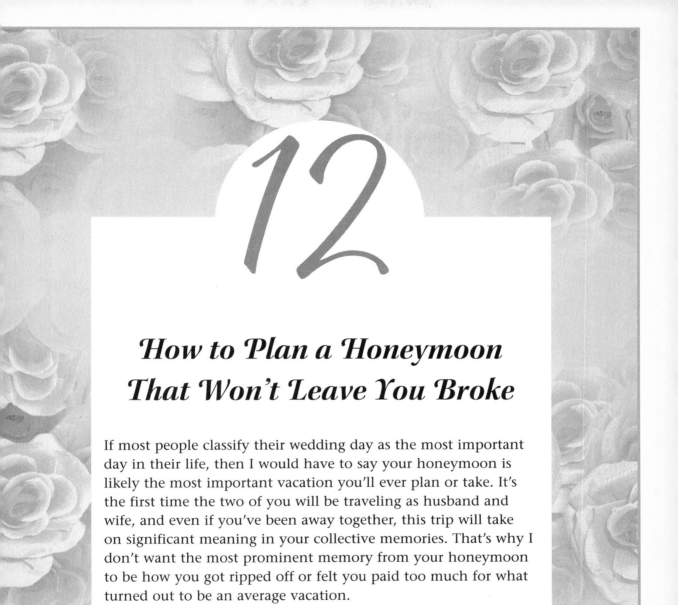

12

How to Plan a Honeymoon That Won't Leave You Broke

If most people classify their wedding day as the most important day in their life, then I would have to say your honeymoon is likely the most important vacation you'll ever plan or take. It's the first time the two of you will be traveling as husband and wife, and even if you've been away together, this trip will take on significant meaning in your collective memories. That's why I don't want the most prominent memory from your honeymoon to be how you got ripped off or felt you paid too much for what turned out to be an average vacation.

In this chapter, I'll help you plan a honeymoon that won't leave you broke. Not feeling broke is important, since the average couple spends about $4,000 on a honeymoon. Among other things, I'll talk about the timing of your trip and how time of year can help you reap financial rewards or wreck your budget.

I'll also give you some good savings ideas—from employee discounts (did you know that some companies offer these to their staff?) to timeshares. I'll also get into the nitty gritty of travel insurance and explain why it's important to make room in your budget for it.

How Time of Year Can Equal Great Travel Deals

Most families vacation during the summer, around Christmas, and during winter or spring break. They often go to Florida or some other family-friendly destination. Because families with school-age children tend to travel during these times and to these places, companies know that during this time of the year, they can charge more for everything from airline tickets to hotel rooms. Want to honeymoon in Disney World? Definitely don't try to go the week of President's Day or around Easter. This is when most schools are off and most families are on the road.

Keep things like time of year in mind when planning your honeymoon, so you won't be paying through the nose for the honor of vacationing with screaming tots. But if you want to go to Florida, September is a great time to go because the weather is still fantastic and all the kids are back in school. Prefer to ski for your honeymoon? I wouldn't recommend doing that in the week between Christmas and New Year's because, guess what, that's where all the snow bunny families will be, too. However, have your wedding in early January and your honeymoon soon thereafter, and you'll likely have the slopes to yourself.

Avoiding crowds and screaming children aside, these off-peak travel times are also when you're going to find the best deals. One bride and groom with a July wedding found that, come high summer, prices to Caribbean destinations get slashed. Fewer people want to go closer to the equator during summer when it's already hot at home, and even more importantly, they don't want to be in the Caribbean during hurricane season.

In fact, hurricane season, June 1st through November 1st, can work in your favor if you prefer honeymooning in the Caribbean. Because of the risk of traveling during this tumultuous weather time, resorts and airlines go the extra mile to attract tourists by slashing prices and offering incentives to lure people into filling their seats and rooms. Of course, if you decide to risk things and visit the Caribbean during this time of year, I strongly suggest you buy travel insurance—just in case. (More about insurance later in this chapter.)

DON'T TRIP
on your SHOESTRINGS

> When budgeting for your honeymoon, don't forget to add in all the taxes that come with airline tickets and hotel stays. They can significantly boost the cost of what you thought was going to be an affordable trip. Case in point: on a recent trip to New York City, I thought I'd snagged a great deal on a hotel room. However, upon checking out, I realized I hadn't budgeted properly, and with all the added taxes, I was actually paying $60 more a night than I thought.

The off-season can work in your favor in non-Caribbean destinations as well. The environment of ski towns become entirely different during the summer, and many of the places you couldn't afford to step foot in when there's snow on the ground suddenly become affordable. The same occurs with beach towns. I can recall vacationing with my husband in the Hamptons after Thanksgiving. While I may not have been able to do the same kind of star watching that's likely going on during the summer, we were able to shop in great stores and dine in fantastic eateries. Also, because it was the off-season, we found that most places we visited had some kind of "two for one" or other incentive deal that made our already affordable trip even cheaper.

You may not want to change your wedding date just to get a great deal on a honeymoon, but no matter when you get married, it's off-season somewhere—and that's the place where you should honeymoon if you're looking to find the best travel deals.

Frequent Flier and Other Affinity Points Programs

Chances are you have frequent flier miles adding up from some traveling you've done or points with a hotel's affinity program that have accrued over time. Now would be a great time to cash those in; miles and points are a fantastic way to "pay" for a honeymoon without laying out a ton of cash.

Dan and Laura took this approach when planning their honeymoon to Tahiti in September. When they first started researching Tahiti, they discovered that flights from Washington, D.C., to Tahiti and back would cost nearly $2,000—per ticket! And the lodging for their weeklong trip would have cost another $3,000. "After paying for our wedding, we simply couldn't afford to lay out $7,000 for our honeymoon," Laura says. Well, who'd want to? That's a big chunk of change on top of the wedding costs. But it turned out that Dan's business traveling paid off for them. With all the points and miles he'd earned on airlines and at hotels, they got their honeymoon free. "Starwood Hotel's points program, in my opinion, is the best because there are no blackout dates or restrictions," adds Dan. "Thanks to that program, our honeymoon was possible." The only things that Dan and Laura ended up paying for were their drinks and food.

Does one of you travel for a living? Have you been saving up all of those frequent flier miles for a rainy day or, in this case, the trip of a lifetime? Well, now would be the time to start looking into how you can use those miles and points to shave costs from your honeymoon. If you do travel a lot and haven't bothered to sign up for any points-based programs, I recommend doing so pronto. Who knows? Maybe by the time your wedding is here, you'll have accrued enough points to be able to plan a honeymoon that's pretty much free.

Money in Your Pocket

From the get go, Dawn, a bride in Los Angeles, understood the value of membership points and how they could go a long way toward helping to pay for her honeymoon. For starters, she paid for everything for her wedding by credit card (smart girl—credit cards provide great protection, which you can read all about in Chapter 1).

And the credit card she used just happened to have been her American Express card, which allowed her to earn membership rewards points. Thanks to her savvy planning, she earned enough points to buy her husband's airline ticket to Paris at a deep discount. Hers cost $2,400—ouch. His? $150. Next, she transferred her remaining rewards points into points at a Hilton hotel and booked three nights in Paris for free. (Had she paid for the room, it would have cost $1,200.)

By the time Dawn and her new husband got to Paris, all they needed to pay for was food, drinks, and shopping during their three-day stay in the City of Lights.

Savings for you: $3,450   **Running total: $69,393.01**

Employee Discounts

Years ago I worked for a company that owned, among other entities, travel agencies. One of our employee benefits was discounted travel from time to time. Usually, once a week we'd get a memo that highlighted any upcoming deals where our employee discount would be eligible, should we be planning a trip. I recall one of my colleagues booking a four-day cruise from New York to Bermuda for only a couple hundred dollars. It was an unbeatable opportunity.

While not every company can offer the kinds of deals that a company with a travel agency arm can, plenty of employers have pre-negotiated travel discounts their employees can use. For example, some companies have aligned themselves with certain airlines and rental cars, which may take 20 percent off a bill because of where you work. Of course, even with 20 percent off, these prices may still not be the best you can get, but if they are, then you should definitely take advantage of them.

One company near Chicago offers a small perk to its employees—$10 to hire a limousine to take them to and from the airport. If you've ever been to the Windy City, you know that a trip in from O'Hare or Midway will set you back $50 or more without traffic. So while a small employee discount like this one won't get you a free honeymoon, it can help cut costs on your transportation to the airport.

Any chance that your employer offers similar discount programs for the people who work there? If you're not sure, pop your head into your human resources office—or send someone in HR an e-mail—and find out if any such discounts exist. You may be pleasantly surprised to learn that your job can help make your honeymoon a little bit more affordable.

Timeshares

Before my husband and I were married, he bought a timeshare in St. Thomas. It cost a couple thousand dollars for two weeks of vacation time a year. At the time, that price seemed exorbitant. However, that timeshare has paid for itself many times over, in that we've "traded" our time from St. Thomas to stay in places as diverse as San Francisco and the Wisconsin Dells. For a mere $150 per trade, we had lodging for a week in each of these locations. You can't get a hotel room in San Francisco for one night for $150.

I'm not writing this to encourage you to go out and buy a timeshare but, instead, to think about someone else's timeshare as a possible honeymoon option. For example, a bride in New Jersey used her uncle's timeshare in Las Vegas for her honeymoon. And instead of paying $1,800 for a week of lodging, she paid $250—the "trade fee" her uncle incurred for giving her that week.

Do you know someone who owns a timeshare in a place where you might like to honeymoon? Are you comfortable asking them for use of that timeshare for your big trip? Don't expect someone to give it to you for free, especially since it usually costs so little out-of-pocket for you to stay in one. However, if you do end up getting it as a gift, that would be fantastic.

Another cost-saving benefit to timeshares that might not be obvious up front is that most timeshares are in an apartment-like setting. That means they'll have a full kitchen or, at the very least, a kitchenette you can use to prepare at least some of your meals. Of course, you'll want to have a dinner or two out on your honeymoon, but with a kitchen at your disposal, you can keep bagels, coffee, and juice on hand and save yourself the $20 or so you would spend on breakfast at a restaurant each morning.

DON'T TRIP
on your **SHOESTRINGS**

Because of changes in security rules, you'll need your passport to travel anywhere outside of the United States—including Canada and the Caribbean, where previously, a passport was optional. If you've never had a passport or need to get yours renewed, give yourself plenty of time to do so. While a new passport costs $97 and a renewed one costs $67, if you leave all of this to the last minute, you're going to pay a $60 fee to expedite your order, plus overnight mailing charges. Visit travel.state.gov/passport for more information on passports.

Borrowing Real Estate

The notion of borrowing real estate for your honeymoon is similar to the idea of using someone's timeshare. Could you do the same with someone's beach house or ski chalet? I'll bet you know at least one person who owns a vacation home somewhere. If you offered that person a nominal fee to "rent" it for a week, do you think that person would go for it?

Of course, this isn't the kind of request that you make at the last minute or for a holiday weekend, when most people travel to their vacation home. However, if you inquired about this rental and you wanted to go during a time when the house would otherwise be sitting empty, what does this person have to lose? I mean, if anything they'll be gaining something—a small amount of income—by granting your request. So if you haven't considered this notion as you try to plan your honeymoon without spending a bunch, you definitely should.

Registering for a Honeymoon

As you know by now, these days couples register for pretty much everything for a wedding—tents at Target, HVAC supplies at Home Depot, and laundry baskets at Linens 'n Things, to name a few. And now you can register for your honeymoon, too. This is a great option if you're trying to plan the trip of your dreams but don't want to pay a fortune for it.

Go Figure

To really know how much your honeymoon is going to cost, it's important to consider everything you're going to need to pay for during your trip. Use the following worksheet to accomplish that task.

Step 1: Cost of airfare for you both   _____

Step 2: Number of nights on honeymoon   _____

Step 3: Price per night of hotel/resort   _____

Step 4: Multiply Step 2 by Step 3   _____

Step 5: Estimated cost per day for food and drinks   _____

Step 6: Multiply Step 2 by Step 5   _____

Step 7: Estimated spending money needed per day   _____

Step 8: Multiply Step 2 by Step 7   _____

Step 9: Other costs (travel to/from departure point, around town on honeymoon, spa visits, entertainment, etc.)   _____

           Total needed for this honeymoon: _____

Most honeymoon or travel registries work through existing travel agencies or travel-related companies who do all of the planning for you. Usually they list all the elements of your chosen honeymoon on your registry, which allows your guests to choose which "part" of your honeymoon they want to pay for as their gift. Or the registry becomes a savings account, if you will, to which your guests can contribute money to help you pay for your honeymoon.

Of the companies offering honeymoon registries, you'll note that the government of Aruba runs one of them. Yes, that's right—the Caribbean nation of Aruba is so serious about attracting honeymooners that they've gone to the trouble of setting up a countrywide registry.

Note: This list of online sites that offer honeymoon registries is just FYI. I have not booked travel with any of these, and therefore cannot vouch for their services.

- ☯ **Aruba.com**   The nation of Aruba lets you register for various activities on the island—from dinner out to scuba diving.

- ☯ **Backroads.com**   Backroads has made a name for itself over the years by focusing on active vacations on bike or on foot. You can register for any of the itineraries they offer. Then you can use whatever amount your guests contribute to the registry to pay for your honeymoon.

- ☯ **Distinctivehoneymoons.com**   This registry program is the brainchild of ProTravel International, an established travel agency, which can do all of the travel booking for you.

- ☯ **Honeyluna.com**   This is one of those registry programs that outlines specific activities the couples have registered for and lets guests contribute accordingly. Even airfare can be included in the desired "activities."

- ☯ **Honeymoonwishes.com**   When you register here, you won't get any travel agency-like benefits or services. This site simply acts as your honeymoon registry "repository" to which guests can send money. You also get a free wedding website.

- ☯ **Sendusoff.com**   A husband and wife, who set up a honeymoon registry for their wedding on their own, launched this company soon after they returned from their trip. You have the option of using their registry services, then booking travel yourself or through one of their travel partners.

- ☯ **Starwoodhoneymoons.com**   The Starwood hotel chain has gotten into the honeymoon registry business by letting you set up a wish list of which Starwood hotel you'd liked to stay in for your honeymoon.

- ☯ **Thebigday.com**   This honeymoon registry offers a free wedding website for registered couples. Through this company, you can book an

African safari or Caribbean cruise as your honeymoon, among your many choices. If you don't book your travel through this site, when you go to "collect" your honeymoon registry loot, you're going to get hit with a hefty service charge.

⌾ **Thehoneymoon.com**   Like other honeymoon registry sites, you can review other couples' registries, in case you're stuck on how to set yours up. This program isn't run through a travel company; they just act as your collection agent for cash donations toward your honeymoon. You get a check five days before you leave on your honeymoon so you can pay off your travel bills.

Are there any drawbacks to a honeymoon registry? Just like when you register for 12 place settings of china, there's no guarantee you'll get all 12, and then you're stuck paying for the remaining settings if you want them. It's the same with your honeymoon registry. If you've planned an elaborate trip and only a few guests have bought into the concept of a honeymoon registry, you're going to have to pay for the remainder of the trip yourselves. At least with china you can put off making those final purchases, but you probably don't want to put off taking your honeymoon.

Also, some companies require a deposit or setup fee up front, and others charge your guests a "processing" fee when they make a financial contribution. Finally, if you cancel your trip or change your itinerary, you may find yourself subject to a penalty fee.

All caveats considered, I still believe that using a honeymoon registry to get your honeymoon for free (or practically free) is a great idea. Just make sure you read the website FAQ and any fine print about how each program works so you know all of the terms and conditions before you sign on the digital dotted line.

Low-Fare Travel

There's more to low-fare travel than airlines like Southwest and Jet Blue. There are many places on the Internet where you can get great deals on airlines, hotels, and more. These sites include Hotels.com, Orbitz.com, Travelocity.com, Priceline.com, and one site I hadn't heard about until a bride told me about it—SkyAuction.com. Here's how that website worked for her.

"We were interested in going somewhere exotic for our honeymoon, like the South Pacific, but we knew we had to spend wisely since we'd just paid for our whole wedding," the bride recalls. A big fan of the eBay model of shopping where you get to bid on auctions, she just happened to stumble upon SkyAuction.com. "It's a site that essentially auctions off everything from vacation packages to airline flights." She and her fiancé had decided to honeymoon on Bora Bora and started watching auctions related to this destination. Though they got outbid a couple of times, they eventually won an auction that really paid off—roundtrip airline tickets and lodging for one week for $1,600. "I discovered that if we'd bought our tickets the traditional way," the bride adds, "we would have paid $1,600 just to fly there one way!"

Sites like Priceline.com work in a somewhat related nature, though you don't bid against others directly. However, you do enter a price you're willing to pay, sort of like an auction. Sure, Priceline.com lets people book travel the traditional way these days, but still, some of the best deals to be found are using Priceline.com the old-fashioned way—telling the site what you're willing to pay and then seeing if your price gets accepted.

If you do go the Priceline.com way, make sure you visit Biddingfortravel. com first. This website and its bulletin boards provide timely information about how others have successfully bid on Priceline.com—such as starting bids and the hotels that likely come up in certain destinations. Whenever I use Priceline.com to book travel, I always stop first at Biddingfortravel.com. Just as an FYI, thanks to this site, I've been able to secure New York City hotel rooms for $75 when Priceline.com said bidding that low was impossible—but then a few screens later told me that my bid had been accepted. And these weren't for dinky hotels, either. They were brand-name hotels in terrific midtown neighborhoods.

Travel Insurance

I was never a big believer in travel insurance until a few years ago. My husband and I had booked our first cruise together, to celebrate our anniversary. A few weeks before we were going to embark, I was diagnosed with gallbladder disease. While my doctor figured my gallbladder still had a good long life ahead of it, he advised me to keep close tabs on my symptoms nonetheless. Well, soon enough I was going to be on the high seas with my honey, and the last thing I wanted was to have my vacation interrupted because I needed emergency surgery.

In addition to the risk of surgery, we were taking a cruise in August to a place known to see hurricanes from time to time—New England and the Canadian Maritimes. While it was unlikely that any hurricane would make its way that far up the East Coast when we were cruising, it was possible. Because my husband is an admitted cheapskate, the idea that we might pay for a week's vacation but only get a few days of it—either because of my gallbladder acting up or a hurricane hitting—was too much for him to handle. So we purchased travel insurance that offered us a number of protections. These included:

- ⚭ Trip cancellation that, should we back out of our vacation before even leaving the port, we would receive a full refund.

- ⚭ Trip interruption, which means just that—if we had to interrupt our trip because my gallbladder was acting up, we could recoup some of our costs.

- ⚭ Travel medical insurance, which we gladly added onto our travel insurance policy in case any hospital we visited wouldn't accept our HMO insurance card.

- ⚭ Medical evacuation, which we also paid for, since we knew we would be out to sea and the cruise ship wasn't going to sail to port because of my gallbladder. In other words, if we wanted off the ship for medical reasons, we were going to have to hire an air ambulance for the job—and we wanted insurance to cover that cost.

Luckily, we never had to use that travel insurance (which, by the way, only added a couple hundred dollars to our travel bill) but we got a first-hand lesson on its importance. On our second day at sea, a man on board the ship had a heart attack and had to be airlifted to shore via helicopter. Later we learned that the man was fine and expected to make a full recovery, but I always wondered if he'd had full travel insurance, too, because I'm guessing it was pretty expensive to have that helicopter fly out to the ship and then back to the mainland.

With my gallbladder situation and this real-life lesson in mind, I now make it a priority to purchase travel insurance whenever I travel. With such an important trip as a honeymoon—and especially if you'll be traveling to a hurricane-prone place during hurricane season—I would say that travel insurance should be a must for you, too. (And the travel insurance companies aren't paying me to say this.)

As far as where and how to get affordable travel insurance, we were able to secure it through the travel company that booked our cruise. Some credit card companies offer travel insurance as part of their benefits. Might one of the cards in your wallet provide this free of charge? I suggest you check it out. Other places to inquire about travel insurance include your local AAA and companies like Travel Guard and Access America.

Shopping for Your Trip

It's important to remember to pack everything you need for your honeymoon, and it's also important not to go overboard with your spending when you arrive at your destination. I always like to hark back to my camp days when preparing for a trip out of town. About a week before I'm set to leave, I start writing a list of all the things I'm going to need to pack. I add to this list over the days as I remember other things I want to take. Then about two days before I leave, I check that list to see what I already own and what I need to buy. I take the list with me to the mall, the grocery store, the pharmacy, or wherever I need to do my shopping, and that list keeps me on track. I recommend you take a similar approach to shopping for your trip.

In addition, I suggest you don't take your upcoming honeymoon as carte blanche to destroy all of the cost-saving measures you've used successfully up to this point. So don't give yourself license to go on a shopping spree. I mean, if you really don't need a new bathing suit, don't buy one. Who are you trying to impress? Your husband loves you for who you are, not the bathing suit you wear. Who cares if it's a year old? If it's in good shape and you already own it (read: free), stick with it. Now, on the other hand, if you're going to a warm-weather destination and you need sunblock, buy it at home, at your local superstore. It and other necessities will cost so much more at your resort.

Dollar-Saving Do's and Don'ts

Hopefully by now you've figured out that you can plan a fabulous honeymoon for not a lot of cash. Here's a recap of some of the dollar-savings do's and don'ts discussed in this chapter:

- Do keep in mind how time of year can affect travel prices—both positively and negatively.

- Don't plan to honeymoon in a location that attracts families at a time when schools are out. That's when prices will be the highest.

- Do consider visiting locations off-season, like a ski resort in summer or a beach town in winter, to get the best deals possible.

- Don't forget to look into using frequent flier miles or hotel rewards points to pay for your honeymoon.

- Don't put off getting a new or renewed passport. If you wait until the last minute, you're going to have to pay hefty expediting fees.

- Do inquire about any employee discounts you might be eligible for, which can help you save money on your honeymoon travel.

- Do ask anyone you know with a timeshare if you can rent it for your honeymoon. Not only are these usually cheaper than hotel rooms, but also they normally have kitchens so you can save money by eating in.

❧ Don't be shy about asking someone with a ski chalet or a vacation home if they would let you stay there for a fee for your honeymoon.

❧ Do make sure to create a tally of exactly how much your honeymoon is going to cost—including airfare, lodging, food, and incidentals—so you have a real sense of how much you're going to have to spend on your trip.

❧ Do consider registering for a honeymoon as a way of getting a portion or all of it free.

❧ Don't register for a honeymoon itinerary that's exorbitantly priced. If your guests don't follow through and "chip in" for your registry, you're going to be stuck footing that very expensive bill.

❧ Don't forget to check out low-fare travel websites like Orbitz.com and Priceline.com for honeymoon deals.

❧ Don't be so cheap as to forego travel insurance. It's a worthwhile investment that, should you need it, will help you recoup any travel costs you would have lost otherwise.

❧ Don't use your upcoming honeymoon as carte blanche to go crazy buying clothes and other accessories. To shatter all your savvy savings efforts this way would be a shame.

13

Taking Care of Your Post-Wedding Expenditures

Congratulations! You've made it through the wedding. Or the wedding still hasn't happened, but you're reading ahead to figure out what else lies in your future. Well, you'll probably have a bunch of things you'll need to accomplish once the wedding is over. This chapter will help you do that—cost-effectively and efficiently.

To begin with, I'll help you figure out a way to send your thank-you notes without spending a ton on stationery and postage. Next, I'll walk you through the process of returning gifts, and show you how where you've chosen to register can help put more cash in your pocket. After that, I'll give you a quick lesson in how to use eBay to sell overruns from your wedding or gifts you can't return. This is a great way to clear out your closets and get some extra cash. Speaking of closets, chances are your gown is hanging in yours, and you're not sure what to do with it. So I'll suggest ways to get it cleaned without spending too much. Finally, I'll help you get pictures from your reception and your honeymoon out of your camera and onto paper in ways that won't leave you broke.

Economical Ways to Handle Your Thank-You Notes and Postage

The first point I want to make is that you should have your thank-you notes written and sent between three and six weeks after your wedding day. I know, that has nothing to do with saving money, but it's good etiquette advice nonetheless.

Now as far as the notes go, there is no reason for you to feel the need to use fancy—and thus expensive—note cards to write your thank-you notes. Earlier in the book I mentioned the importance of stocking up on inexpensive note cards whenever you see them, and I hope you've followed my advice. If not, then I suggest you drive over to a Marshall's, TJ Maxx, Nordstrom Rack, or whichever discount store you prefer and check out the stationery section to see if they have note cards on sale. Shoot to pay less than $1 per card—50 cents per card if you can swing it. Remember—no rule says all your thank-you notes have to match or must have your name printed on them. The most important thing is to make sure you write them and send them in a timely manner.

As far as saving money on postage, you should do the same thing you did with your invitations way back when—take a note inside an envelope to the post office and have it weighed. If you're planning to enclose a picture of your new spouse and you, make sure you've included one of them with the card set, as that will affect the weight, too. This way, you'll know how much postage you need to buy to mail each card.

Want to save money on both the cards and your postage? Send postcards as your thank-you notes. You can pick up postcards for as little as 10 cents each, and mailing a postcard costs significantly less than sending a letter via first class. You could really shave a decent amount of dollars off your spending by going the postcard route.

Money in Your Pocket

I just mentioned how using postcards can save you big bucks on thank-you notes and postage. Given that the average couple spends about $102 getting this task done (that number is for note cards and postage), I'm confident you can do it for significantly less. Here's how it might work for a bride who has to write 100 thank-you notes.

If she goes the postcard route and picks up 100 postcards for 25 cents (these would be pricey postcards, of course), she's spent $25. Then with postcard postage, at 24 cents a pop (current as of 2006), she's spent an additional $24. Taken together, she'll have purchased all the supplies she needs for her thank-you notes for only $49. Now all she needs to do is write the actual notes and mail them.

Savings for you: $53 **Running total: $69,446.01**

Getting the Most (Dollars) out of Returning Gifts

Even couples who register carefully usually end up with duplicate gifts or items that weren't purchased off the registry and just don't work for their lifestyle. This is where store returns come into play—and how your registry can help or hurt you in this respect.

I hope you heeded my advice from Chapter 2 in choosing your gift registry stores wisely. Do you recall the story of the bride who registered at Bed Bath & Beyond? She was able to get cash back for her returns. To me that is the best-case situation, and I hope it's one you'll find yourself in when returning gifts, though her situation is probably the exception rather than the rule.

Before you can take anything back, you'll probably have to do a little bit of homework. Most stores won't take returns without one of three key pieces of information, which you'll need to have. These are:

⌀ Price sticker on box or item

⌀ Gift receipt

⌀ Updated copy of your registry list

Let me explain how each of these items can work in your returns favor.

To begin with, a price sticker will show where the item came from, and hopefully it will show that it was purchased in the store where you're trying to return it. If the sticker has the bar code on it, all the better, because a cashier can scan the code and let you know how much the return is "worth."

A gift receipt will help you in a similar manner, but sometimes it's better than a price sticker alone. That's because many stores these days won't take items back and refund the full amount spent without receipts—even if they have a sticker on the box. I know at stores like Target, for example, if you take something back that was clearly bought at Target but you don't have a receipt, you'll get a credit for however much that item is selling for now. If that item has gone on clearance since your guests purchased it, you're out of luck. Without a receipt, you have to accept this lower price. However, if you have a receipt—gift or otherwise—you are more likely to get credit for the full amount your guest spent.

DON'T TRIP on your **SHOESTRINGS**

> Usually, brides and grooms open their gifts in a rush of adrenaline, right after the reception has ended or they've returned from their honeymoon. If you start coming across gift receipts with your gifts, don't just toss them aside. These little slips of paper could turn out to be the barrier between getting the full price or nothing at all for any gifts you need to return. If you're concerned about receipts getting separated from gifts, jot down on the receipt which gift it came with—if it isn't clearly printed on it. You may even want to tape it to the actual box, so that should you have to make returns, the receipt will be right there.

Finally, if you bring a copy of your updated registry list, you can use it to "prove" to a store that you registered for the item. For example, let's say that you registered for four sets of bath towels, and your registry shows that all four had been purchased for you. Maybe some of your guests bought the same towels at another store, leaving you with too many towels. Regardless of where the towels came from, if they're the same brand you registered for, you should be able to return them at the store where you're registered.

If you have a list to prove that you had four towels on your list and four were bought, I would think that the store would willingly take them back. Again, without a receipt you may have to accept credit for the item at a lower price, but at least you'll be getting something for it.

Keep in mind that this sticker, receipt, and registry list advice is just overall ideas to keep in mind. It's up to you to investigate ahead of time what kind of return and exchange policies stores have, and you should know going into your registering process what to expect when you get to this point—the point of returns. I can't promise that Target's gift receipt policy will remain the same forever or that Bed Bath & Beyond will continue to give cash back for registry returns. That's why I implore you to do your homework so you don't feel cheated. It's your job to be an informed consumer—and an informed bride as well.

Selling on eBay Can Help You Make Money on Your Wedding

A few years ago, I wrote a book (titled *Buying and Selling Your Way to a Fabulous Wedding with eBay*) that focused entirely on using eBay to buy stuff for a wedding as well as using the online auction site to get rid of stuff you don't want or need after your wedding. If you're a big eBay fan and don't want to deal with store returns, putting up for auction extra gifts or items you don't really need anymore is a great idea. This way, you can clear your home of piles of gifts and, hopefully, earn some money in the process.

Plenty of people turn to eBay to buy gifts for a wedding. Maybe that crystal bowl you got two of—and now you're selling one—will make the perfect gift for another wedding guest to buy.

You can also use eBay to recoup some of your wedding costs by selling any accessories or supplies that you used on the big day but that are still in perfect condition. In my eBay book, I talked about brides and grooms who sold leftover tulle for making pew bows, cake toppers, and even wedding dresses.

You may be surprised by what people will buy. Some of these folks sold their items on their own; others turned to eBay resellers—the kind that have set up brick-and-mortar storefronts that are the modern-day version of the consignment shop. These stores are a terrific option for people who don't have the time to deal with eBay sales or simply would like someone else to do the selling for them.

The important thing to remember when trying to sell your wedding overstocks, if you will, on eBay is that not everything is going to bring in big bucks. I recently sold a bridesmaid gown that I purchased for $100 for a friend's wedding. I only got $25 on eBay for it, plus $15 in shipping, which means, obviously, I did not recoup my costs. However, that was money I wouldn't have otherwise had in my pocket, and I've cleaned out some space in my closet.

Sometimes, though, fate works in your favor on eBay. Last year I changed my mind at the last minute on a wedding gift I wanted to give a girlfriend. The gift was a linen-covered photo album that I thought she'd really like, but then I found out she was doing her entire wedding album digitally and that she'd registered for her honeymoon. I reasoned that a traditional wedding album would be little good to her when all the pictures were going to be on her computer and she obviously wanted people to chip in for her honeymoon.

I sent my check off to the honeymoon registry and put the photo album up on eBay. Well, my timing must have been impeccable because before long I had 12 bids on the album. I'd started at $6.99 and soon was up to $27. By the time the auction closed five days later, that album sold for $58. (I'd spent $30 on it.)

Keep in mind that the best way to make eBay work for you is to not get greedy as you put things up for auction. Sure, you may think your headpiece is worth $40, but if similar headpieces are selling for a lot less, then you're going to have to start the bidding at a lower price.

In fact, there is often this collective mentality on eBay that people will only start bidding on items when they are priced tremendously under market—like a headpiece for 99 cents—and when people feel they're getting a great deal. Once people start bidding, they usually get into a frenzy that drives the prices up. Sometimes you'll end up selling the item for closer to the full price you wanted, simply because people couldn't control themselves. This doesn't work every time, but I've found that when you start your bidding lower, your items will get more attention.

Cleaning Wedding Garments Doesn't Have to Cost a Fortune

I'm sure you went through sticker shock when you first started looking at wedding gowns and realized that one dress could cost thousands of dollars. Well, prepare yourself again—you may be in for more sticker shock as you begin investigating where to get your gown cleaned. Because of the intricate detailing on typical wedding gowns, cleaners usually charge a couple hundred dollars to do the job.

Don't think you can get away with not cleaning the gown as a way of saving money. You may not be able to save the gown if you leave it as is. That's because sweat, oils from your skin, and any food on the fabric can, over time, eat away at the dress or cause permanent stains. If you have any hopes of having that dress as a keepsake or handing it down to someone, someday, to wear, then you really need to have it professionally cleaned.

A good place to find a cleaner for the job is the website of the trade association of wedding gown cleaners—www.weddinggownspecialists.com—which lists dry cleaners in your area who are equipped to clean a gown. Call around first to compare prices, so you won't faint when you're handed the bill later on.

Keep in mind your corner dry cleaner may not be the best place to take your gown, even if it is the cheapest. Many of these cleaners don't clean a wedding gown in a special way—they just throw it in with the rest of the garments they're dry cleaning. Because of this, there's no guarantee your gown will come back in good condition. If it doesn't, it will lose all of its value, meaning you've lost your investment in it.

Another option for finding a cleaner is the store where you bought your gown. In fact, you may want to think about negotiating dress cleaning into the price of your wedding gown purchase. That's what one bride I know did, just on a fluke. "I knew it would cost so much to clean the gown that I figured it wouldn't hurt to ask," this bride recalls. "I mean, what's the worst they can say? No." Lucky for her, they said "Yes," and instead of shelling out $300 to get her gown cleaned later on, she paid $100 extra for her gown and then took it back to the store when her wedding was over.

The store where you bought your gown may also be a good resource if they use a cleaner on a regular basis and would be willing to pass along their discount to you.

If you negotiate the price for cleaning when you buy the dress, make sure you get this agreement in writing with the store. Should the store change hands or the employee who agreed to this leave his job, you'll be out money and still have a dirty gown on your hands.

Finally, if your husband wore his own suit or tuxedo, you'll want to get that cleaned, too. I recommend you try to negotiate some kind of discount with the company you hire to clean your gown. Maybe if you ask, they'll give you some kind of two-for-one deal. Then again, maybe they won't, but you'll never know unless you inquire.

How to Get Your Wedding and Honeymoon Photos Developed Affordably

You're likely to come away from your wedding celebration with two sets of photos that you need to develop. Those are the pictures your guests took with the disposable cameras at the reception and any pictures you took on your honeymoon. Also, if you worked out a deal with your wedding photographer whereby you develop your own pictures, you'll need to take care of those as well.

It doesn't matter whether you shot digital or film images; you can still get them onto photo paper for a good price.

For starters, if you shot your pictures digitally and you own a photo printer, you're in the best of all situations. You can upload your files to your computer and print them out with supplies you already own. Photo paper can get pricey, though, so it's important to decide ahead of time which images you want to print and which you want to leave on your hard drive. This way, you don't end up wasting any paper on pictures that will end up in the trash at the end of the day.

Another affordable way to get digital pictures onto paper is to use those self-serve kiosks at superstores like Target and Wal-Mart or your local supermarket. Usually, you can get prints for pennies apiece.

Go Figure

If you decide to let someone else do your photo developing and/or printing, it's important to figure out if there's going to be a per-print charge and how much it's going to be. This worksheet will help you with that:

Step 1: Cost for film developing   _____

Step 2: Number of prints on roll/on disk   _____

Step 3: Price per print for printing   _____

Step 4: Multiply Step 2 and Step 3   _____

Step 5: Cost for postage, if mailing   _____

Step 6: Add Steps 1, 4, and 5 for printing total   _____

                              Total amount you expect to spend   _____

You can also go online to get your pictures printed. I know plenty of people who swear by web-based photo services like Shutterfly.com, Snapfish. com, Flickr.com, Photoworks.com, Pickle.com, and Kodakgallery.com, among others. Again, you can get prints for just pennies. Also, when you register on these sites, you can expect to receive coupons and other e-mailed discounts from time to time. So hold on to any of those to use when you get your wedding pictures printed.

And if you want to pass on the cost of printing to your family and friends, you can share your photos online. For a small fee, you can upload your images and then e-mail them to the folks you'd like to see the pictures. Then, if they're interested, they can print them out on their dime.

Even people who shoot photos traditionally—with film—can benefit from the cheap prices at these web-based companies. Just look on the sitemap for "pricing" so you can see if they offer cheaper services than you might find at your local superstore or supermarket. These days, getting film developed and pictures printed doesn't have to be a huge financial ordeal.

Dollar-Saving Do's and Don'ts

You've a ton of things on your post-wedding to do list, but don't freak out about your finances. Here's a recap of ways to get all of those tasks completed in a cost-efficient manner:

- Do stock up on inexpensive and "on sale" thank-you notes and avoid paying for pricey cards when you need them.

- Do consider using postcards for your thank-you notes. Between the cost of the postcards and their required postage, you can save a bundle.

- Do prepare wisely for any gift returns you have to make. Make sure you have a price sticker, gift receipt, or your registry list at the ready.

- Don't discount the importance of gift receipts. Without one, you might not get the full credit for the gift's price.

- Do consider putting gifts up for sale on eBay if you can't or don't want to return them to the store.

- Do think about selling on eBay any other leftover items or supplies from your wedding as a way to recoup some of your wedding costs.

- Don't forget the cost of cleaning your wedding gown when thinking about your total wedding budget.

- Do try to pre-negotiate a good price on cleaning from the boutique where you bought your gown or to at least inquire about using their volume discount with a cleaner.

- ❧ Do find a professional cleaner who specializes in delicate garments, so you don't end up with a ruined dress that's worth nothing.

- ❧ Do ask about any discounts you may be eligible for if you get your husband's tuxedo or suit cleaned at the same time and at the same place as your gown.

- ❧ Don't let your photos sit inside a camera for months on end. If you don't develop the prints, you'll have wasted money on film and/or disposable cameras.

- ❧ Do print digital shots at home if you've got a photo printer. That way you can control how many you print.

- ❧ Don't get reckless with your at-home printing—photo paper can get pricey over time.

- ❧ Do think about taking your pictures to a superstore or sending them to a web-based photo service for affordable developing and printing.

- ❧ Do consider the ultimate photo cost-savings—sharing your pictures online for free.

Appendix A
Glossary

Throughout your wedding planning, you may come across words or sayings you've never heard before. Although you don't have to sign up for a foreign language class in order to walk down the aisle, getting a quick, crash course in wedding speak would be helpful for you. That's why I've put together this glossary of some wedding terms and other words in the wedding lexicon you may come across. That way, when, for example, you look at a gown with an empire waist, not only will you know how to pronounce empire—it's ahm-peer, not em-pihr, like the Empire State—but you'll also know what it means.

"A" list Usually followed by "B" and "C" list, this is how brides and grooms "rank" the people they invite to their wedding when space or money is tight. That is, they'll mail invitations to the "A" list first and then, based on how many "A"-listers decline, they mail invitations to folks on the "B" list. Word of caution: never let anyone know on which list he or she appears, especially if it's not the "A" list. That's because being on anything but the "A" list can seem like a slap in the face to some.

baron's table A fancy way of describing the head table, reserved for the bride and groom to sit at during the reception. Many baron's tables are round, but they don't have to be. Also sometimes referred to as a sweetheart's table.

barter   The act of receiving goods or services from someone in exchange for goods or services. In other words, a transaction where skills, rather than money, is the preferred "currency."

boutonnière   A small flower that a man wears on a jacket's lapel. At a wedding, the groom, the men in the bridal party, the fathers, even the ringbearer might wear a boutonnière on his jacket.

bridal train, or train   The part of the bridal gown that trails behind the bride and is usually held up by a junior bridesmaid. Usually a train is removable, so the bride doesn't have to drag it around at her reception.

charger   An oversize plate or flat, circular object used as a place setting and onto which dinner plates are placed. You'll usually find chargers in the most formal of settings, though I've heard of music-loving brides using old record albums as chargers at their reception tables.

chuppah   A canopy under which a Jewish bride and groom are married. A chuppah is traditionally a prayer shawl that is secured to and held up by four poles, which people hold over the couple. However, some couples use wisteria branches or other articles from nature to fashion a chuppah. May be spelled *chuppah* or *huppah*. Pronounced "hup-ah."

civil ceremony   A nonreligious ceremony that doesn't involve clergy. A civil ceremony is as legally binding as a religious one, as long as a marriage license is involved.

crinoline   A petticoat-like slip made of stiff material that is worn underneath a gown to create a bell shape to the skirt.

cummerbund   A sash-like belt a man wears with a tuxedo, it's an optional accessory with a tuxedo, though traditionalists swear by them. Never wear a cummerbund when wearing a vest with a tuxedo—it's one or the other, never both.

disposable cameras   Also known as one-time-use cameras, couples put these cameras on their reception tables for guests to take pictures with. When all the film is shot, the entire camera set gets shipped off for developing and printing.

DIY   Stands for do-it-yourself.

empire waist   Pronounced "ahm-peer," it describes the waist on a dress or gown with a waistline that rests just below the bust.

end caps   The shelves at the end of each aisle where stores stock inventory on clearance; a must-troll part of any retailer if you're on the prowl for bargains.

escort cards   At your reception, this little card will tell your guests at which table they are sitting. Often mistaken for the place card, which is used exclusively with assigned seating. Also, place cards are already set out at specific places at each table, to tell guests exactly where to sit; escort cards are displayed on a table when you first walk into a reception, and guests are supposed to take theirs to "escort" them to the proper table where they may sit in any available seat at the table.

favor cards   Placed on your reception tables or with your favors, these cards explain the significance or meaning of favors. Favor cards are useful if you choose to forego traditional favors altogether and make a donation to charity instead.

favors   Little gifts you give to your guests, normally at the reception, to thank them for coming to your wedding.

FIL   Stands for father-in-law; *see also* MIL.

FOTB   Stands for father of the bride; *see also* MOTB.

gift receipt   A receipt you can request when buying a gift that shows what you bought and where you purchased the item but not how much you paid for it. The receipt usually includes a bar code that when scanned reveals the original price. A gift receipt can help you get a full refund should you need to return a gift.

groom's cake   Typically a Southern tradition, though appearing at more weddings nationwide, the groom's cake is an entirely different style and design from the wedding cake, and is usually made to reflect the groom's tastes. It may be served as dessert along with the regular wedding cake.

headpiece   A generic term that describes something the bride wears on her head during the wedding, usually to secure her veil. A headpiece may be a tiara, hair clip, headband, or some other accessory worn on the head.

inner envelope   The envelope that holds the invitation set and on which you write the names of the invited guests. It is tucked inside the outer envelope you use to mail the invitation.

MIL   Stands for mother-in-law; *see also* FIL.

MOH   Stands for maid of honor.

MOTB   Mother of the bride; *see also* FOTB.

multi-camera setup   Terminology that describes having multiple video cameras at a wedding ceremony and/or reception to capture the action from different angles. Usually a more expensive video option and unnecessary at smaller weddings.

off the rack   Usually refers to a dress that is purchased from existing stock in a store, or "off the rack." In other words, it's a garment that doesn't have to be special ordered.

officiant   The person who officiates at a wedding. Could be a rabbi, priest, minister, or justice of the peace, or another ordained or official person who can legally perform a wedding.

one-time-use cameras   *See* disposable cameras.

open bar   A bar at which the guests at your wedding do not pay for their drinks. It is also usually the most expensive option at a wedding.

outer envelope   The envelope that holds the invitation set and on which you write a guest's address and place the stamp. Basically, it is the envelope you use to mail the invitations.

per-head or **per-person prices**   Literally, the amount you will pay for each person who attends your wedding reception. Most caterers, for example, charge on a per-head or per-person basis.

place card   The card at a reception table that indicates a specific seat in which a guest should sit; used with assigned (not open) seating at a table and often mistaken for escort cards.

rider   An addition to an insurance policy, which usually covers an expensive item that a traditional policy would not take care of. Some expensive engagement rings require insurance riders because their value is more than a homeowner's insurance policy would include.

RSVP card   The card your guests will use to "RSVP" or respond to your invitation to attend your wedding. It usually arrives with a self-addressed, stamped envelope for easy reply.

save-the-date card   A note or card that arrives soon after your engagement and asks the guests to please "save the date" on their calendar for your upcoming wedding.

sponsored wedding   A wedding in which the bride and groom secure advertisers or sponsors to pay for their wedding. In return, the couple promises to promote each company to their guests during the wedding.

table card   The card in the middle of a reception table that explains which table it is and how it relates to a guest's escort card. Most weddings use numerals to note tables, though your table card can reflect any manner you choose to identify them—favorite songs or names of states or food groups, for example.

timeshare   A real estate option whereby you own "time" at a resort as opposed to actual property.

trousseau   Directly translated from the French, it means the bride's personal possessions. Typically associated with lingerie for the wedding night, you can have a trousseau of stationery, housewares, or shoes, or anything else where you have a "collection" of like items. It can also include the clothing for the honeymoon and a getaway outfit for your departure from the reception.

tussy mussy   A bouquet holder or small vase, usually made of metal.

Appendix B
Caribbean Primer

In Chapter 5, I wrote exclusively on planning a destination wedding, and as you'll recall, much of that chapter focused on destinations in the Caribbean. In addition, when reading Chapter 12 about honeymoons, the thought of planning a Caribbean honeymoon may have crossed your mind.

While clearly not every newly married American couple will honeymoon in the Caribbean, a large percentage do. That's why I've devoted this appendix to the Caribbean.

In the following pages, I'll give you basic information on nearly all the countries within the Caribbean region. You'll notice I haven't included countries like Cuba or Haiti, because these are destinations most Americans can't or won't travel to for political reasons.

Note: I've included Bermuda, The Bahamas, and Turks and Caicos in this Caribbean section, even though, technically, none of them is in the Caribbean Sea—rather, they're all in the Atlantic Ocean. The same is true for Belize, which sits just under Mexico on the Yucatan Peninsula. However, when you search travel sites for travel information on the Caribbean, these destinations often get lumped right into that Caribbean category.

For general information on traveling to the Caribbean, visit the website of the Caribbean Tourism Organization at www.doitcaribbean.com.

Country: Anguilla
Official Language: English
Currency: Eastern Caribbean dollar
Time Zone: Atlantic
Physical Facts: Only 35 square miles in size, Anguilla is one of the smallest and least developed islands in the Caribbean—so much so that the island has only one road. Although small, you'll discover 33 separate beaches on this island.
Website for More Information: http://anguilla-vacation.com

Country: Antigua and Barbuda
Official Language: English
Currency: Eastern Caribbean dollar
Time Zone: Atlantic
Physical Facts: The dual islands of Antigua and Barbuda form a single nation, which lies in the eastern Caribbean Sea, southwest of Puerto Rico.
Website for More Information: www.antigua-barbuda.org

Country: Aruba
Official Language: Dutch
Currency: Aruban florin
Time Zone: Atlantic
Physical Facts: Aruba's closest neighbor is the South American country of Venezuela, and 20 percent of this island is a national park.
Website for More Information: http://aruba.com

Country: Bahamas
Official Language: English
Currency: Bahamian dollar
Time Zone: Eastern
Physical Facts: The Bahamas actually contains 700 different islands, though only 30 of these islands are inhabited. The biggest island is Andros, but the best known is probably New Providence, where you'll find Nassau.
Website for More Information: http://bahamas.com

Country: Barbados
Official Language: English
Currency: Barbados dollar
Time Zone: Atlantic
Physical Facts: Barbados is the easternmost Caribbean nation, jutting out into the Atlantic Ocean near the southernmost tip of the Windward Islands.
Website for More Information: www.visitbarbados.org

Country: Belize
Official Language: English
Currency: Belize dollar
Time Zone: Central
Physical Facts: Belize is part of Central America, located on the Caribbean side, between Mexico and Guatemala.
Website for More Information: www.travelbelize.org

Country: Bermuda
Official Language: English
Currency: Bermuda dollar
Time Zone: Atlantic
Physical Facts: Bermuda lies in the Atlantic, nearly due east of North Carolina, and is best known for its pink sand beaches.
Website for More Information: www.bermudatourism.com

Country: Bonaire
Official Language: Dutch
Currency: Netherlands Antilles guilder
Time Zone: Atlantic
Physical Facts: Coral reefs surround Bonaire, making it a diver's paradise. Part of the "ABC" Dutch islands, just off the coast of Venezuela, its neighbors include Aruba and Curacao.
Website for More Information: www.infobonaire.com

Country: British Virgin Islands
Official Language: English
Currency: U.S. dollar
Time Zone: Atlantic
Physical Facts: A collection of 60-plus islands, the best known in the BVI include Virgin Gorda, Tortola, and Necker Island—the latter is owned by Sir Richard Branson of Virgin Airlines, but it is available for rent.
Website for More Information: http://bvitourism.com

Country: Cayman Islands
Official Language: English
Currency: Cayman Island dollar
Time Zone: Eastern
Physical Facts: There are three main islands of the Caymans—Grand Cayman, Cayman Brac, and Little Cayman. This archipelago lies just south of Cuba and to the west of Jamaica.
Website for More Information: www.caymanislands.ky

Country: Curacao
Official Language: Dutch
Currency: Netherlands Antilles guilder
Time Zone: Atlantic
Physical Facts: Like the other ABC islands, Curacao lies very near to the South American coast. However, due to its proximity to the equator and other geological factors, the island gets very little rain and, despite being surrounded by water, has a more arid landscape than other Caribbean islands.
Website for More Information: http://curacao.com

Country: Dominica
Official Language: English
Currency: Eastern Caribbean dollar
Time Zone: Atlantic
Physical Facts: Tiny Dominica, one of the Leeward Islands, has a little of nearly every kind of landscape—volcanoes, rainforests, sulphur springs, and waterfalls.
Website for More Information: http://dominica.dm

Country: Dominican Republic
Official Language: Spanish
Currency: Dominican peso
Time Zone: Atlantic
Physical Facts: The Dominican Republic sits on the eastern side of the island of Hispanola; the western portion of the island is Haiti.
Website for More Information: http://dominicanrepublic.com

Country: Grenada
Official Language: English
Currency: Eastern Caribbean dollar
Time Zone: Atlantic
Physical Facts: Grenada is nearly the last in the Windward Islands chain, so far south that it's almost in Venezuela.
Website for More Information: http://grenadagrenadines.com

Country: Guadeloupe
Official Language: French
Currency: Euro
Time Zone: Atlantic
Physical Facts: Guadeloupe is like two entirely different places in one island—one portion of the island is rocky and volcanic while the other portion is smooth with sandy beaches.
Website for More Information: http://antilles-info-tourisme.com

Country: Jamaica
Official Language: English
Currency: Jamaican dollar
Time Zone: Eastern
Physical Facts: Jamaica is the third largest island in the Caribbean; its nearest neighbors are the Cayman Islands, Cuba, and Haiti.
Website for More Information: http://visitjamaica.com

Country: Martinique
Official Language: French
Currency: Euro
Time Zone: Atlantic
Physical Facts: Thanks to the island's volcano—which erupted once, killing everyone nearby—you can find black sand on Martinique's beaches.
Website for More Information: www.martinique.org

Country: Montserrat
Official Language: English
Currency: Eastern Caribbean dollar
Time Zone: Atlantic
Physical Facts: Tiny Montserrat, the southernmost nation in the Caribbean's Leeward Islands, has had its share of volcano problems in the past few decades—so much so that its biggest city is now a ghost town. However, the north side of the island, where everyone had to move, is still vibrant with beaches, birds, and bougainvillea plants.
Website for More Information: http://visitmontserrat.com

Country: Puerto Rico
Official Language: Spanish and English
Currency: U.S. dollar
Time Zone: Atlantic
Physical Facts: Puerto Rico's beaches offer something for everyone—snorkeling, sailing, sunbathing, and, in the winter, surfing for visitors who are looking for warm water in which to catch a wave.
Website for More Information: www.gotopuertorico.com

Country: St. Barthelemy, a.k.a. St. Barts
Official Language: French
Currency: Euro
Time Zone: Atlantic
Physical Facts: Though only eight square miles in size, St. Barts has 22 beaches from which to choose. St. Barts is so underdeveloped that you'll need a boat to get to some of its beaches because there are no roads.
Website for More Information: http://st-barths.com

Country: St. Eustatius, a.k.a Statia
Official Language: Dutch
Currency: Netherlands Antilles guilder
Time Zone: Atlantic
Physical Facts: Statia is an island that's an eco-traveler and a diver's heaven—protected lands abound and virgin dive sites surround this 11.8 square mile spit of land nestled just south of St. Barts.
Website for More Information: http://statiatourism.com

Country: St. Kitts and Nevis
Official Language: English
Currency: Eastern Caribbean dollar
Time Zone: Atlantic
Physical Facts: This dual-island nation of St. Kitts and Nevis is lush and green, and with plenty of golf courses to boot.
Website for More Information: http://stkittstourism.kn

Country: St. Lucia
Official Language: English
Currency: Eastern Caribbean dollar
Time Zone: Atlantic
Physical Facts: St. Lucia has two mountain peaks—well, the Caribbean version of a mountain peak—called the Pitons, which are really volcanic formations. The island is also home to a waterfall with a 1,000-foot drop.
Website for More Information: www.stlucia.org

Country: Sint Maarten
Official Language: Dutch
Currency: Netherlands Antilles guilder
Time Zone: Atlantic
Physical Facts: Two nations exist on this one island—Dutch Sint Maarten to the south and French St. Martin to the north. Sint Maarten is the smaller part of the island, at 17 square miles, though it is home to 37 beaches.
Website for More Information: http://st-maarten.com

Country: St. Martin
Official Language: French
Currency: Euro
Time Zone: Atlantic
Physical Facts: As mentioned above, two nations exist on this one island—Dutch Sint Maarten to the south and French St. Martin to the north. This is the smallest island in the world where two nations share one home.
Website for More Information: http://st-martin.org

Country: St. Vincent and the Grenadines
Official Language: English
Currency: Eastern Caribbean dollar
Time Zone: Atlantic
Physical Facts: St. Vincent is the largest in this string of nine islands, eight of which comprise the Grenadines. These less inhabited islands of the Grenadines include Bequia, Mustique, Petit St. Vincent, and Tobago Cays.
Website for More Information: www.svgtourism.com

Country: Trinidad and Tobago
Official Language: English
Currency: Trinidad and Tobago dollar
Time Zone: Atlantic
Physical Facts: Years ago this twin island nation was attached to nearby South America, but over time that land connection was washed away. Today, you'll find the islands to be as diverse as the people. Trinidad is a more urban, populated, and fast-paced place, while Tobago is more reminiscent of other laid-back Caribbean islands.
Website for More Information: http://visittnt.com

Country: Turks and Caicos
Official Language: English
Currency: U.S. dollar
Time Zone: Eastern
Physical Facts: You'll find this string of 40 Turks and Caicos islands at the southern end of The Bahamas. Only eight of the islands are inhabited and even those eight aren't very built-up.
Website for More Information: http://turksandcaicostourism.com

Country: United States Virgin Islands (USVI)
Official Language: English
Currency: U.S. dollar
Time Zone: Atlantic
Physical Facts: Situated just to the east of Puerto Rico, the USVI are made up of the islands of St. Thomas, St. John, and St. Croix. There are also 50 uninhabited islands and reefs within this island chain.
Website for More Information: http://usvitourism.vi

Appendix C
Resources

You may want more information about a number of companies I've cited in this book. Please refer to the following resources list, which appears in alphabetical order, for a brief recap of most of the companies or services and how each might benefit your wedding on a shoestring. Whenever possible, I've included a website with each mention so you can log on for more information.

AboutFlowers.com
The Society of American Florists, a professional organization or floral designers, offers a consumer-oriented website at www.aboutflowers.com. It's a fantastic resource for learning about different kinds of flowers, and it's a must-see website before meeting with a florist.

AC Moore
A national craft store, check out AC Moore's website at www.acmoore.com, where you can find an entire section devoted to wedding crafts.

Amazon.com
Originally known as a bookseller only, these days Amazon.com is a place to buy just about everything you could need for a home or a hobby. Amazon also offers a registry program, which

is ideal for couples that don't want to travel to a brick-and-mortar store to register for their wedding. Check it out at www.amazon.com.

Ann Taylor
Ann Taylor has recently expanded its clothing line to include special-occasion garments. Called the "Celebrations Collection," dresses in this line could easily pass for a laid-back bridal gown or something an attendant would wear. You can preview the collection at www.anntaylor.com.

Apple.com
If you're considering purchasing or registering for an iPod to avoid hiring a deejay for your event, do your homework first on Apple's website. Also, you can learn more on this website about Apple's photo editing software called iPhoto and video/film software called iMovie. Log onto www.apple.com for more on each of these programs.

Aruba.com
The nation of Aruba lets you register for various activities on the island—from dinner out to scuba diving—via its website at Aruba.com. It's a great option if you were hoping to honeymoon on the island anyway. You can start your planning at http://aruba.com.

Backroads
Backroads has made a name for itself over the years by focusing on active vacations on bike or on foot. Now you can register for a Backroads honeymoon and have your guests contribute funds to pay for it. Learn more about the honeymoon registry program at www.backroads.com.

Bed Bath & Beyond
With more than 700 locations in the United States, Bed Bath & Beyond is a soup-to-nuts housewares store with an extensive registry program. The store also has a generous return policy that allows you to choose between a refund, a store credit, or an even exchange when you return a gift there. You can get more information on the registry program or the store at www. bedbathandbeyond.com.

Biddingfortravel.com

Bidddingfortravel.com is a free website run by Priceline.com enthusiasts. It's a must-see website for anyone considering bidding on travel on Priceline. The message boards here outline what prices have "won" on Priceline lately and what those wins have resulted in. You'll get great tips for selecting neighborhoods, for example, when bidding for hotel rooms in cities and the lowest prices you can get away with entering on the Priceline site. You will have to register on the site before you can use it. Visit www.biddingfortravel.com for all of the details.

BJ's

BJ's is a wholesale club where you can buy items in bulk at a discount. Many of the clubs have bakeries, florists, and photo departments on location, where you might just find a great deal for your DIY wedding. You'll have to buy an annual membership to have access to BJ's great prices. Annual membership prices vary. Visit www.bjs.com for more information or to find a club near you.

BlueNile.com

An online jewelry retailer, BlueNile.com is best known for selling high-quality diamonds at lower-than-retail prices. These days, though, you can get more than diamonds at Blue Nile. You'll also find all kinds of jewelry that you might need for a wedding. Visit www.bluenile.com.

Cafe Press

Cafe Press is a web-based business that lets you personalize hats, mugs, t-shirts, and more without spending a bundle in the process. If you're looking to give out novelty items as favors, you should check out what Cafe Press has to offer at www.cafepress.com.

California Cut Flower Commission

The California Cut Flower Commission is a trade association of flower growers located in California, but its website at www.ccfc.org offers information about flowers that anyone nationwide might find of interest. Probably the best resource on the website for brides is a searchable database of flowers, which can tell you when certain blooms are in season and therefore more affordable.

Carnival Cruise Lines
Carnival Cruise Lines calls its fleet of ships "fun ships" for the ongoing, onboard merriment. Carnival offers cruising itineraries in The Bahamas, Caribbean, Mexican Riviera, Alaska, Hawaii, Canada, New England, Bermuda, and Europe. Visit its website at www.carnival.com to learn more about weddings at sea.

Chelsea Premium Outlets
Chelsea Premium Outlets own and run outlet centers, under the "Premium" name, in more than 20 states. You can find an outlet near you by visiting www.premiumoutlets.com.

The Conde Nast Bridal Group
Conde Nast is a publisher of many national magazines, including three of the biggies in the bridal market: *Brides, Elegant Bride,* and *Modern Bride* (and all of the regional versions of *Modern Bride*). While not everything that appears in these magazines may fit with your shoestring budget, you can still get great ideas paging through these magazines. Visit www.brides.com for links to all of the company's wedding magazines.

Costco
Like BJ's, Costco is a wholesale club that allows you to buy items you would find in a regular supermarket, but in larger quantities and at a discount. Annual memberships start at $50. Besides being a place to buy food and flowers, you can also book travel through Costco. Visit www.costco.com to learn more about the club.

Craigslist
A free, online community, Craigslist has local versions in more than 150 U.S. cities and a handful of foreign locations. On Craigslist you can find everything from a job to free junk. But for your purposes it's also where you might find a wedding gown, photographer, or other vendor to hire for your wedding. As always, check references before hiring anyone you find on Craigslist or elsewhere. Visit www.craigslist.com, find your city (or the nearest city to you) on the right-hand side of the screen, and click on it for your localized version of Craigslist.

Cruises Only

Cruises Only is a Boston-based travel agency that specializes in cruise packages. You needn't live in the Boston area to work with them, though. You can book your travel through the company's website at www.cruisesonly.com.

CVS

National drugstore chain CVS can be a great resource for your pre- and post-wedding purchases. For starters, make sure you sign up for the CVS Extra Care card. With it not only do you get day-of discounts on your purchases but also, from time to time, you'll get ready-to-use coupons that print out right on your sales receipt. These coupons are a way to save money in the future on things you are going to buy anyway. Besides the traditional drugstore offerings, CVS also has a photo center, which you may want to check out for any wedding picture developing and printing. Log onto www.cvs.com to find out all about the store's offerings.

DailyCandy.com

DailyCandy.com is a website and e-newsletter that provides the inside scoop on fashion and shopping in Atlanta, Boston, Chicago, Dallas, London, Los Angeles, Miami, New York, Philadelphia, San Francisco, and Washington, D.C. You can visit the website to check out deals and to search for past information on a certain topic, such as bridal. In addition, you can sign up for "daily deals" that are delivered via e-mail to your inbox every day.

David's Bridal

A renowned bridal store, David's Bridal offers one of the largest selections of wedding gowns and bridesmaids' dresses, not only in a rainbow of colors but also in a range of sizes—right in the store. No more will you have to hold up a sample-size gown to your body and try to imagine what it looks like on you. At David's Bridal you can try everything on. To find a store near you, visit www.davidsbridal.com. Also, David's Bridal owns After Hours Formalwear, an affordable store for the groom's attire.

Distinctivehoneymoons.com

Distinctivehoneymoons.com is a honeymoon registry program run through ProTravel International, an established travel agency. Not only can the company collect funds to put toward your honeymoon, but they can also do all of your honeymoon travel booking for you. Go to www.distinctivehoneymoons.com for more information.

eBay.com

If you don't know what eBay is in this day and digital age, then you must check it out. eBay is an online auction site where you can find just about anything for sale. It is an awesome tool for anyone trying to plan a wedding on the cheap. What's important to remember, though, is before you bid, you must check a seller's feedback. Anyone without a good rating is a seller you don't want to do business with. One hundred percent feedback is ideal. Besides buying stuff for a wedding here, you can also put items up for sale on eBay after your wedding is over. It's a great way to get rid of unwanted or unreturnable gifts and make some cash in the process. Log onto www.ebay.com to learn more about how eBay works.

Elegant Hotels Group

The Elegant Hotels Group is comprised of five properties on the island of Barbados. Elegant Hotels offers a range of wedding ceremony and reception programs, which you can find on its website, www.eleganthotels.com, under "elegant romance."

Flickr.com

Flickr.com is an online site for uploading, storing, and sharing of digital images. It has a nifty search function for checking out others' photos that are stored there, too. Take a tour at www.flickr.com.

Freecycle.org

Freecycle is a grassroots organization that encourages people to give away or recycle their used goods rather than throw them in the trash. There are thousands of local versions of Freecycle, usually broken out by county, and inventory changes daily. Visit www.freecycle.org to see if there is a group near you or to use the website's search feature to see if someone locally is giving away something you might be able to use for your wedding.

Harry and David

This specialty food and gift retailer made its name selling succulent pears from Oregon. These days you can find all kinds of goodies at Harry and David—through its catalog, retail stores, and website at www.harryanddavid. com. Harry and David often sells towers of wrapped candy boxes as gifts. These towers, when on sale, are something to consider for your table center-pieces. That's because they can be taken apart at the end of the night, and each box handed out as a favor.

Honeyluna.com

Honeyluna.com is a registry program that outlines specific activities couples have registered for, such as breakfast in bed for two, and then lets guests contribute according to which activity they hope to cover on the couple's honeymoon. Even airfare can be included in the desired "activities." You can use the Honeyluna.com registry in one of two ways—register for your activi-ties and let the company make your travel plans; or register and then take the cash you've received to pay for a honeymoon you plan yourself. Visit www.honeyluna.com for more information.

Honeymoonwishes.com

When you register at honeymoonwishes.com, you won't get any travel agency-like benefits or services. This site simply acts as your honeymoon registry "repository" to which guests can send money. Later, before your big trip, they'll send you the balance of funds received, which you can apply to your travel plans. One of the benefits of this registry is that you get a free wedding website. See for yourself if this registry plan is right for you by log-ging onto www.honeymoonwishes.com.

Hotels.com

Hotels.com is a travel website that lets you book more than just hotel rooms at a discount. Run by Expedia.com, you can search this site for flights, resort packages, and even discounted rooms at bed and breakfasts. Check out the details at www.hotels.com.

The I Do Foundation

The I Do Foundation is a philanthropic organization that allows brides and grooms to turn their wedding into a charitable affair. The I Do Foundation works with couples in three distinct ways. One, it lets couples register for a charity and then funnels donations from guests to the charity on the couple's behalf. Two, it has developed working relationships with traditional retailers where couples may choose to register for "regular" gifts. These retailers then give a portion of that couple's registry gift sales to charity. And three, it helps couples choose a charity and make donations to it in lieu of giving guests traditional favors at the reception. Visit www.idofoundation.org for more information.

InterfaithOfficiants.com

This website at www.interfaithofficiants.com works as a referral service for couples looking for an interfaith officiant to perform at their wedding ceremony. The website defines interfaith as any couple where neither person shares a religion, and can offer referrals to ordained individuals who represent nearly every world religion.

International Freeze Dry Floral Association

The International Freeze Dry Floral Association is a trade group for florists that specializes in dried flowers, a floral option you may want to consider for your wedding because it's often cheaper than fresh flowers. You can visit the association's website at www.ifdfa.org to find a florist near you that works with freeze-dried flowers.

iPrint.com

Iprint.com is an online printer that offers the same kinds of services you'd expect from a traditional printing shop. It can also help with your wedding plans, in that you can order invitations, print postcards, and request personal stationery, among other items. Visit www.iprint.com.

J.Crew

No longer is retailer J.Crew for casual, weekend wear only. In the "wedding and party shop" section of its website, you'll find plenty of wedding-worthy options for the bride, the groom, and their attendants. Log onto www.jcrew.com to give the wedding wear a once over.

Jet Blue Airlines

What sets Jet Blue apart from other airlines is that it offers an upscale in-flight experience for a bargain-basement price. These days you can fly Jet Blue from its hub at New York City's JFK airport to cities across the continent and to international destinations as well, including Aruba, the Bahamas, and Bermuda. You can view a flight map and fares at www.jetblue.com.

Joann Fabric and Crafts

Joann's started out as a place where seamstresses could get good deals on fabric. While the store still sells fabric, it has become a fantastic resource for craft supplies as well as craft classes. Check out its offerings at www.joann.com, where you can also search for the store closest to you.

Kinko's

Technically known as FedEx Kinko's (since FedEx bought the company some years ago), this copy and printing chain first burst onto the scene in college towns nationwide, where copying syllabi and other materials is an almost daily event. For your wedding, Kinko's can be a terrific resource for any custom printing or copying you need done for DIY invitations, programs, or similar items. Quick savings tip: FedEx Kinko's offers a 15 percent educator discount to teachers, administrators, and academics, so if you work in education, make sure you take advantage of this discount when getting anything for your wedding (or otherwise) printed at FedEx Kinko's. Log onto www.kinkos.com for more information. Note: Don't freak if you get redirected to the FedEx website; you'll still find the information you need on printing stuff at Kinko's.

TheKnot.com
An online wedding resource, TheKnot.com offers free wedding websites for its registered users. The Knot's local "channels" can be a great place to track down recommendations for and warnings about local wedding vendors. At www.theknot.com.

Kodak Easy Share Gallery
Kodak, one of the original makers of celluloid film, has gotten into the digital picture business through its online venture at kodakgallery.com. Here, you can upload photos from a digital camera or camera phone and then share them, via its online gallery, with friends and family. You may also order traditional prints and other personalized items through the website. Learn more by visiting www.kodakgallery.com.

MAC Cosmetics
MAC Cosmetics is the makeup brand that actors and models swear by. MAC makeup stores or department store counters are where you might be able to track down a freelance makeup artist who can make you look beautiful on your big day—that is, if you wear MAC makeup and have worked with this makeup artist before and know that she can do a good job. To find a MAC retail location you can visit, check out www.maccosmetics.com.

Marshall's
Marshall's is a discount store where you can find great deals on thank-you notes, potential centerpieces, and more. Visit www.marshallsonline.com to locate a store near you.

Mary Kay
Mary Kay can be a great resource for a bride who is planning to do her own wedding-day makeup. Visit www.marykay.com to find a consultant who lives nearby, and then book a home party so you can shop. Even better, you can plan to have a party with your girlfriends or bridesmaids so that they, too, can buy new makeup. Finally, the Mary Kay website has an entire section devoted to bridal beauty, including tips for looking your best on your big day.

Men's Wearhouse
Men's Wearhouse is a national men's attire chain that sells and rents tuxedoes. Find a Men's Wearhouse location near you by visiting its website at www.menswearhouse.com.

The Mills Outlets
The Mills Corporation owns more than a dozen outlet malls around the country, all of which have "Mills" in their names. To view a map of its malls log onto www.themills.com.

National Gardening Association
If you're interested in taking a do-it-yourself approach to your wedding flowers, the National Gardening Association's website at www.garden.org is a great place to learn about flowers, pick up tips for planting and arranging, and find links and referrals to local garden clubs, in case you want to rub shoulders with fellow green thumbs.

Nordstrom Rack
The discount arm of the Nordstrom department store, Nordstrom Rack stocks tons of marked-down items you may have just seen, at full price, in the regular store. Nordstrom Rack has an extensive stationery and toiletries section, where you can find great gifts for your attendants or guests or plenty of paper for writing thank-you notes. Visit www.Nordstrom.com, and then scroll down to the bottom of the page for a link to the Nordstrom Rack store information, including how to search for a nearby location using your zip code.

Office Depot
Office Depot is primarily an office-supply chain, but you can find do-it-yourself invitation kits, plus specialty papers, here, too. To find an Office Depot location near you, visit www.officedepot.com.

Orbitz.com
You'll find Orbitz's origins to be with five airlines—American, Continental, Delta, Northwest, and United—which got together some years ago to start

a website where customers could search for flight information on these airlines. It was a way to spread the wealth, if you will, among travelers looking to compare prices and book their travel online. These days Orbitz, owned by the Cendant Corporation, a biggie in the travel business, lets you search for flights along with rental car deals and cruises. Visit www.Orbitz.com to see what deals are available now.

Paper Direct

Paper is all they do at Paper Direct, which has an online component as well as a printed catalog from which you can order. This is a great place to get supplies for do-it-yourself invitations, place cards, and menus. Price things carefully, however, because Paper Direct isn't always the cheapest paper source in town. Log onto www.paperdirect.com to request a catalog.

Party City

Best known for its party supplies, Party City can also be a great resource for inexpensive wedding invitations. Many Party City locations offer the same invitation-ordering books you'd find in upscale stationery stores, but those same invitations cost significantly less at Party City. While you can't order custom invitations on Party City's website, www.partycity.com, you can use the site to find a Party City location near your home.

Payless Shoe Source

Payless offers discounted shoes nationwide, including a line of dyeables that are perfect for a wedding. Even if you're not interested in dyeing shoes to match a dress, you can find tons of great-looking footwear for a great price at one of their locations. Visit www.payless.com to shop online or to find a nearby store.

Photo Works

Online photography and printing company Photo Works specializes in taking digital images and creating professional-looking, bound photo books that look like something a professional photographer would have ordered. However, the company doesn't charge the kinds of prices that you'd expect to pay with a professional photographer. You can see for yourself what Photo Works has to offer at www.photoworks.com.

PhotoShop

PhotoShop is a photo-editing software program that can make amateur pictures look professional, and it allows you to add special effects to any image you can upload to a computer. Not cheap by any means, Photoshop is likely available to anyone working in the graphic design industry who might have free access to it at work. Created by Adobe Systems, you can learn more about PhotoShop at www.adobe.com.

Pickle.com

Pickle.com is one of the newest online photo companies on the block. Like the other websites in this niche, you can upload your photos to the Pickle.com website, and then share them with friends and family. What sets this site apart from the crowd is that it was one of the first to offer digital video uploading and sharing. Check it all out at www.pickle.com.

Priceline.com

Priceline is the original "name your own price" travel website, though it has recently added a more traditional travel booking option. Still, some of the best deals to be had on Priceline are by telling it what you want to pay for a hotel or flight, for example, and then seeing if it accepts your price. Always check on www.Biddingfortravel.com (mentioned earlier in this appendix) before bidding on www.Priceline.com.

Prime Retail Outlets

There are Prime Retail Outlet centers in 17 states and Puerto Rico. Find one near you by visiting www.primeoutlets.com.

Rabbinic Center & Research Counseling

The primary focus of the New Jersey-based Rabbinic Center & Research Counseling is to research interfaith marriage among Jews and non-Jews. A small part of what the organization does is help interfaith couples find a rabbi to officiate at their wedding. Log onto www.rcrconline.org for more information. Note: the address is R-C-R-C-ONLINE.ORG—RC repeats.

The Rag Shop

The Rag Shop is a regional craft store, whose prices rival the Joann's and AC Moore's of the world. Currently, you'll find Rag Shop locations in Connecticut, Florida, New Jersey, New York, and Pennsylvania. If you live in one of these states, get your Sunday paper before you go shopping—the Rag Shop usually has a discount coupon in each week's paper. Visit www.ragshop.com to learn more about this retailer.

RomanticFlowers.com

This website's name is a bit of a misnomer, since it's a retail site that sells wedding favors and not flowers. However, if you log onto the site using this URL—www.romanticflowers.com/flower_chart (that's slash flower underscore chart)—you'll find an extensive chart of flowers. This chart includes flower names, when they're in season, what they look like, and if they're typically affordable or expensive.

Royal Caribbean International

When you visit the website of cruise line Royal Caribbean International (www.royalcaribbean.com), click on the "All About Cruising" button to find a link to information about weddings. There you'll find wedding guidelines, reception pricing, and details on how to personalize a wedding on board one of the company's ships.

Sam's Club

Sam's Club is a warehouse club run by the folks who own Wal-Mart. Like Costco and BJ's, it can be a treasure trove of great deals for a wedding—from cakes to corsages. Annual memberships start at about $40. Visit www.samsclub.com to find a location near you or to check out the services available.

Sandals Resorts

Sandals Resorts has 12 properties in four tropical locations: Antigua, The Bahamas, Jamaica, and St. Lucia. Sandals' wedding program, called Weddingmoons, includes ceremonies and receptions that celebrity wedding planner Preston Bailey designed. For more on getting married at a Sandals resort, visit www.sandals.com.

Sendusoff.com

A husband and wife who set up a honeymoon registry for their wedding loved the concept of a honeymoon registry so much that they decided to launch Sendusoff.com soon after they returned from their honeymoon. You have the option of using their registry services to collect funds for your honeymoon and then using that money to pay for travel you've booked yourself. Or you can book your honeymoon travel through one of the company's travel partners. Get the details of how this honeymoon registry works at www.sendusoff.com.

Sephora

Sephora stores were one of the first to take department store-quality cosmetics brands, like Nars, Smashbox, and Stila, and bring them to a traditional storefront, the Sephora store. Here you can find makeup, fragrances, and other beauty products you may need to look gorgeous on your big day. You may also find a makeup artist to hire for the job if this person has applied your makeup before and you like what you saw. You can also set up a gift registry at Sephora, which is a great way to get your cosmetics for free. Use the Sephora website at www.sephora.com to find a store you can visit in person.

Shutter Fly

Shutter Fly is an online photo store that does way more than just send you prints of the images you've uploaded from a digital camera. It allows you to share photos online, turn those photos into custom-printed cards, and create professional-quality photo albums without ever having to slip a photograph into a sleeve. Visit www.shutterfly.com for more about how the service works.

SkyAuction.com

SkyAuction.com is to travel what eBay is to everyday shopping—a place you can go on the Internet to bid on everything travel-related. Also, like eBay, you can purchase using a traditional auction and bidding model, or you can buy on the spot, using a "buy it now" approach. Check out the details at www.skyauction.com.

Snapfish.com

Computer peripherals giant Hewlett-Packard owns Snapfish.com, an online photo printing and sharing company. Like similar online photo services, you can upload digital images to the website and receive traditional prints in return or share them with friends via e-mail. You can also order personalized gifts, like coffee mugs. Snapfish can even develop traditional film like you would find in your one-time-use cameras. Take the site's tutorial at www.snapfish.com to learn all about how the company works.

Southwest Airlines

Southwest Airlines has made a name for itself by offering no-frills air travel for a no-frills price. Currently, Southwest flies to United States destinations only. If you're planning a wedding or honeymoon within the continental states and don't want to pay a lot getting to and from your destination, you may want to look into flying Southwest. Recent fare sales let you fly coast-to-coast for $39 (plus tax) each way. Visit www.Southwest.com for more information on routes and fares.

Staples

Most people think of Staples as an office-supply store, which it is. But for the bride and groom on a budget, Staples is also the place where you can purchase paper and envelopes for DIY printing projects, find discounted thank-you notes, and even use a copy shop for any copying you need done for directions or other items. If you're going to be doing a lot of wedding-related or other shopping at Staples, make it pay off for you—literally. Sign up for the Staples Rewards program, and from time to time, Staples will send you a check to reward you for shopping there. Visit www.staples.com for more information.

Starwood Hotels

The Starwood Hotels' Preferred Guest program is this chain's affinity offering that allows guests to earn points with each stay at a Starwood property. Supposedly, it is the most generous of these programs, in that members earn points more quickly than with other programs and can redeem them with no blackout dates. Also, if you're short points to meet a minimum requirement for a flight or hotel stay, you can purchase additional points for a fair fee. If you travel a lot for business and tend to stay in the Starwood family of hotels (W, Westin, and Sheraton, for example), it probably makes sense for you to join the program so you can use points toward your honeymoon. Starwood also has a honeymoon registry program, which you can learn more about at www.starwoodhoneymoons.com. Visit www.Starwoodhotels.com for more information on hotel properties and the Preferred Guest program.

Talbot's

A traditional women's clothing retailer, you can often find bridesmaid-like or flower girl-inspired dresses for sale here. Talbot's has separate sections for petite and woman-size customers, too. To see what I'm talking about, visit www.talbots.com.

Tanger Factory Outlet Centers

You'll find Tanger factory outlet centers in 23 different states. When you visit the company's website at www.tangeroutlet.com, you can download a coupon book for your use. You can also use the site to search for a nearby outlet center.

Target

Target is the kind of store where you can find just about anything you need for a wedding or real life. You can stock up on paper products, goodies for welcome baskets, and more. But what I like best about Target are the deals you can find on the end caps—literally, the shelves at the end of each aisle where the store stocks stuff on clearance. Check here for marked-down thank-you notes and other stationery supplies that might come in handy for a wedding. You've got to visit an actual store to benefit from end-cap bargains, but you can visit www.target.com to find a store near where you live or work.

Thebigday.com

Thebigday.com is a honeymoon registry that a travel agency of the same name (The Big Day Travel) uses to promote its travel packages and specials, which range from African safaris to Caribbean cruises. Register here and you'll get a free wedding website. However, if you don't book your travel through The Big Day, when you go to "collect" your honeymoon registry loot, you're going to get hit with a hefty service charge. Make sure you read the fine print at www.thebigday.com to fully understand how this honeymoon registry program works.

Thehoneymoon.com

Thehoneymoon.com registry program isn't run through a travel company—the website just acts as your collection agent for cash donations toward your honeymoon. You get a check five days before you leave on your honeymoon so you can pay off your travel bills. Get the details at www.thehoneymoon.com.

TJ Maxx

Like Marshall's, this is a discount store where you can find great supplies for your wedding, at great prices. FYI, the same company owns TJ Maxx and Marshall's, so you may find similar items on sale in both stores. Check out www.tjmaxx.com to find a store location close to you.

Travelocity.com

Travelocity is a soup-to-nuts travel website, run by Sabre, the company that handles most airlines' reservations. Like other discount travel websites, you can search for deals in all aspects of your travel plans, including flights, hotels, and rental cars. You can compare prices at www.travelocity.com.

United States Postal Service

With postage changing on what feels like an almost annual basis, it's important for you to bookmark the United States Postal Services (USPS) website at www.usps.com. Not only can you find the latest information on postal increases here, but also, if you know how much your invitations or thank-you notes weigh and don't want to schlep to the post office to buy stamps, you can order all of your supplies here. Most USPS supplies will be delivered for free or only a nominal charge. Also, the website lets you preview that year's "wedding stamps" offerings.

Universal Life Church

This multi-denominational church based in Arizona gives out free ordination papers to anyone who takes the time to register on the website—meaning, if you wanted to get ordained to perform at someone's wedding, the Universal Life Church allows you to do that instantaneously via its website at www.ulc.org. Usually, though, once you have your "papers," you need to take them to your local county courthouse to get certified to perform a wedding in that county.

Vistaprint

An online printing company, Vistaprint.com first made its name in providing affordable business cards. Now it has expanded its wares into note cards and invitations. See what they've got to offer for a wedding at www.vistaprint.com.

Wal-Mart

Most people think of Wal-Mart as just a super-size store that competes with the likes of Target. What you may not realize is that many Wal-Mart locations have extensive craft departments, including fabric, making it a great resource for the DIY bride. These days you can even register at Wal-Mart. Check it all out at www.walmart.com.

Wedding Gown Specialists

The website www.weddinggownspecialists.com is the online portal of the Association of Wedding Gown Specialists, a trade association of companies that clean, preserve, and restore delicate garments like wedding gowns. Not only do these businesses clean special-occasion clothing, but also these are the folks that theaters and museums call when they need their costumes and collections cleaned. You can search for a specialist near you by visiting the website and using the pull-down menu to find your state.

WeddingOfficiants.com

This website at www.weddingofficiants.com is sort of like a dating service for engaged couples looking for someone to officiate at their wedding. In order to tap into the website's referral service, you must register with the site and answer a questionnaire. Once that information is in the system, the folks that run the website will try and match you with an appropriate officiant in your area.

Yahoo! Photos

Website giant Yahoo! does everything—e-mail, online groups, and now, printing. If you visit http://photos.yahoo.com, you can get a sense of the kinds of personalized t-shirts, mugs, tote bags, and other goodies you can customize by uploading digital images to the site and then placing an order.

Appendix D
Sample Vendor Contract

I can't stress enough how important it is to get everything in writing when dealing with wedding vendors. If for some reason your vendor doesn't have a contract to offer, that doesn't mean you're off the hook. Instead, you need to present a contract for him to sign. If he balks, you walk and find another vendor for the job. No upstanding businessperson should have a problem with signing a contract. If he does, that's a red flag in my book, and it should be in yours, too.

In case you find yourself needing to be the person generating the contract, here is a sample you can use.

Vendor Agreement

This is an agreement between (name of vendor, vendor mailing address, vendor phone number, fax number, and e-mail), herein known as "vendor," and (name of bride and groom, bride and groom mailing address, phone number, fax number, and e-mail address), herein known as "buyer," for the following services: (fill in blank for services in as much detail as possible. For example, a photographer who will shoot for six hours and provide the buyer with at least 400 exposed images.), known hereafter as "services." (Note: if the vendor you're hiring is a specific company with many employees, and you want to book a specific employee within that firm, list his or her name here so they can't just send anyone for the job.)

Vendor promises to provide services on this date: (fill in date), beginning at this time (fill in time) and ending at this time (fill in time). Services will be provided at this location (fill in address of location or locations where vendor will be working).

Buyer promises to pay vendor (fill in amount) for services, payable as follows: 25 percent upon signing contract; 25 percent one week before event; 50 percent upon completion of job, within seven business days. Vendor promises that he will accept a credit card for these payments.

In the event that vendor must cancel agreement with buyer, vendor will do so in writing and refund all monies to buyer within seven business days.

In the event that buyer must cancel agreement with vendor, buyer will make cancellation known in writing. Vendor will refund all monies, if notified before second 25 percent payment or before one week ahead of the event. If buyer cancels after that time, no money will be returned.

In exchange for agreed-upon fee, vendor promises to arrive wearing wedding-appropriate attire (specify clothing if necessary) and to stay for time period stated above.

Vendor acknowledges that the agreed-upon fee will cover any and all expenses vendor incurs in taking on this job, including but not limited to travel, food, and hiring additional people to work for vendor. Buyer will not be responsible for these additional costs.

Buyer will provide vendor with (fill in the blank) breaks at (fill in the blank) intervals as well as a meal during the reception.

Please sign and date the agreement below.

_____   _____
Vendor signature with date   Buyer signature with date

Appendix E
Wedding Checklist

Between getting engaged and returning from your honeymoon, you're going to have a lot on your "to do" list—tasks ranging from choosing a wedding date to finding a wedding location to figuring out what you're going to wear. It would be easy to let things fall by the wayside, or for you to get waylaid and overwhelmed, simply by the amount you need to accomplish.

Don't sweat it, though. The purpose of this appendix is to provide you with a "to do" checklist from each of the chapters in the book. Even after you've read the book cover to cover, you can turn to this appendix and see exactly what you need to do for each part of your wedding.

I hope that these checklists will keep you on task—and on budget—as you go from engaged couple to husband and wife.

Chapter 1

Here's your "to do" checklist from Chapter 1:

❏ Begin crunching some numbers to see how you can make a $5,000 wedding budget work for your needs.

❏ Approach one or both sets of parents to see if they are able or willing to contribute toward your wedding.

❏ Start acting frugal in your everyday life—like making coffee at home instead of buying it, or brown-bagging your lunch—so you can begin socking away money for your wedding.

❏ Think about how you will prioritize the various parts of your wedding—meaning which aspects you will be willing to pay more for and which aspects you can spend less on.

❏ Bone up on contracts, deposits, and vendor agreements as you get ready to hire wedding pros by asking any recently married friends how they handled these elements of their wedding plans.

❏ Decide how you're going to pay for your wedding—cash, check, debit, credit, equity, or a mix of many of these options—and the pros and cons of each.

❏ Investigate whether bartering for wedding goods and services is an option for the two of you.

❏ Begin asking around to see if you know—or anyone you know knows—anyone in the wedding business who might be able to give you a discount on goods and services.

❏ Decide if it's worth it to consider a sponsored wedding, whereby people donate goods and services to your wedding in exchange for advertising and promotion to your guests.

❏ Do the math to determine how certain pre-wedding celebrations might adversely affect your budget, such as clothing needed for a bridal shower.

Chapter 2

Here is your "to do" checklist from Chapter 2:

❏ If you've decided to have an engagement photo taken, schedule time with a professional photographer or arrange to have a friend take the picture.

❏ Outline where you want to send your announcement, such as local or hometown papers and alumni magazines.

❏ Order or desktop publish your announcement.

❏ Book a weekday evening or weekend day when you can assemble your announcement and photo, and send them out to interested parties.

❏ Draft a guest list with your fiancé.

❏ Ask your parents to draft their "perfect world" guest list as well.

❏ Have everyone compare guest lists so you can get rid of duplicates, then get a sense of where you're heading as far as the size of your guest list.

❏ If the first draft of your guest list feels too big, break down names into an "A" and "B" list.

❏ As you work on your guest list, don't forget to figure out if you're going to include children or not at your wedding—and how your decision either way will affect your head count.

❏ Do an inventory of your home to see what you might want to register for shower and wedding gifts.

❏ Start checking out stores, businesses, or online sites where you might want to register, based on your needs or wants.

❏ Before you commit to a store, make sure you understand its return policies.

❑ If you decide that you don't need any more "stuff," look into registering with a charity (a website like idofoundation.com can help bring you up to speed on this modern registry alternative).

❑ If you haven't already done so, get your engagement ring appraised.

❑ See if your homeowner's insurance will cover your engagement ring. If not, purchase a rider.

❑ Decide how you're going to handle a wedding website—if you're having one at all—and which one of you is going to be responsible for setting it up and keeping it up-to-date.

❑ Register your wedding website domain, if you want an original one. Otherwise, set one up for free using a website like The Knot.

Chapter 3

Here is your "to do" checklist from Chapter 3:

❑ Discuss and decide whether you're going to have a religious or civil ceremony.

❑ Begin checking out ceremony location options, such as your house of worship, someone else's house of worship, or a third-party location where clergy can officiate, if you've decided on a religious wedding.

❑ Get recommendations for officiants and arrange meetings with those you might consider hiring or using.

❑ Compare the prices of various officiants and locations.

❑ Book your ceremony location and officiant.

❑ If any deposits or payment plans are necessary for your ceremony location, update your calendar now for when those payments are due so that you don't miss any deadlines and forfeit your reservation.

❑ Choose attendants for your wedding.

❑ Begin shopping for wedding rings.

❏ Consider the price differential between rings made of various metals—gold versus silver versus platinum.

❏ If you live near a city with a jewelry district, set aside time to visit the shops there to hunt for bargains.

❏ Figure out if you're going to write your own vows.

❏ If you are going to write your own vows, begin drafting what you may want to say to each other at your wedding ceremony.

❏ If your officiant is going to supply you with vows, ask him or her to let you see them ahead of time.

❏ Determine your wedding colors.

❏ Decide what kind of flowers you would like to have at your ceremony—and in which shape, form, and, of course, color, based on the colors you've chosen for your wedding.

❏ Once you've chosen your attendants and know how many people will be participating in your ceremony, you can begin estimating how many corsages and boutonnières, and the like, you'll need to order.

❏ Think about the kind of bouquet you'd like to carry—including which kind of flowers you'd like to see in it.

❏ Begin visiting florists so you can get a sense of how much flowers will cost for your wedding.

❏ If florists seem too expensive, comparison shop by visiting warehouse clubs, home improvement centers, supermarkets, and other non-florist shop venues that sell flowers.

❏ Visit your ceremony location so you can see what kind of decorations it needs for a wedding, if any.

❏ If you're having a Jewish wedding, see how much it costs to order personalized yarmulkes versus the generic kind—and then determine which best fits into your budget.

❏ Also if you're having a Jewish wedding, begin making plans for your chuppah or marriage canopy. Will you make, buy, or borrow it?

❏ If you're getting married in a house of worship, ask if there is a wedding before yours that will let you reuse their flowers.

❏ Find out if there is a way that your church or synagogue can extend its congregation discount to your flower order.

❏ Pay your deposit for your flowers, if that is necessary, and if any payments are due in the coming months, mark those on your calendar now so you don't miss any payments.

❏ Think about how you're going to get to and from the ceremony—and which mode of transportation you'd like to take.

❏ If you've got your heart set on a limousine, begin calling around to companies to get price estimates.

❏ While you're at it, call local car rental agencies and see how their prices compare to limousine companies.

❏ Make a deposit on your chosen mode of transportation and be sure to find out when final payment is due—then mark that date on your calendar.

Chapter 4

Here is your "to do" checklist from Chapter 4:

❏ Use the Internet to investigate reception location options, including some that may be considered offbeat.

❏ Schedule time after work or on a weekend when you can visit some reception location options in person.

❏ If you're getting married in a place where you don't live, such as the town you grew up in, book a weekend or take a few days off from work so that the two of you can travel to check out ceremony and reception locations in person.

❏ If you're having a house-of-worship wedding, take a walk through the fellowship hall to see if it might be just right for your reception.

❏ When interviewing reception location managers, ask them to spell out the price differential depending on time of year, time of day, and day of the week.

❏ If you're computer savvy, set up a spreadsheet so you can compare all of these numbers from the reception locations. (You may even want to add columns and rows for the other aspects of your wedding, too.)

❏ Put a deposit down on your reception location. Make notations on your calendar when other payments are due.

❏ Since stocking your own bar is often a great way to save money at a reception, take a day and bring your calculator with you to the local liquor store so you can crunch some numbers on how much bottles of alcohol cost—and how those costs might affect your budget.

❏ Comparison shop the cost of wedding cakes by contacting private bakers, the corner bakery shop, and your local warehouse club.

❏ While you're in number-crunching mode, set aside time to price check nontraditional centerpiece options, including bowls of candy, topiaries, and clusters of candles.

❏ See if your reception location will be providing centerpieces, linens, and other extras as a part of the fee you pay.

❏ Make a note to ask your reception locale if they'll have an extra table available that you can set up as your gift table.

❏ If your reception place won't be able to give you a table for gifts, you're going to have to provide one yourself.

❏ Assign the task of bringing and setting up the gift table to a responsible and reliable friend or family member, who can also be responsible for transporting your gifts home from the reception.

❏ Shop around for price quotes on transportation from the ceremony to the reception and then to your hotel. (If possible, piggyback this to-do task onto the similar task for transportation to the ceremony, which was mentioned in the previous section.)

Chapter 5

Here is your "to do" checklist from Chapter 5:

❏ Talk about whether or not a destination wedding makes sense for the two of you.

❏ If so, look into which Caribbean or other "exotic" location seems the most feasible.

❏ Spend time looking around websites like doitcaribbean.com, the website of the Caribbean Tourism Organization, which offers a clearinghouse of information on destination weddings in the Caribbean.

❏ If you're unsure which warm-weather destination might be appropriate for your wedding, visit each of the country websites mentioned in Chapter 5 so you can educate yourself on the pros and cons of getting married in each of these places.

❏ If you've decided to get married in a destination wedding and need to have any documents translated into a foreign language, begin looking now for a translation service.

❏ Get your documents translated and make sure you ask when they will be ready for pickup.

❏ If you've decided to get married in a foreign location and you need to have medical exams and blood tests done, make appointments with your respective doctors now to avoid any last-minute rushing around for test results.

❏ If you've decided to get married in a foreign location and one of you needs to establish residence there, speak to someone in your human resources office to find out how much vacation or personal time you are able to take for this purpose.

❏ Once you've identified a resort where you want to tie the knot, call their wedding coordinator/banquet manager to find out exactly what the resort can cover for you as far as officiants, meals, and ceremony details.

❏ If either of your passports is set to expire within the next year, take a day and get new ones. Many foreign locales won't allow you to visit if your passport will expire soon—they're probably worried that once you arrive, you won't leave.

❏ Don't forget to get new passport photos, too.

❏ If a wedding at sea rocks your boat, call around to cruise companies, and travel companies that specialize in cruises, to see what your options are for an ahoy wedding.

❏ If you've decided to have a destination wedding—whether in the Caribbean or at sea—send in your deposit as soon as you make your decision so you don't risk losing your spot.

Chapter 6

Here is your "to do" checklist from Chapter 6:

❏ Research wedding dresses in bridal magazines to get a sense of styles you like and where they might be available locally.

❏ Book a day when you can take a friend or family member with you to visit local bridal salons. Call ahead to see if you need an appointment.

❏ Since many bridal salons do not have a range of sizes in the dresses you try on, see if there is a David's Bridal near you where you can try on dresses in all kinds of sizes. This will give you a better sense of how wedding dresses will look on you.

❏ Check in the newspaper, in regional magazines, or online to see if any bridal stores near you will be having trunk, sample, or clearance sales that you can attend to look for bargains on bridal attire.

❏ Set aside time to visit nontraditional stores that often carry bridal-like attire, such as Talbot's, Ann Taylor, and J.Crew.

❏ Don't forget to check out what's available in the "evening" department at your local department store in terms of dresses or gowns that might work for a wedding.

❏ Visit the websites of outlet mall owners to see if there is one near you that has a bridal or prom store outlet.

❏ Make time to check out websites like Freecycle, eBay, and Craigslist for great deals on wedding attire.

❏ If you live near consignment, thrift, or resale shops, pop in to see what they've got available in the area of wedding attire.

❏ If you've decided to wear your mother's or another relative's wedding gown, make an appointment with a seamstress and specialty cleaner to have its condition evaluated and any fittings done to make sure the dress looks right on you.

❏ If you're ordering your gown, place a deposit on your purchase as soon as possible to get your dress order into the system.

❏ Find out the timeline for when your dress will be in and when you'll need to go to the salon for fittings—and then add those dates to your calendar so you don't forget.

❏ Once you find a dress that fits you well—and fits your budget—figure out the other kinds of accessories you'll need to wear with it.

❏ Make a list of these accessories and set aside time to shop for them—whether it be online or in a brick-and-mortar store.

❏ Encourage your fiancé to make time to visit formal wear shops to investigate renting or buying his wedding attire.

❏ Visit a local craft store like JoAnn's or AC Moore to see if you can sign up for a crafting class to make wedding accessories, such as your headpiece.

Chapter 7

Here is your "to do" checklist from Chapter 7:

❏ Contact musical friends or family members to see if they might lend their talent to your ceremony and/or reception.

❏ Investigate the faculty and staff at your local college or university to see if they have musicians there who perform at weddings.

❏ Contact any recently married acquaintances to see if they can recommend talented and affordable musicians for your wedding ceremony and reception.

❏ Check out the websites of recommended bands and deejays.

❏ Call or e-mail the bands and deejays you're interested in so you can get more details on how they work with weddings.

❏ Make appointments to meet face-to-face with the musicians and/or deejays you're considering hiring for your ceremony and reception.

❏ Once you've chosen the entertainment for your ceremony and reception, be sure to put a deposit down to save your spot.

❏ Find out when other payments may be due—and mark those on your calendar.

❏ When booking your band for your reception, see if any members of the ensemble might be available to play at the ceremony as part of the entire fee you're paying them for the event.

❏ If you've decided to go with a digital deejay—i.e., an MP3 player or iPod—for your ceremony and/or reception, begin shopping for and downloading the music you'd like to use on the big day. Don't leave this task to the last minute.

Chapter 8

Here is your "to do" checklist from Chapter 8:

❏ If you've decided to send save-the-date cards, begin checking out your options for them. You can visit stationery stores and look online to see the various kinds of cards you can order.

❏ Order your save-the-date cards as soon as you set your wedding date. These cards are key if you're having a wedding on a holiday weekend or in a destination that requires nearly everyone to travel to.

❏ If you've decided to make your save-the-date cards and invitations, investigate where you're going to get paper stock for the project, and then give yourself at least three weeks to complete the project.

❏ Before you buy paper and envelopes à la carte, check out the invitation kits that stores like AC Moore, Bed Bath & Beyond, and Office Depot sell.

❏ As soon as the details (time, date, location) of your ceremony and reception are finalized, order your wedding invitations.

❏ Mail your invitations 12 weeks ahead of time if you're having a destination or holiday weekend wedding, otherwise 8 weeks ahead of time is sufficient.

❏ Once you've got your ceremony planned and your attendants lined up, investigate the cost and time of ordering ceremony programs versus doing it yourself.

❏ Once your reception plans are in order and RSVPs have all come back, order or plan to print all of the reception-related printed goods—escort cards, table cards, menus, and more.

❏ Before you begin your printing project, check the status of your printer's cartridge. You don't want to be in the middle of printing only to discover that your printer has run out of ink.

❏ Start shopping around for a guest book—that is, if you've decided you want to have one available for guests to sign.

❏ Check out the cost of buying disposable cameras to place on your reception tables.

❏ If you've decided to buy these cameras, make sure you order in one fell swoop enough for all of the tables so you can save on shipping charges, key if you've ordered them off of the Internet.

❏ When ordering or buying supplies for your invitations, purchase your thank-you notes, too—that is, if you want all of the paper stocks to match.

❏ Visit the post office or go to their website to purchase stamps for invitations, RSVP cards, and thank-you notes.

❏ Double-check that there won't be any postage hikes between now and when your invitations go out. If there is a postage hike looming, purchase additional postage to use on your invitations and RSVP cards, just in case.

Chapter 9

Here is your "to do" checklist from Chapter 9:

❏ Ask any recently married people you know if they can recommend a photographer.

❏ Visit the website of each recommended photographer so you can look at his or her work.

❏ Call each photographer whose work you like and make an appointment for a face-to-face meeting and so you can review his or her portfolio.

❏ When meeting with photographers, find out how much they charge for shooting a wedding, and what you get for the prices they quote.

❏ Take a similar approach with investigating videographers.

❏ When you find the photographer and videographer you like, put down a deposit.

❏ Find out when the rest of your payment will be due to the photographer and videographer—then mark that date on your calendar so you don't forget.

❏ If you've decided to let your guests be your collective photographer at the ceremony and reception, make sure you buy enough disposable or digital cameras for each guest to use.

❏ Print up a card to place on each reception table that will explain to the guests how you hope that they will have fun taking pictures of your wedding in lieu of a professional photographer.

❏ Before the big day, figure out which service or online site you'd like to use to get your film developed and pictures printed.

Chapter 10

Here is your "to do" checklist from Chapter 10:

❏ Ask your girlfriends for recommendations for a makeup artist, if you've decided to hire one to do your hair and makeup for your big day.

❏ If your girlfriends come up blank with recommendations, ask your photographer if he knows someone, since photographers often work closely with makeup artists for other kinds of photography work they do.

❏ Call beauty schools and your local salon to find out if any of the instructors or technicians do hair and makeup on a freelance basis for weddings.

❏ Visit the beauty counter at your local mall to see if you can track down a good makeup artist.

❏ Call and talk with each recommended artist to find out how much experience she has with weddings and how much she charges.

❏ When you find one or two artists you like, book a session with each to have them do a test run of makeup and hair. (Note: You will have to pay for this separately from any price you'll pay for your wedding-day hair and makeup services.)

❏ If you've decided to do your makeup on your own, set aside time to shop for new cosmetics—and to get a free makeover or makeup lesson at a cosmetics counter at a department store or makeup store like Sephora or MAC.

❏ If you like the idea of getting your teeth whitened for your wedding, make an appointment today with your dentist, since they often book out months in advance. (You should be getting a pre-wedding cleaning anyway.)

❏ If you've decided to do your teeth whitening yourself, read up on the various over-the-counter products available.

❏ Buy and use a tooth whitening kit well in advance of your big day—in case you have an adverse reaction to the treatment. This will give you plenty of time to recover.

❏ Buy whitening toothpaste to maintain your whiter and brighter smile.

❏ Book your pre-wedding manicure and pedicure at a reputable and clean salon.

❏ Book any waxing or eyebrow-shaping services you'd like to have done before your wedding—or hone your skills on doing all of this yourself.

❏ Make a list of the products you'll need to stock in your wedding emergency kit and the toiletries baskets you'll put out in the bathrooms at the wedding.

❏ Go shopping for these supplies.

Chapter 11

Here is your "to do" checklist from Chapter 11:

❏ Outline the people for whom you will need to buy gifts for your wedding—your attendants, your parents, and so on.

❏ While you're in the brainstorming mode, crunch the numbers on how many favors you're going to have to buy for your guests—and begin thinking about what you'd like to give to them.

❏ Brainstorm ways you can be frugal and practical in the gifts you choose.

❏ Investigate double-duty favors, such as potted plants that can serve as centerpieces during the reception and which guests can take home afterward as favors.

❏ If you're going to serve up food favors, like caramel apples or freshly baked cookies, map out your shopping, baking, and packaging schedule now to ensure that you don't leave this task for the last minute.

❏ If you're interested in making donations to charity in lieu of traditional favors and gifts, spend some time looking around www. idofoundation.com, which helps couples find good causes they can make a donation to in their guests' names.

❏ If you decide to make a donation to charity instead of giving out favors, plan a time now when you can make or order cards you can place on the reception table that explain your decision. You don't want to leave your guests scratching their heads when it appears that they will be going home from your reception empty-handed.

Chapter 12

Here is your "to do" checklist from Chapter 12:

❏ Investigate the most affordable locations where you can honeymoon, given the time of year when you're going to be getting married.

❏ Keep in mind that off-season one place may be considered high-season somewhere else.

❏ If you will be honeymooning between June 1st and September 1st, think about targeting your honeymoon to places other than the Caribbean, Atlantic, and Pacific, where it is prime hurricane season this time of year.

❏ Set aside time to check in with the frequent flier programs where you've earned miles or any other affinity program where you've earned points so you can use these points or miles to get a discount on your honeymoon.

❏ If you work for a company that has a travel arm to it, use your lunch hour to place a call or send an e-mail to that division to see if you are eligible for any travel discounts.

❏ Outline any friends or family members who own a timeshare and who might be willing to let you use that timeshare for your honeymoon.

❏ Call or e-mail to inquire of these timeshare-owning friends or family members.

❏ Double-check the expiration date of your passport.

❏ If your passport is set to expire within the next 12 months, get it renewed.

❏ Have passport pictures taken at a local shop or do them yourself with a digital camera and your PC.

❏ Plan a day when you can visit your local passport agency to get a new passport—or budget enough time to get your new passport renewed through the mail.

❏ Look into registering for a honeymoon, if that makes sense to you.

❏ Visit the websites of organizations and travel companies that offer this honeymoon registry option.

❏ Book your honeymoon.

❏ Make a note on your calendar the last day on which loved ones can purchase a "gift" from your honeymoon registry. (You need to know this date so that if you've booked a honeymoon through your registry, and then not all of it was covered through gift purchases, you have enough time to pony up extra funds to cover the trip.)

❏ Pay the balance on your honeymoon.

❏ Purchase travel insurance.

❏ Create a packing list for your honeymoon.

❏ Spend a weekend day purchasing any odds and ends on your packing list that you don't already own.

❏ Pack for your honeymoon a few days before your wedding so you allow yourself a grace period to remember any forgotten items that didn't make it onto your packing list.

Chapter 13

Here is your "to do" checklist from Chapter 13:

❏ Compile your gift list from the wedding.

❏ Decide how you're going to handle thank-you notes. Will you sit down and write them together in one fell swoop or will one of you write the notes while the other addresses envelopes?

❏ Double-check that you have enough thank-you notes, envelopes, and stamps to get the job done.

❏ If you're running short on any supplies, go to the store now to stock up. Don't leave it to the last minute.

❏ If you're going to be including a photo of the two of you in your thank-you notes, touch base with your photographer to find out when those images will be ready.

❏ Organize your gifts, gift receipts, and any other information on gifts that you need to return.

❏ Locate a copy of your registry list from each store where you registered—and from where your guests bought your gifts.

❏ If you don't have a copy of the list, see if you can print it off the Internet. If not, set aside extra time when you visit each store to print one out from a store kiosk before hitting the return department.

❏ Cluster gifts by the stores where you need to return these items, including the registry list.

❏ Book a weekend day or take a day off from work to devote to returning gifts.

❏ If you registered via online stores and need to return items, make sure you have enough mailing supplies to send everything back. Or take everything to a shipping depot like the UPS Store and let someone else handle it for you efficiently and affordably.

❏ Decide if there are any gifts you'd like to sell on eBay.

❏ If selling on eBay, first research how well (or poorly) similar items have sold in the past—and in which categories.

❏ Devote a block of time for taking digital pictures of all of your items, and then create the eBay listings you need.

❏ After you've posted your auctions online, check your "My eBay" inbox regularly to deal with any questions about your products.

❏ Investigate a dry cleaner where you can take your wedding gown to get cleaned.

❏ Once you've found someone you can trust with your garment, set aside a time when you can bring it in.

❏ Find out when the dress will be ready, and then mark that date on your calendar so you can check back in on the status of your gown.

❏ When your gown is ready to be picked up, go get it. The longer it stays at the cleaner, the greater the chance that it could get damaged or lost.

❏ Drop off your film or disk at a photo store to get your honeymoon pictures developed and printed. While you're at it, bring any disposable cameras from your reception in for developing, too.

❏ If you've gone the digital route with your pictures, set aside an afternoon to upload them to your computer or your favorite photo site, then e-mail links to friends and family.

Index

C

D

ℛ

S

T